Democracy Without Justice in Spain

PENNSYLVANIA STUDIES IN HUMAN RIGHTS

Bert B. Lockwood, Jr., Series Editor

A complete list of books in the series
is available from the publisher.

DEMOCRACY WITHOUT JUSTICE IN SPAIN

The Politics of Forgetting

Omar G. Encarnación

PENN

UNIVERSITY OF PENNSYLVANIA PRESS

PHILADELPHIA

Published by
University of Pennsylvania Press
Philadelphia, Pennsylvania 19104-4112
www.upenn.edu/pennpress

Printed in the United States of America
on acid-free paper

10 9 8 7 6 5 4 3 2 1

Library of Congress Cataloging-in-Publication Data

Encarnación, Omar Guillermo, 1962–
Democratization without justice in Spain : the politics of forgetting / Omar G. Encarnación. — 1st ed.
p. cm. — (Pennsylvania studies in human rights)
Includes bibliographical references and index.
ISBN 978-0-8122-4568-4 (hardcover : alk. paper)
1. Democratization—Spain. 2. Transitional justice—Spain. 3. Criminal justice, Administration of—Spain. 4. Spain—Politics and government—1975–. 5. Spain—History—Civil War, 1936–1939—Influence. I. Title. II. Series: Pennsylvania studies in human rights.
JN8221.E525 2014
320.946'09047—dc23 2013021881

CONTENTS

Introduction

William Faulkner's famous dictum that "the past is never dead; in fact, it is not even past" aptly captures how the past looms over contemporary Spanish politics. In 2007, the Congress of Deputies approved the Law of Historical Memory with the intention of reconciling the dark legacy of the Spanish Civil War (1936–1939), that epic interwar showdown between democracy and fascism generally regarded as a dress rehearsal for World War II, and the dictatorship of Generalissimo Francisco Franco, whose 1936 coup against the popularly elected Second Republic set the Civil War in motion. Scores of mass killings committed by both sides of the conflict (the right-wing Nationalists and the left-leaning Republicans) earned the Spanish Civil War worldwide infamy. But the violence of the Franco dictatorship, less known outside Spain, was just as brutal and horrific. Franco ruled Spain with an iron fist for nearly four decades, from his declaration of victory over the Republican army on April 1, 1939 to his death of natural causes on November 20, 1975, with the bulk of the violence falling disproportionately during the early years of the dictatorship. With the major democracies of the day (Britain, France, and the United States) at war with Germany's Nazi regime, Franco undertook a vicious policy of *limpieza* (cleansing) that resulted in the execution and imprisonment in concentration and labor camps of hundreds of thousands of left-wing sympathizers. This bloody campaign gave Franco bragging rights of being the Cold War's most successful anticommunist crusader.

Spain's encounter with the past in 2007 was long overdue given the unorthodox handling of the political excesses of the Civil War and the Franco dictatorship during the 1977 democratic transition. To coincide with the restoration of democracy, the national parties from the right and left negotiated the so-called "Pact of Forgetting" with the intention of letting bygones be bygones. As a consequence of this informal agreement no one was put on trial for the political crimes of the old regime or disqualified from playing a role in the politics of the new democracy, since the pact was accompanied by a broad amnesty law that granted immunity for all political crimes committed prior to 1977. The contrast with Spain's sister Southern European dictatorships, Greece and Portugal, whose transitions to democracy roughly coincided with the Spanish transition, is striking. The members of Greece's Colonels' regime (1967–1974) were hauled off to court on charges of high treason, resulting in death sentences for the top military leadership, sentences later reduced to life in prison. Portugal's Salazar-Caetano regime (1932–1974) was subjected to a policy of "lustration" intended to purge the state and society of authoritarianism. The purging began with the military and was gradually extended to the civil service and authoritarian collaborators in the business community, the media, and the Catholic Church.

Another consequence of the Pact of Forgetting was to thwart any attempt at "truth-telling" like Argentina's *Nunca Más* (Never Again), the report by the National Commission on the Disappearance of Persons that chronicled the human rights abuses of the military dictatorship between the years of 1976 and 1983 and that launched several analogous efforts across South America, and South Africa's landmark Truth and Reconciliation Commission (TRC), which examined the sins of apartheid. Furthermore, the pact to forget effectively precluded an official condemnation of Franco's military coup in 1936 and even a memorial and an official apology to the many victims of the old regime. Adding insult to injury, the pact facilitated the survival of numerous monuments across the Spanish territory honoring Franco, including the infamous El Valle de los Caídos, Franco's megalomaniacal monument on the outskirts of Madrid to his Nationalist crusade, which today houses his remains and those of José Antonio Primo de Rivera, founder of the Spanish fascist organization Falange, who was executed by the Republicans during the Civil War.[1] The upkeep of Franco's burial site is underwritten by the Spanish state, including, until 2007, a mass held by Benedictine monks on the anniversary of his death.

Instead of justice and truth, forgetting and moving on prevailed in Spain. For decades into the new democracy the memory of the past, especially that of the Civil War, appeared to have vanished among the usually contentious Spanish political class. The only occasion that merited a reference to the past was to stress the importance of not talking about it. In 1977, in anticipation of the first democratic elections since 1936, communist leader Santiago Carrillo, the most prominent member of the democratic opposition to the Franco regime, noted that "In our country, there is but one way to reach democracy, which is to throw out anyone who promotes the memory of the Civil War, which should never return, ever. We do not want more wars, we have had enough of them already."[2] Yet more unexpected is that the pact to forget succeeded in turning the past into a taboo among ordinary Spaniards, by making discussions of the violence of the Civil War from either side of the conflict and the political repression of the Francoist era inappropriate and unwelcome in almost any social context. Commenting on the apparent disappearance of the memory of the Civil War among the Spaniards, the *Economist* noted in 2006: "The pact of forgetting has meant that mere mention of the Civil War has been kept of out everything, from politics to dinner-party conversations."[3]

Oddly enough, for a piece of legislation generally seen as an act of deferred justice against the Franco regime (Aguilar, Balcells, and Cebolla-Boado 2011), the 2007 Law of Historical Memory is remarkably short on accountability. Indeed, the law left in place much of the status quo about the past introduced by the Pact of Forgetting. Although the law offered reparations to those victimized by past injustices and condemned the Franco regime as "illegitimate," it did not overturn the 1977 amnesty law, making it highly unlikely that anyone associated with the old regime will ever face prosecution on human rights charges. Ironically, today in Spain only those seeking to bring former Franco officials to justice are risking prosecution in connection to the crimes of the Franco regime. In 2010 a court indicted "Super Judge" Baltazar Garzón, the maverick magistrate who gained worldwide fame in the late 1990s for his audacious indictment on human rights abuses of Chilean General Augusto Pinochet, on charges by the conservative group Manos Limpias that Garzón had abused the powers of his office by attempting to use the Law of Historical Memory to prosecute former Francoist officials.[4] Garzón was eventually acquitted, but other charges forced him to relinquish his judicial post, thereby ending all meaningful efforts to bring justice to the Franco regime.[5]

More striking is that the Law of Historical Memory did not automatically nullify the verdicts of those sentenced by Francoist tribunals, including the kangaroo courts created after the end of the Civil War in 1939, which convicted thousands of people for simply having supported the Republican government, nor did the law call for the organization of a truth commission to examine the human rights abuses committed during the Civil War and the Francoist period. To its credit, the law mandates removal from public spaces of monuments that glorify either of the sides that fought the Civil War (a stipulation that applies mostly to the numerous monuments honoring Franco and his regime, including those in Catholic churches, a reflection of the symbiotic relationship that developed between the old regime and the Catholic Church), but it protects monuments that possess "historical and cultural significance," including Franco's burial site at El Valle de los Caídos.

The Lines of Inquiry

The rise and persistence of the politics of forgetting in Spain pose important questions about how nations settle a "dark" past and the consequences of the polices put in place to deal with that past for the emerging democratic regime. Foremost among these questions is why the reluctance to adopt conventional means for dealing with the political excesses of the old regime, such as political trials and a truth commission? What explains this apparent case of Spanish exceptionalism? And what has been the legacy for Spanish democracy and society at large of the deliberate repression of the memory of the violence and political excesses of the Civil War and the Franco dictatorship entailed in the pact to forget? Did the absence of justice and truth prove to be a hindrance to democratization in Spain? These questions gain much significance when we consider, first, the bundle of contradictions, ironies, and paradoxes embedded in the case itself.

Given its troubled history, Spain was an unlikely candidate for adopting a strategy of forgetting and moving on. A voluntary agreement to repress the memory of a violent past would be remarkable for any society, but especially for Spain, a country notorious for its anarchic character, polarized parties, and rebellious civil society, and hence a longstanding scholarly reputation for being "different," a euphemism for unfit for democracy that darkly hinted at the Spaniards' propensity for violence, revenge, and recrimination (Wiarda 1973). Predictably, the forecasts issued by scholars for Spain around the time of Franco's death failed to foresee the rise of a collective will to forget. By and large, these forecasts warned about the return of the old habits that for centuries have nourished the well-known myth of the two Spains: a country tragically divided into two halves that can never find a way to get along. These sentiments were perfectly captured by historian Richard Herr (1971: 27), writing in the twilight of the Franco era:

> Spain's future is still wrapped in mystery. Like every country that has been ruled recently by a strong man, it is subject to the question, after he goes what? For Spain this anxiety is especially keen because it has a long history of political instability, going back to the nineteenth century. Spaniards have appeared by nature rebellious and politically mercurial. Indeed their recent striving for economic betterment has been interpreted as a sublimation of the energy that they would normally devote to political agitation, a sublimation forced upon them by the ban on politics. Should the ban end, many persons, both friends and enemies of Franco, anticipate that Spaniards will return to their former habits.

Moreover, social science theories would have predicted that Spain after Franco was destined for a robust encounter with some form of reckoning with the past. Arguably, the most reliable variable for understanding whether justice against the old regime would be part of the transition is the extent to which state-sponsored violence and repression penetrated the social fabric (see Borneman 1997; De Brito et al. 2001; Hite and Cesarini 2004). From this perspective ensues the popular hypothesis that the more violent and repressive the legacy of the previous regime, the more vigorous and comprehensive the attempt at justice will be. There is much logic to this thinking, since an especially repressive regime is likely to embolden citizens to demand justice from the new democratic regime during the transition while creating a powerful incentive for the new government to want to hold the old regime accountable for its crimes.

Assumptions linking the legacy of violence and repression of the old regime to the dispensation of justice during the transition are powerfully challenged by Spain, which under Franco endured far more violence and repression than either Portugal and Greece or South America's infamous bureaucratic authoritarian regimes (Argentina, Brazil, Chile, and Uruguay), countries that all underwent some kind of reckoning with the past. To be sure, the lion's share of the violence and repression that gave Franco notoriety took place in the early 1940s, so that by the mid-1970s the worst memories of the Franco regime were receding into history. But the regime remained repressive and violent through its last days, a point often overlooked by studies of the late Franco era (Townson 2007). As will be seen later, in its final years the Franco regime turned quite repressive, especially after the 1973 assassination of Admiral Carrero Blanco, Franco's designated political heir, which triggered the return of political executions and restrictions on civil society organizing and public mobilization not seen in decades.

Also noteworthy is that while stubbornly refusing to look into the dark history of human rights abuses under Franco, Spain since the democratic transition has accumulated an outstanding record of complying with international human rights conventions. Spain is a signatory to all the major international human rights accords, including the International Covenant on Civil and Political Rights, the accord that tabulates the first half of the rights and freedoms enshrined in the Universal Declaration of Human Rights, which Spain signed in April 1977, in the midst of the transition to democracy, and the European Convention on the Prevention of Torture, which it signed in 1987. A plethora of national laws prevent torture and inhumane treatment, including a ban on the death penalty, which has not been carried out in Spain since Franco's passing.

On some human rights fronts, such as expanding the rights of ethnic and sexual minorities, Spain has led rather than followed the international community. It has been a leader in extending home rule to culturally distinct communities such as the Basques and the Catalans, arguably the most autonomous of Europe's "stateless peoples," a development that ensued from the recognition of different nationalities within the Spanish territory in the 1978 Constitution. In 2005, Spain became only the fifth country in Western Europe, and the first Catholic-majority country in the world, to enact same-sex marriage legislation that makes no distinction in the right to marry and adopt between homosexual and heterosexual couples. This landmark law influenced the expansion of gay rights in the Iberian-Latin world, including, most notably, legalization of same-sex marriage in Argentina and Portugal in 2010 and in Uruguay in 2013.

Most ironic of all, however, is the prominent role Spain has played in popularizing the practice of prosecuting former despots. Judge Garzón's 1998 indictment of General Pinochet established the principle of "universal jurisdiction," which holds, in a nutshell, that some crimes are so heinous that they offend all of humanity and are therefore prosecutable by any nation. In 2005, the Constitutional Court, Spain's highest court, ruled that a lower court could proceed in investigating crimes of genocide, murder, and torture committed by the military during Guatemala's Civil War, arguing, to the delight of human rights activists everywhere, that "The principle of universal jurisdiction takes precedence over the existence of the national interest." These actions further burnished Spain's reputation as a human rights trailblazer while highlighting an apparent double standard (if not outright hypocrisy) in how Spain regards the issue of the crimes of an old regime: forgetting for itself and prosecution for everybody else.[6] Wilder Tyler, legal and policy director for Human Rights Watch, highlighted this double standard when noting: "Spain is an obligatory reference to many countries in the process of democratic transition. I do not understand why Spain does not apply to itself the same standards of justice that it demands of other countries."[7]

But it is the manner in which the Spanish experience so boldly flies in the face of the "transitional justice" movement that makes any investigation into the rise and consequences of Spain's politics of forgetting so compelling. Transitional justice refers not only to the measures undertaken during the period of democratization to bring accountability to the previous regime for its human rights abuses, but also, as seen next, to a set of normative theories about the importance of "coming to terms with the past" (see Kritz 1995; Ignatieff 1996; Rosenberg 1996; Crocker 1999; Tutu 1999; Teitel 2000; Boraine 2006). Due to this movement's influence—it has largely shaped an international consensus on the need for emerging democracies to confront their past—leaving the depravity of the old regime unpunished or unexamined is no longer an acceptable option for any respectable member of the international community.

Unsurprisingly, given the impunity embedded in the 1977 Pact of Forgetting and the 2007 Law of Historical Memory, Spain has been denounced in international forums as something of a transitional justice outlaw.[8] In 2002, the United Nations cited Spain as a state that has yet to properly address its past and urged the country to lift its amnesty law, arguing that it contravened state duties to prosecute, prevent, and punish human rights abuses. Major human rights organizations including Amnesty International, Human Rights Watch, and the International Commission of Jurists have criticized the 2007 Law of Historical Memory for failing to conform to international justice standards. In the view of these organizations, the shortcomings of the law, especially the persistence of legal protections against prosecutions, "prevent the truth from emerging and treat the victims of human rights abuses as passive elements."[9]

The Age of Transitional Justice

Although often thought of as a new phenomenon, transitional justice is as old as the rise of democracy in the modern world. During the French Revolution, an era of unprecedented democratic ferment, the newly declared Republican government agonized over the fate of King Louis XVI, before finding him guilty of "crimes against the people" and handing him the most gruesome of sentences: death at the guillotine. What is new about transitional justice is its emergence as the linchpin of a new morality in international politics, one that regards human rights as above domestic laws, customs, and conditions and respect for human rights around the world as a matter of concern for the international community as a whole. Such developments explain talks about the advent of "the age of transitional justice" (Philpott 2007: 2), sustained by an expansive "transitional justice industry" (Theidon 2009) led by human rights activists, leading political theorists and legal experts, multilateral organizations like the United Nations and the International Criminal Court (ICC), NGOs such as Human Rights Watch, Amnesty International, the International Commission of Jurists, and the American government, which under the George W Bush administration made justice against the Saddam Hussein regime a centerpiece of its democratization policy in Iraq.

More important, the rise of transitional justice has generated widespread claims about the advent of universal standards of justice and accountability for departing authoritarian regimes. Benhabib (2009: 695) notes that transitional justice exemplifies "the transition from *international* to *cosmopolitan* norms of justice." Whereas norms of international law "emerge through treaty obligations to which states and their representatives are signatories," cosmopolitan norms, according to Benhabib, "accrue to individuals considered as moral and legal persons in a worldwide civil society." In this way, "cosmopolitanism" self-limits or self-binds the sovereignty of states by obliging them to treat their citizens in accordance with human rights standards. This willingness of states to conform to the postulates of transitional justice is thought to take place in a variety of ways, but almost all of them emphasize the role of international norms and values in shaping domestic practices and behaviors.

While some scholars emphasize how the willingness of governments to sign international law treaties empowers domestic human rights stakeholders to press for accountability for outgoing authoritarian regimes (Simmons 2009), others emphasize the phenomenon of contagion in the international arena. Sikkink (2011) highlights a "cascade of justice" in international politics in the years since the end of the Cold War prodded along by countries copying one another and by multilateral institutions such as the ICC and ICTJ. Others highlight the international "diffusion" of human rights norms that takes place through "socialization," defined as "the crucial process through which a state becomes a member of the international society" (Risse and Sikkink 1999: 11). Socialization emerges "not in isolation but in relation to and in interaction with other groups of states and international non-state actors," and its goal is "for actors to internalize norms, so that external pressure is no longer needed to ensure compliance." Such external pressure includes "strategic bargaining," "moral consciousness-raising," and "shaming" (11–13). Key to the success of socialization is the work of "transnational action networks" that operate across national boundaries in creating and enforcing human rights norms and practices by linking international and domestic actors (Keck and Sikkink 1998).

There is, to be sure, no consensus within the heterogeneous transitional justice movement on what bringing accountability to an old political regime actually entails. But at least two very distinct models can be identified. These models represent the two intellectual wings that dominate the transitional justice movement: "retribution" and "reconciliation." Although often deemed polar opposites, both models make the case for coming to terms with the past as a democratization imperative, by linking retribution and reconciliation to such outcomes as helping to consolidate the rule of law, enhancing democratic values, bringing dignity to those victimized by political violence or repression, purging the body politic of the memory of political trauma, and preventing history from repeating itself. Failure to confront the past, out of political expediency or societal apathy, is presumed to lead to the emergence of a weak or flawed democracy, one unable to garner much support among the citizenry because of the impunity afforded to the old regime, and vulnerable to painful eruptions of memory that ensue from having repressed a past that was never properly examined and exorcised.

Retribution Versus Reconciliation

As the name itself implies, retribution promotes vigorous prosecution of the old regime. "Crimes against humanity" is usually the charge, which places the genesis of retribution in the landmark Nuremberg International Tribunal, the ad hoc court convened by the victorious Allies in 1945–1949 to prosecute former Nazi officials for the horrors of the Holocaust. At the conclusion of the trials, Nuremberg prosecutors were successful in obtaining verdicts that included the death penalty for 12 high-ranking Nazi officials, 10 of whom were hanged on gallows erected at the courthouse where the trials were held, and in putting on trial lesser actors such as doctors, lawyers, and industrialists affiliated with the Nazi regime. This achievement accounts for Nuremberg's reputation as having served "an important exemplary and jurisprudential function" for how nations should confront the misdeeds committed or sponsored by a prior regime (Judt 2002: 161), even as the legacy of the trials remains the subject of debate among historians (Rabkin 1999; Hirsch 2008; Rodden 2008).[10]

Foremost among the virtues linked to retribution is strengthening the rule of law by boosting the principle of equality under the law and due process for all parties in society since it demonstrates that no one is above the law. The absence of prosecution, by contrast, is thought to undermine the rule of law by perpetuating tolerance of a culture of impunity and disregard for human rights. Garton Ash (2002: 269) notes that "the fact that the torturers or the commanders go unpunished, even remain in office, compromises the new regime in the eyes of those who should be its strongest supporters." At a more practical level, making former despots pay for past political misdeeds is thought to serve as a deterrent against future human rights abuses. According to this view, trials not only enforce moral norms, they also drive home the point about the consequences of wrongdoing. This was a key rationale behind the staging of the Nuremberg trials in the first place. At the end of World War II, several British and American politicians, including Winston Churchill, favored swift execution of the main architects of the Nazi regime without due process. But as U.S. Secretary of War Henry Stimson, a strict legalist, observed in making the winning argument in favor of political trials over extrajudicial killings, "We should always have in mind the necessity of punishing effectively enough to bring home to the German people the wrongdoing done in their name, and thus prevent similar conduct in the future" (Cooper 2009: 92).

Prosecuting the previous regime is also seen as necessary for rooting democratic values in society and encouraging ordinary citizens to support these values. Behind this association of justice and democracy is the belief that dispensing justice against an old regime can act as a teaching moment capable of transforming public attitudes. According to Teitel (2000: 3), transitional justice contributes to the "defining feature" of democratic transitions by grounding within society "a normative shift in the principles underlying and legitimizing the exercise of state power." Accordingly, it is widely assumed by transitional justice proponents that "the better the transitional justice, in the sense of having more vigorous, morally engaged and pedagogically adequate trials, the better the democratizing outcome will be" (Pendas 2008: 58).

Reconciliation's chief concern is establishing an official record of the human rights abuses of the old regime rather than prosecuting that regime. South Africa's TRC is widely regarded as the paradigmatic example of reconciliation.[11] Because of the primacy accorded to truth-telling, reconciliation advocates have been known to support partial or full amnesty for members of the old regime, something generally regarded as anathema by retribution advocates. As noted by Benomar (1993: 5), "tactical and prudential considerations," such as whether new democracies can survive convicting and punishing the previous regime, generally underpin any decision to forgo prosecution. But the driving force of reconciliation resides in truth-telling itself, as a means to shift attention in the dispensing of justice against the old regime away from the perpetrators of human rights abuses and toward their victims, with trials often seen as too legalistic to adequately convey the suffering of the victims. Aukerman (2002: 71) contends that "while trials may have moments of high drama, their formalism and rigidity can also make them excruciatingly boring."

A desire for truth-telling also stems from the belief that only a complete accounting of the horrors of the past can bring about societal catharsis from the trauma inflicted by large-scale human rights abuses. "The truth will set you free" is a popular refrain among reconciliation advocates that features prominently in the work of transitional justice organizations. According to Boraine (2006: 20), "Documenting the truth about the past, restoring dignity to victims and embarking on the process of reconciliation are vital elements in the creation of a just society." The catharsis that the truth is meant to achieve is also generally seen as a precondition for forging ahead with the future, with that future usually a stand-in for democracy. Rosenberg (1996: xviii) has argued that "nations, like individuals, need to face up to and understand traumatic past events before they can put them aside and move on to a normal life."

Reconciliation is also animated by the idea that developing a consciousness about past abuses can prevent future abuses. Analyzing the importance of remembrance to the transitional justice movement, Garton Ash (1998: 35) notes that many scholars have made coming to terms with the horrors of the past a necessity for "redemption" for past wrongs and for avoiding "the recurrence of evil." Such arguments echo the post-Holocaust German concept of *Vergangenheitsbewältigung*, broadly understood to stand for "mastering" the past for the purpose of avoiding its reoccurrence (Maier 1988; Herf 1997; Langenbacher 2005). Analogous views are evident in Western political philosophy running from Greek philosophers (Plato in particular) to the Spanish-American philosopher George Santayana, who is credited with the popular aphorism "Those who cannot remember the past are condemned to repeat it."[12]

Last, but not least, reconciliation is premised on the view that justice is intrinsically intertwined with forgiveness, an assumption that draws from the Christian tradition and that has granted religion and reconciliation "an elective affinity" (Philpott 2007: 2). Indeed, for some, the use of religion in discussions of reconciliation represents one of the most overt displays of "public religion in the modern world" (Casanova 1994). According to South African archbishop Desmond Tutu (1999: 52), the TRC's charismatic chairman, "justice is being served when efforts are being made to work for healing, for forgiveness, and reconciliation." From this thinking emerged what has been termed "restorative justice," a victim-centered process of political reconciliation that aims to empower and restore the dignity of victims (Braithwhite 2002). It requires that human rights abusers assume responsibility for their misdeeds by offering the kind of apology that leads to a dialogue between the offender and the victim. In doing so, restorative justice brings "victim, perpetrator and community together to determine what is needed to put right what is wrong" (Nagy 2002: 325).

Whether they favor retribution or reconciliation, transitional justice advocates are in agreement that the transition to democracy is the most appropriate time for nations to confront a difficult and painful past. The core message from what has been termed "the transitional justice culture" is that "the moment of transition is the golden opportunity to forge a new, democratic social contract, and that the new democratic future envisaged by that contract will be possible, and will last, only by using the law to confront and overcome the repressive and abusive past" (Golob 2008: 127). This view is underpinned not only by the obvious symbolic importance of the transition to democracy as a marker of a new political destiny but also by the realization that the transition could well be the only opportunity for confronting the past. "It's now or never" is another ubiquitous phrase among transitional justice activists in making the case for attending to the past during the transition to democracy. Behind this popular claim is the worry that delaying or deferring justice can result in neglecting to confront the past by allowing other problems to crowd the political agenda (like fixing the economy or drafting a new constitution). There is also the fear that the passage of time can weaken societal resolve for justice by allowing time to claim the memory and lives of those most directly affected by the crimes of the old regime.

Transitional Justice and Its Critics

Both as a theory and as practice, transitional justice has invited a host of controversies. Among the most compelling critiques of transitional justice is the philosophical view that some crimes are so heinous and incomprehensible as to be beyond the capacity of the law to find ways to repair the damage they cause and/or to overcome the traumatic legacy they leave in their wake, an argument echoed in Hannah Arendt's eloquent contention in *The Human Condition* (1958: 214) that "we are unable to forgive what we cannot punish and we are unable to punish what has turned out to be unforgivable." Certainly, Arendt was not arguing against confronting evil deeds—far from it. Rather, she was warning about the limitations of man-made mechanisms to cope with such heinous crimes as genocide. As such, Arendt's views on prosecuting human rights abusers stand at odds with the perception of transitional justice as a transformative force capable of bringing closure about a difficult and painful past.

Most criticisms of transitional justice, however, are more precise and tend to focus on one of the two models above for coming to terms with the past. Arguably, the most noted criticism of retribution is the potential danger of morphing into revenge, which in turn can make transitional justice the source of conflict and recrimination rather than peace and reconciliation. For this reason, many advocates of criminal prosecution for human rights abusers support the principle of "selective prosecution" when deciding whom to go after for punishment for the old regime's crimes. Inaugurated with the Nuremberg Tribunal, and revived by the military trials in Argentina in the mid-1980s, selective prosecution aims at bringing justice to the individuals most directly responsible for the violence and abuses of the old regime (usually heads of state, high-level military officers, and directors of security and intelligence) rather than everyone involved in the repression of society.

Criticism of reconciliation has been more widespread, a reflection, perhaps, of the popularity of truth commissions. Some have decried the abrogation of justice entailed in the exchange of truth for amnesty that characterizes South Africa's TRC, while others have lamented the conflation of religion and politics injected into the process of reconciliation, another legacy of the TRC. Crocker (2000: 6) has noted that Archbishop Tutu's ideal of "social harmony" is not only "impractical" and "unrealistic" but also "morally objectionable," because no truth commission or any other government body should "force people to agree about the past, forgive the sins committed against them, or love one another" (6). In voicing these concerns, Crocker implicitly advocates for the right of those on whom irreparable moral harm has been inflicted to withhold forgiveness and perhaps even harbor bitterness and resentment toward their abusers.

A more general criticism of reconciliation is that it is a very poor substitute for justice. By and large, this criticism reflects the structural nature of truth commissions. These bodies are generally defined as much for what they do—to establish the "official" truth about specific historic events—as for what they do not do (see Rotberg and Thompson 2000; Rosenberg 1996; Hayner 2001). Truth commissions usually lack the power to punish or prosecute human rights abusers; they also are seldom empowered to implement whatever recommendations are issued in the final report. The extent to which recommendations for reforms and reparations made by a truth commission make it into law is usually left to the discretion of the politicians, who often have little incentive to see them implemented since this often entails significant political risks. All of this has led many to downgrade expectations about what truth commissions can actually accomplish. Ignatieff (1996: 112) writes that, at most, truth commissions can be expected "to reduce the number of lies that can be circulated unchallenged in public discourse."

Another criticism of reconciliation is whether the ambitious objective of creating a national narrative about the past that is supported by a broadly shared collective memory about historical events is of actual use to democracy. As observed by Müller (2002: 19), "In the end we may have to accept that contested, conflicting, and competing memories are an inevitable legacy of transitions to democracy. But that in itself might not be such a bad thing; after all, democracy itself is a form of contained conflict—and as long as memories remain contested, there will be no simple forgetting or repression *tout court*." Müller adds (19) that "rather than aiming for some elusive social consensus in which one narrative of the past is enthroned, arguing about the past within democratic parameters and on the basis of what has been called an 'economy of moral disagreement' might itself be a means of fostering social cohesion."

Truth commissions have also been criticized for the troubled conjoining of history and memory, as suggested most pointedly in the popular concept of "historical memory," which falsely implies that history and memory are always comfortably aligned. Those responsible for compiling the final report of a truth commission generally base their findings on personal testimony rather than on rigorous historical research. The former is prone to manipulation and politicization, and, in any case, is highly subjective and notoriously fallible. This privileging of personal testimony over actual historical fact-finding generally reflects the desire of truth commissions to serve as a vehicle for victims' voices to be heard and recorded for posterity. As argued by Jelin (2003: 54), articulating victims' voices is an essential part of the reconciliation process since it works against the image of those abused by the old regime as "passive victims." But for others, reliance of truth commissions on personal testimony poses the risk of memory replacing history, which in turn can lead to misrepresenting rather than representing the past. For Müller (2002: 19), "memory has turned into a secular religion, or at least an 'ersatz metaphysics,' which feeds on a new emotionalism, and gives rise to endless grievance claims couched in the language of personal memories." A "soft-therapeutic concept of memory," even a kind of "boundless mnemonic subjectivism," takes the place of "traditional, hard historical approaches and truths."

A harsher indictment of truth commissions is that an excessive emphasis on memorializing the past can effectively prevent countries from moving on. Augé (2004: 88) has theorized that humans, either as individuals or as a community, have a duty to remember as well as to forget: "Those who were subjected to it (a traumatic past), if they want to live again and not just survive, must be able to do their share of forgetting, become mindless, in the Pascalian sense, in order to find faith in the everyday again and mastery over their time." Analogizing remembering to gardening, Augé contends that memories are like plants: "there are those that need to be quickly eliminated in order to help others burgeon, transform, flower." In a similar vein, the political commentator David Rieff has decried the emergence in the transitional justice movement of a "memory fetish" that can create historical distortions that do little to bring about political reconciliation and can in fact help perpetuate discord and war, while praising the capacity of forgetting for allowing countries to move forward.[13]

A different type of critique of transitional justice comes from within the movement itself and calls attention to zero-sum arguments in which retribution is seen as preferable to reconciliation and vice versa, by arguing that no single model of transitional justice can deliver a successful coming to terms with the past; that this can only be secured through a combination of things. The ICTJ advocates a "holistic approach" to transitional justice, a proposal that incorporates not only criminal prosecution of the leaders of the old regime and a truth and reconciliation commission, but also reparation for the victims of human rights abuses, reformation of state institutions, such as the courts, the police, and the security apparatus, the erection of museums and memorials intended to "preserve public memory of victims and raise moral consciousness about the past abuse," and even "gender justice," defined as challenging "impunity for sexual-and gender-based violence" to ensure "women's equal access to readdress of human rights violations."[14]

A Case That Challenges the Rules

Spain, a case of almost complete noncompliance with transitional justice, significantly expands on the critique of transitional justice laid out already by highlighting several important challenges that so far have gone largely unnoticed. First among these is the assumption that coming to terms with the past, through retribution and/or reconciliation, is a prerequisite or precondition for successful democratization. This claim is implicitly stated in the bleak scenarios that have been painted for nations that neglect to dispense justice for the old regime—from undermining the consolidation of the rule of law by perpetuating a culture of impunity, to preventing society from moving forward, haunted by the memories of unaddressed collective traumas, to, worst of all, inviting the recurrence of evil. But there is little in the Spanish experience to support these contentions.

The de facto impunity institutionalized in Spain with the Pact of Forgetting has led some to criticize Spanish democracy for its "impure genesis" (Cardús i Ros 2000: 19), and to link the rise of the politics of forgetting to some of the most unsavory aspects of post-Francoist politics—like a penchant for secret bargaining among the political class, corruption of public officials, militarization of the police force, and even breaches of the rule of law, such as the creation of the Grupos Antiterroristas de Liberación (better known as GAL), the extrajudicial military force that battled Basque separatists during the 1980s (see Ballbé 1983; Buck 1998; Amnesty International 1985). But these claims do not detract from the overwhelming success of democracy in the post-Francoist era. Paradoxically, Spain is one of the most (if not the most) celebrated cases of democratic transition of recent times, with the case becoming something of an obligatory point of reference for democratization scholars. "Spain is a miracle," marvels Przeworski (1991: 8), while positing Spain as a model for Latin America and post-communist Europe. Linz and Stepan (1996: 5) note that Spain is the paradigmatic example of "democratic consolidation," understood to mean that juncture in politics when democracy becomes "the only game in town," just as interwar Germany can be regarded as the paradigmatic example of "democratic breakdown."

A second challenge to the transitional justice orthodoxy afforded by the case of Spain is the apparent but seldom recognized compatibility between forgetting and democratization. While the transitional justice scholarship sees forgetting as undermining democratization, the Spanish case suggests the very opposite. Interestingly enough, for much of the scholarship on contemporary Spanish politics, democracy consolidated in Spain not in spite of the fact that the past was put aside during the transition but rather because of it (see Share 1986; Di Palma 1990; Gunther 1992; Linz and Stepan 1996; Gunther, Montero, and Botella 2004; Gunther 2007; Encarnación 2008a). The decision not to delve into the past is credited with minimizing political uncertainly about the outcome of the democratic transition, helping integrate the political class around the project of democratic consolidation, especially those forces most likely to disrupt democratization, such as the military, and ending a vicious cycle of hate and recrimination that for centuries had kept stable democracy at bay. These positive by-products of the pact to forget suggest that forgetting and moving on can actually serve as a foundation for democratization.

Third, the Spanish experience pointedly questions the assumption that a legal or ethical treatment of the past during the transition to democracy is always possible and in the best interest of the process of democratization. Instead, Spain suggests that in some cases a political solution that abridges, circumvents, and delays justice against the old regime might be preferable. This hard truth gets us to the question of why forgetting flourished in Spain in the first place. In Spain, the question about what to do about the past was approached not as an ethical or legal challenge, as the transitional justice movement is prone to do, but rather as a political dilemma. This entailed doing what was possible rather than what was right. As seen next, conditions on the ground dictated this overtly political calculation, especially a sociopolitical environment that provided no room for questions about the past to emerge. On the one hand was societal resistance to any revisiting of the past; on the other was the political dynamics and legacy of a state-led democratic transition.

The Traumatic Past

The most popular explanations for the rise of forgetting in Spain all relate to how the traumas of the past affected the political mindset of the Spanish political elite and society at large around the time of the democratic transition. The best known among these "psycho-political" explanations is the theory of *memoria traumática* (traumatic memory), which stresses that during the transition the Spaniards willed themselves into political amnesia as a direct consequence of the collective traumas inflicted by the Civil War and the postwar period. In essence, this Freudian-inspired theory analogizes Spain to an individual afflicted with a severe case of Post-Traumatic Stress Disorder (PTSD), a condition whose symptoms include reexperiencing the original traumas through flashbacks or nightmares, and avoiding situations or potential situations associated with traumatic past events for fear that they may reoccur. Reams of studies in the Spanish psychological literature support the PTSD diagnosis (Ruiz-Vargas 2002; González Duro; 2003; Mínguez Villar 2004). A comprehensive review of this literature concludes that "the brutal repression imposed upon the losers of the Civil War not only impeded the possibility of overcoming the traumas of the war, it also added an abusive burden of suffering. The politics of terror and silence imposed by the dictatorship created an environment that engendered a veritable epidemic of post-traumatic stress" (Ruiz-Vargas 2006: 1).

Fears about repeating the past, specifically falling back into civil war and dictatorship, were induced not only by the memory of the past but also by how the past had been manipulated by the Franco regime. According to Aguilar (2002: 25), "Francoism instilled a ferocious, obsessive, and omnipresent fear of any repetition of the Civil War," from which arose a national consensus on *nunca más* (never again), a phrase meant to convey that Spain would go to any length to avoid becoming embroiled in a similar conflict. A corollary of the *nunca más* discourse promoted by the Franco regime was the deliberate association of democracy with anarchy and divisiveness and of dictatorship with peace and prosperity. The intention was to legitimize Franco's contention of having saved Spain from chaos and destruction, a founding myth of the dictatorship, while planting doubts in the public's mind about the country's capacity to comport itself under democracy.

Further exacerbating fears about repeating the past was the political violence surrounding the transition. Although the Spanish transition is remembered for a proliferation of elite pacts, like the pact to forget, political violence was quite characteristic of the era. In fact, Spain witnessed more acts of political violence and terror during the transition to democracy than any other nation in Southern Europe or South America, including "revolutionary" Portugal. Especially notable in affecting the collective psyche of the Spanish public was a wave of political assassinations—more than 200 between 1979–1980, most of them perpetrated by Euskadi Ta Askatasuna (ETA, the armed branch of the Basque separatist movement), which eerily resembled the one that preceded the advent of the Civil War. Understandably, as will be seen later, public opinion in Spain for much of the post-transition period suggests that the public has been more concerned with order and stability than with justice and accountability, and regarded the latter as a threat to the former.

Another popular psychopolitical explanation for forgetting revolves around how the general public constructed its memory of the Civil War and its consequences and how this "collective memory" worked to dissuade confronting the past and actually actively encourage a culture of political forgetfulness. A central feature of the public memory of the Civil War during the transition to democracy was the notion of "collective culpability," which argued, in a nutshell, that both sides of the conflict were equally guilty.

Aguilar (2002) has compellingly argued that while at the inception of democracy Spaniards could not agree on the causes of the Civil War, they shared an understanding of the war as a national tragedy, and more specifically as a *guerra fraticida* (fratricidal war), a conflict between brothers that had torn the nation apart and for which everyone bore equal blame. This problematic view of the Civil War—it overlooks Franco's violent military coup in 1936 and the fact that the Nationalist side committed the bulk of the killings, to say nothing of the postwar repression imposed by Franco—made revisiting the Civil War during the transition seem redundant and even counterproductive.

The notion of collective culpability was given considerable credibility after it was embraced by the democratic opposition to the Franco regime to justify its acceptance of the politics of forgetting. Around the time of the transition, leading left-wing leaders promoted the idea that the Civil War was best understood not as a result of Franco's assault on a popularly elected government or of the ideological struggles of the era, but rather as *un error histórico* (a historical error) that grew from an act of collective madness that produced no winners or losers, only victims. As seen later, although the left nowadays no longer subscribes to the idea of collective culpability—in fact, it generally deems it a myth—the idea remains central to the opposition of many Spaniards, especially but not exclusively those of a right-wing persuasion, to any revisiting of the past, including a truth commission.

Yet another psychopolitical school of thought regards forgetting as a necessity for moving forward, and more concretely as an imperative for constructing a *tabula rasa* on which to build a democratic future. This argument, which applies most directly to the behavior of the political class during the transition, echoes what Nietzsche (1983: 62) referred to as "active forgetting," which he defined not as a simple failure of memory but rather as a concerted effort to repress the memory of selective events from the past in order to envision possible futures. More specifically, for Nietzsche (61), active forgetting entailed purging the mind of those traumatic events that are likely to "return like a ghost and disturb the calm of a later moment." Santos Juliá—Spain's leading intellectual historian, who has vigorously defended the decision of the political elites to set the past aside during the transition against the criticism that this amounted to an act of wanton disregard for history and truth-telling—is most closely associated with this line of thinking.

According to Juliá (2003), forging a democratic project in Spain hinged on the capacity of the political class to *echar el pasado al olvido* (cast the past into oblivion) by enacting the 1977 amnesty law. Yet this action did not mean the politicians were condemning Spain to political amnesia. Amnesia, Juliá argues, implies involuntary loss of memory; amnesty indicates a decision to forget the past, arrived at after deliberate consideration of that past. Therefore, in defending forgetting Juliá has characterized as "grotesque" the idea that in the post-transition period Spain has lived under "a pact of silence" and that the history of the Civil War and the Franco dictatorship has been turned into a taboo.[15] Juliá has also criticized memory activists, such as the Association for the Recuperation of the Historical Memory, for failing to recognize that even before the transition all the political forces had come to the realization that a general amnesty was indispensable for getting democracy off the ground, and for failing to appreciate that amnesty was essential for creating the democracy that today allows society to press demands for remembering the past.[16]

Last but not least is the provocative notion that political forgetting in Spain is rooted in the country, especially the political elite, having emerged from dictatorship with pointed lessons about past political mistakes and ready to apply these lessons to the present. This view draws heavily upon the theory of "political learning," which sustains that "all people, followers and leaders alike, are capable of learning from experience, and political actors rarely weather economic depressions, internal wars, or the violent collapse of a form of government unchanged" (Bermeo 1992: 274). The most talked-about lesson that the politicians drew from history as they undertook to democratize Spain in 1977 was that too much bickering and too little compromising aborted the previous attempt at democratization during the interwar Second Republic. Thus, a pact to forget was embraced by both left and right as an insurance policy against a similar outcome. According to García Cárcel, the agreement to "disremember recent history," embodied an agreement of "prudence" and "auto-controls" about the perils of looking backwards arising from an obsession with "historical failure."[17]

A less self-evident historical lesson was that Spain had indulged in revenge and retaliation in handling the sins of the old regime in previous instances of regime transition. Therefore, when confronted with the conundrum of what to do about Franco's political crimes, an effort was made to correct past excesses of transitional justice. It is notable, as Aguilar (2001: 98) points out, that the democracy established in 1977 is the only political regime in the twentieth century in Spain "that has not called prior regime leaders to account." The Second Republic held the leaders of the Primo de Rivera dictatorship

(1923–1930) accountable, as did Franco, with the leadership of the Republic, and as did General Miguel Primo de Rivera's regime with the Restoration regime (1874–1931). Especially notable is the retribution policy implemented by the Republicans in 1931, which ended both the Restoration period and the Primo de Rivera dictatorship. The Republicans denied amnesty to the leaders of the Primo de Rivera dictatorship, forced the abdication of King Alfonso XIII, charged him with high treason, and created a commission to establish political responsibilities (as a prelude to future trials) that even some Republicans criticized as "too harsh" (Payne 1993: 40–42).

Not surprisingly, the psychopolitical explanations highlighted above are suggestively echoed, whether directly or indirectly, by the rationalizations offered by the politicians for their decision to forgo justice toward the Franco regime. Virtually all the major political figures of the transition stressed the need to avoid *abrir viejas heridas* (opening old wounds), a surgical metaphor intended to convey both the pain and the danger of engaging in any revising of the past and the benefit of forgetting and moving on in securing both democracy and peace. No other occasion proved itself more adequate for making these justifications than the parliamentary debate that led to the enacting of the 1977 amnesty law, the legal-institutional backbone of the Pact of Forgetting. Politicians of every political stripe made the point that forgetting was the only way to break the cycle of violence, war, and recrimination that for centuries had defined Spanish politics and to consolidate peace. One of the most moving speeches was that of labor leader Marcelino Camacho, who, speaking on behalf of the Spanish Communist Party, observed (Aguilar 2002: 196):

> How could those of us who had been killing each other have made the peace if we had not erased the past once and for all? For us, in the same way as in the settlement of the injustices committed over these forty years of dictatorship, amnesty is a national and democratic policy, the sole measure which might close that chapter of civil wars and crusades. We, that is to say, the Communists, who have suffered so many outrages, have buried our dead and our resentments.

Nor it is surprising that the politicians' justifications for overturning the Pact of Forgetting in 2007 were couched in terms of the nation having finally overcome the traumas of the past due to thirty years of peaceful democratic co-existence. As Carlos García de Andoin, federal coordinator of the

Roman Catholic wing of the Spanish Socialist Party, noted before the vote that enacted the 2007 Law of Historical Memory, "During the transition remembering the past meant re-opening divisions that we were not ready to deal with. The era was delicate and we needed to concentrate on reconciliation and leaving the past behind. Thirty years later things are very different, remembering no longer threatens the stability of the democratic system."[18]

Those who today champion a more truthful and ethical treatment of the past have expressed similar sentiments. Carlos Castresana, the lead prosecutor in the Pinochet case, and today an internationally renowned human rights lawyer, noted around the time of the parliamentary debate about the Law of Historical Memory:[19]

> The years of democratic transition were spent in a permanent state of anguished necessity of having to choose the least bad of bad options, which culminated in the untruthful process that gave us back our freedom. But is has been a while since that situation of emergency has been overcome. The prosperous democracy of today is sufficiently mature to handle the truth, in spite of those who deny this with their words and deeds. Our silence today is no longer mandatory, as it was during the transition. The truth about the past is the compensation that we owe those who made the miracle of our transition possible with the sacrifice of their silence.

The Nature of the Transition

A second driving force behind the rise of forgetting in Spain was the nature of the transition, a far less studied factor and arguably a more compelling one than the traumatic past. For one thing, psychoanalytical explanations derived from the traumatic past cannot explain why, after fears about the past had vanished from the public consciousness with the consolidation of democracy by the early 1980s, both the government and the general public remained firmly wedded to forgetting. Ironically, the heady days of forgetting came not when public opinion showed Spaniards to be most fearful about the future (the earliest years of democratic transition, between Franco's death in 1975 and the enactment of a new democratic constitution in 1978), but during the long reign of the Spanish Socialist Party during the

1980s and 1990s, when unprecedented political stability and economic prosperity prevailed.

Several aspects of the democratic transition of great consequence to how matters about the past were handled in Spain are highlighted in this study, the first being the limitations on political justice imposed by a transition to democracy born in the very structures of the authoritarian regime. Unlike other transitions to democracy that preceded it in Southern Europe (Greece and Portugal), and subsequent ones in Latin America and the post-communist world, the authoritarian regime in Spain was not defeated or humiliated in a foreign war, toppled from power by its foes in civil society, or brought to its knees by economic failure or external pressure. Instead, Spain's authoritarian regime was gradually transformed into a democracy from the inside out by reformers operating within the authoritarian government, including, ironically enough, Franco's hand-picked successor, King Juan Carlos, and relying on the authoritarian regime's own legal and political institutions, many of which survived the transition to democracy virtually intact (see Carr and Fusi 1981; Maravall 1981; Malefakis 1982; Gunther 1992).

The ramifications of the democratic self-reformation of the authoritarian regime for the disposition of the past after Franco's passing were significant. Implicit in the left's acceptance of a democratic transition orchestrated by the authoritarian regime and assisted by existing legal and political frameworks was willingness to forgo retribution against the old regime. This exchange of "amnesty for democracy" was introduced with the 1976 Law of Political Reform, enacted by the Francoist parliament (without representation from the opposition), which simultaneously ended the authoritarian regime and put the country on the path toward democracy by legalizing political parties and independent trade unions and scheduling free elections, Spain's first in four decades. Predictably, the law had nothing to say on the issue of political justice against the old regime. Amnesty for the old regime was institutionalized with a law by the new democratic parliament in 1977. The timing of this law in Spain is significant because, unlike other cases, it meant that amnesty was enacted not by the outgoing authoritarian regime but by its democratic successor.

A second focus of our analysis is the ethos of political consensus that permeated the transition to democracy and that accounts for Spain's reputation as the paradigmatic example of a "pacted," "brokered," and "negotiated" transition (Share 1986; Linz and Stepan 1996; Gunther 2007; Encarnación 2008a). Numerous factors underscored elite consensus during the transition, starting with the urgent need for intra-elite collaboration in order to confront all the intractable problems that over the course of centuries had made democracy an uphill struggle—from finding a constitutional role for the monarchy, to meeting the Catholic Church's demands for some kind of public function in the polity, to accommodating demands for self-governance from nationalist-separatist regions. The latter was especially taxing; after all, granting limited autonomy to the Basques and Catalans was a leading cause behind Franco's uprising against the Second Republic in 1936, by projecting the sense that Spain was coming apart at the seams. Regional autonomy was even more explosive an issue during and after the democratic transition since Franco's repression of Spanish ethnic minorities had engendered a separatist, terrorist movement in the Basque Country anchored around ETA that was determined to engage the state in a prolonged armed conflict with the goal of establishing an independent Basque state.

But the main inducement for consensus may well have been the desire of the political class to make the democratic transition an unambiguous marker between "old" and "new" Spain, with the old representing anything associated with pre-transition Spain and the new focused on democracy and Europe. This desire for remaking Spanish political identity was most intense within the left, which explains why the politics of forgetting flourished not during the transition during the late 1970s (when Spain was ruled by a center-right government led by former Francoist leaders who had every reason to fear any process of transitional justice), but rather under socialist rule during the 1980s and 1990s. During those years, the socialist administration endeavored to reimagine Spain as a modern, forward-looking European nation. The pact to forget aided this dual project of modernization and Europeanization by obscuring the things that for decades had set Spain apart from the rest of Europe, especially the Civil War and the Franco dictatorship, and by encouraging a forward-looking culture that did not appreciate remembrances of the past, especially things in Spanish history—like the Civil War and the Franco dictatorship—that stood in the way of Spaniards' perception of themselves as Europeans.

The Organization of the Study

The rest of this book is organized as follows. Chapter 1 provides an overview of the Pact of Forgetting that stresses what the pact stood for, how it was made to operate, and what historical events it sought to obscure from the public memory. Chapter 2 revisits the years of democratic transition (1975–1981) for the purpose of illustrating how the transition to democracy conditioned the rise of the Pact of Forgetting by limiting the capacity of the democratic opposition to make justice demands against the old regime and by enhancing the ethos of consensus born with the transition. Chapter 3 examines the endurance of the Pact of Forgetting under the socialist administration of Prime Minister Felipe González (1982–1996), which implemented the policy of *desmemoria* (disremembering) to modernize political institutions and reinvent national identity.

Chapter 4 looks at the puzzling absence of civil society opposition to the rise of the Pact of Forgetting throughout the transition and consolidation of the new democratic regime, a discussion that emphasizes both societal complicity with the political class and the legacy of the transition. Chapter 5 explores the birth of the movement for the recuperation of the historical memory, an unintended consequence of General Pinochet's arrest in London in 1998 on orders from Spain. Chapter 6 discusses the enactment of the 2007 Law of Historical Memory, a dramatic reversal of a three-decade-old commitment to forgetting the past led by a new generation of left-wing leaders not politically socialized in the struggle against Francoism and not beholden to the political compromises of the democratic transition.

Chapter 7 mines the Spanish experience with coping with the past, together with comparative evidence from other democratizing states in Latin America and post-communist Europe, for lessons about scholarly debates on transitional justice and democratization. Much of the discussion emphasizes the need to adopt a more nuanced and pragmatic understanding about justice in times of transition. For all its virtues, and there are many, transitional justice is not the panacea for democratization many of its advocates make it to be—in some cases alternative approaches or a mixture of approaches might in the end yield better results. Transitions to democracy come in many forms, some more compatible with transitional justice than others, and they leave in their wake different configurations in the balance of power of the new regime and divergent stocks of residual authoritarian power profoundly affecting what is possible with respect to the political excesses of the old regime; to say nothing of the fact that public attitudes about an anguished past can vary dramatically from country to country.

CHAPTER 1

History, Politics, and Forgetting in Spain

Spain's Pact of Forgetting conforms to the definition of a "political pact" offered by the democratization literature as "an explicit, but not always explicated or justified, agreement among a select set of actors which seeks to define (or better redefine) rules governing the exercise of power on the basis of mutual guarantees for the vital interest of those entering into it" (O'Donnell and Schmitter 1986: 37). As such, political pacts bring together a small number of elite actors for the purpose of settling issues that bring them into conflict with one another. Traditionally, the making of political pacts in the context of democratization has been done behind closed doors, with nary an opportunity for the general public to weigh in on the decisions being negotiated on their behalf by the political elite (see Encarnación 2005). This unappealing aspect of political pact-making can lead to important decisions about the emerging democratic regime being made before a single free vote has been cast. Not surprisingly, political pacts have been linked to a host of negative and unintended consequences for democratization, from marginalizing civil society groups, such as the labor movement (Karl 1987), to allowing for the transfer of authoritarian vices into the new democratic regime (Hagopian 1992), to promoting corporatist, exclusionary and even undemocratic modes of policy-making (Przeworski 1991).

Yet Spain's Pact of Forgetting is unique. Unlike most political pacts negotiated during a democratic transition—including Spain's own Moncloa pacts, the landmark set of accords that committed the government, the national parties, and elements in civil society such as the labor movement and employers' groups, to collaborate in the making of economic policy—the Pact of Forgetting was never formalized and publicly discussed. No text was ever drafted by those entering into the pact, and no mechanisms were ever stipulated to facilitate its enforcement, including penalties for those choosing not to obey the pact or to walk away from it. Therefore, notwithstanding some legal underpinnings such as the 1977 amnesty law, the Pact of Forgetting is best regarded as an "informal institution," understood as norms that regulate political conduct (Helmke and Letvisky 2006). More tenuous than formal institutions, informal institutions nonetheless create considerable predictability in the behavior of political actors.

At the heart of the Pact of Forgetting was not forgetting per se (such a goal would have been unattainable under almost any circumstances), but rather a desire by the political class to prevent the memory of certain historical events from encumbering the transition to a new democratic regime. In the wake of Franco's death in 1975, this objective was to be achieved, first, by not holding anyone accountable for any political crime committed prior to the transition to democracy. This is the most formal (and controversial) part of the pact since it was backed by a comprehensive amnesty process that offered immunity from prosecution to anyone associated with the authoritarian regime and elements within civil society that opposed the authoritarian regime. Another component of the pact committed the government and its opposition to refrain from pursuing public policies that would awaken longstanding historical controversies, such as who bore ultimate responsibility for the Civil War: the Nationalists or the Republicans.

Another component of the pact was not to use the past as a weapon in political deliberations by committing political actors to treading carefully in situations that could be politically divisive, such as the observation of an important historical anniversary like the start of the Civil War. Making an issue of anyone's past political affiliations (such as attempting to disqualify someone from participating in the politics of the new democracy because of having belonged to a political organization deemed offensive to democratic sensibilities) was also implicit. Former members of the old regime have benefited the most from this provision, since they have been allowed to participate in democratic politics without having their Francoist past thrown back at them. But the provision has also been useful to the left by obscuring the radical background of many leftwing leaders.

More generally, the Pact of Forgetting aimed at arriving at something of a consensus about Spanish history, especially the Civil War. Although the memory of the Civil War remained polarized, for the main actors of the democratic transition the conflict came to be understood as a *guerra de locos* (war of collective madness) that produced no winners and losers, only victims. In this problematic formulation, both sides bore equal responsibility for the Civil War, which made it redundant to ascribe blame to any particular group in society. The important thing was to ensure that a similar conflict would never happen again, and the best way to achieve that result was to forget and to look to the future. Building a consensus about the past also entailed recognizing that partisan bickering rested deeply in Spain's past democratic failures and that keeping disagreement to a minimum was the best way to ensure a stable democratic regime. In the democratic period, this consensus about the Civil War was embraced by the entire political class save for extremist elements, such as ETA, for whom the memory of the Civil War became a tool to rationalize its continuing use of political violence against the Spanish state. ETA's "war memory," according to Muro (2009: 667), was anchored upon the brutality of the Franco regime against the Basques but also on notable historical distortions, such as the view that "the Basques had suffered a bloody war that did not concern them."

To be sure, there was less of a historical consensus among those agreeing to the terms of the pact to forget about the Franco dictatorship. Unlike the Civil War, the dictatorship had a clear oppressor (the right) and a clear victim (the left). As observed by Humlebaek (2005: 78), "while the pact of silence with regard to the Civil War was based on equilibrium between the parties, since both sides had taken part in the atrocities of the war, the pact was not characterized by the same harmony insofar as it concerned the Franco regime." This reality made the Pact of Forgetting inherently fragile and vulnerable to a defection from the left, as was eventually the case. It also explains how the pact itself would be characterized during the years of forgetting. While those on the left have been more prone to refer to the Pact of Forgetting as a "pact of silence," a necessary evil induced by the traumas of the past and the exigencies of the transition, those on the right have been more inclined to refer to the pact as "a pact of reconciliation" intended to prevent repetition of past political mistakes.

None of what the Pact of Forgetting stood for, however, entailed official censorship or restrictions on intellectual inquiry into the Civil War or the Franco dictatorship by the general public, journalists, and academics; in fact, such inquiry has actually thrived in the post-transition years, a point readily conceded by academics, even those whose works have a liberal bent.[1] In stressing the point that the Pact of Forgetting has not entailed censorship, Juliá (1999a: 117) has observed that cultural policy in post-Franco Spain has been "unhampered by ideological compromise" and that historians have been able "to delve into the past as they saw fit." Valls (2007: 156) writes that after the democratic transition "historians were able to investigate the Civil War and the Franco dictatorship freely, and publications on both periods grew in number and established numerous factual and interpretative approaches that are accepted today by the vast majority of the professional community of historians in Spain." Boyd (2008: 135), noting the surge in interest in the Civil War since Franco's passing, estimates that by 1986 the bibliography of the Civil War in Spanish included some 15,000 titles.

Forgotten: Democratic Collapse, Civil War, and Dictatorship

As far as the political class was concerned, the Pact of Forgetting relegated to the dustbin of history some of the most tumultuous happenings of twentieth-century Spanish history, beginning with the traumatic collapse of democracy during the interwar years. Franco's Nationalist uprising of July 18, 1936, triggered the fall of the Second Republic, a legally constituted democratic government widely considered to be Spain's first real experience with democracy. Unabashedly liberal policies—such as abolishment of the death penalty, civil marriage and divorce, suffrage for females, secularization of schools and cemeteries, and home rule for Spain's national ethnic minority communities—explain the Second Republic's reputation for political radicalism among its detractors and for political progressivism among its defenders. The liberalism for which the Second Republic is famous mirrored the political orientation of its founding fathers, which, according to Crow (1985: 292), were "as heterogeneous a mixture as has ever appeared in the pages of European history," incorporating "intellectuals, liberals of various shades and colorings, some of whom were Catholics but most of them were not, Catalan and Basque separatists to whom the Republic meant local autonomy, and the Spanish left composed of the anarchists, the socialists, and the communists."

A prolonged and bloody civil conflict rather than a successful takeover was the result of Franco's attack on the Second Republic. On the Nationalist side were the constituencies most vigorously opposed to the policies of the Republican government: the military, rural oligarchs, industrialists, the Catholic Church, and an assortment of right-wing organizations, including the Falange (Phalanx), a fascist organization whose motto, "One, Great, and

Free," and "strong Catholic sentiment" suited Franco "admirably" (Crow 1985: 348), and the Carlists, defenders of the Spanish monarchy. Popular organizations, such as the socialist Unión General de Trabajadores (UGT), the anarchist Confederación Nacional del Trabajo (CNT), and the communist Partido Obrero de Unificación Marxista (POUM) were the face of the Republican resistance. The left-wing orientation of these organizations permitted Franco to frame the Civil War as a Christian crusade to save Spain from the godless Republicans, a struggle not unlike the holy battle for the soul of Spain that medieval Christian monarchs waged against Muslim infidels. In this second crusade, "the enemy was not Islam but a hydra of social and political revolution that had flourished with the Republic" (Grugel and Rees 1997: 11).

While at war in 1936–1939, Nationalists and Republicans fought with complete conviction in the righteousness of their respective causes, which explains the Civil War's reputation as the quintessential conflict between freedom and fascism. By the time of Franco's coup, the political center had disappeared, and politics had been reduced to a zero-sum game dominated by political groups at opposite ends of the ideological spectrum.[2] Under the last government of the Second Republic, the Popular Front (elected into office in 1936 and headed by labor leader Largo Caballero), Spain took a decisive turn toward the extreme left, backed by a "workers' alliance" embracing socialist, communist, and anarchist unions. The opposition, the National Front, a coalition of right-wing parties led by the Confederación Española de Derechas Autónomas (CEDA), a fascist-leaning party, represented its own kind of political extremism. Unsurprisingly, an intense ideological battle fueled the violence of the Civil War. As Crozier (1967: 216) put it, "The revolutionaries massacred the bourgeoisie because this, as they saw it, was their mystical and exalted class duty. The counter-revolutionaries killed because the 'Marxists' whose death they ordained represented the 'anti-Spain'."

Franco declared victory over the Republican army on April 1, 1939, and soon thereafter all hostilities came to a halt. Aiding in the Nationalist victory was a significant military advantage: the most experienced troops in the Spanish army were those under Franco's command. These troops, made up of many lower-echelon and young military officers, began to defect en masse to the Nationalist side as soon as the war started. The Republicans also made many tactical errors, and none more prominent than the decision to concentrate on a socio-economic revolution rather than on developing a strategy to defeat Franco and his army of rebels. At the inception of the Civil

War, the CNT and UGT devoted much of their energies to collectivizing industry and farmland while ignoring the military conflict. Despite dealing a big blow to urban capitalists and the oligarchs, the socioeconomic revolution left the Republican side ill-prepared to defend itself against Franco.[3] As noted by Payne (1985: 15): "What was left of the Spanish army in the Republican zone was largely disbanded in favor of leftist militia battalions that were full of revolutionary zeal and reasonably well-equipped but lack discipline, leadership, and military skill."

The Civil War's international dimensions also favored a Nationalist victory. Sympathetic foreign leaders such as Hitler and Mussolini supported Franco's uprising from the start of the Civil War by providing the military weapons (aircraft in particular) and expertise that proved critical to crushing the Republicans. Britain, France, and the United States, despite "the intense degree of psycho-emotional solidarity with the struggle of the Spanish left" on the part of hundreds of thousands of French, British and American citizens, decided to sit out the war in Spain fearing that their involvement would trigger a European-wide conflict (Payne 1970: 275).[4] Such fears left the International Brigades, the foreign, volunteer army that gathered in Spain to fight Franco, which organized some 40,000 soldiers, including 2,800 members of the American Lincoln Brigade, as the main source of foreign support for the Republicans (Richardson 1976: 11). Abandoned by its fellow democracies, the Second Republic turned to the Soviet Union for help in the form of aircraft, tanks, and political and military advice.[5] But this assistance in the end proved incapable of overcoming Franco's rebellion.

The Human Toll of the War

How many people perished during the Civil War remains highly debated among historians, and it may well be the case, as noted by Richards (1996: 157), that "we will never know the true figure." One million is the popularly accepted figure in Spain since it was adopted, for very different reasons, by both the Franco regime and its opposition. For Franco, the figure of one million dead underscored his claim of having saved Spain from bloodshed, chaos, and destruction. For the opposition, it highlighted the grotesquely violent nature of the Franco dictatorship. Historians of the Civil War, however, have questioned the veracity of the figure. Arguably, the most respected accounting comes from Jackson (1965: 539), in no small part because it comes

Table 1. The Spanish Civil War in Comparative Perspective

Country	*Outcome*	*Winners' coalition*	*Losers' strategies*	*Casualties*
Ireland (1922–23)	Democracy	Divided	Moderation	800–3,000
Finland (1918)	Democracy	Divided	Moderation	30,000
Greece (1943–50)	Hybrid	Divided	Little Moderation	60,000
Hungary (1919)	Hybrid	Unified	Moderation	5,000
Spain (1936–39)	Authoritarianism	Unified	Little Moderation	500,000+

Source: Kissane and Sitter (2005: 186–88, 196).

from a foreigner. This study puts the total number of the Civil War dead at 580,000. But even this greatly reduced figure, as seen in Table 1, makes the Spanish Civil War the deadliest by far of all European civil conflicts of the interwar era. Jackson (1965: 539) estimates that between 1939 and 1943 100,000 Spaniards were killed in direct combat, 10,000 in air raids, 50,000 from disease and malnutrition, 20,000 from Republican "reprisals," 200,000 from Nationalist "reprisals," and 200,000 "red" prisoner deaths resulting from execution and disease.

Republican violence targeted the sectors of society that sided with the coup's plotters: the business community, landed oligarchs, and clergy. Of these targets, the clergy are probably most closely associated with Republican violence, given the deep-seated anti-Catholicism of the Republican leadership. "Spain is no longer a Catholic country, even though there are many millions of Spanish Catholics," declared Manuel Azaña, the Second Republic's first prime minister, as he launched an unprecedented attack on the church that ended state financial support for the clergy and nationalized the church's vast property holdings (Amodia 1976: 11). The estimated number of clergy murdered by the Republicans, however, remains in dispute. After the end of the Civil War, the Nationalist side claimed that 7,937 religious persons were killed out of a total community of around 115,000, but this figure is probably inflated.[6] That noted, there is little doubt that "wanton cruelty" was imposed on the clergy, with some reports stating that some priests were "burned to death in their churches" while others were "buried alive after being made to dig their own graves" (Beevor 1982: 70).

Nationalist violence is considered to have been more indiscriminate than the "red terror" imposed by the Republicans (Balcells 2007: 5). Obtaining control of Republican strongholds or areas of the country thought to have been infiltrated by "reds" often involved air raids intended to eradicate entire villages and towns as a prelude to a Nationalist occupation. Territories "conquered" by the Nationalists were also often subjected to *limpiezas* (cleansings) designed to "flush out internal enemies," and frighten the civilian population from aiding the Republican resistance (Vincent 2007: 151). The "cleansings" often degenerated into orgies of killing and abuse, involving raping women. General Gonzalo Queipo de Llano, Franco's main propagandist during the Civil War, famously urged his troops to rape Republican women, a fact that helps explain a common piece of graffiti that appeared in towns and villages conquered by the Nationalist rebels: "Your women will give birth to fascists" (Treglown 2009: 21). Ironically, the eradication of "reds" was often most brutal in areas where there was no large-scale resistance to the Nationalist rebellion, such as Castile, where known left-wing sympathizers were easily picked up and treated to enforced "purging and purification" by Franco's army (Vincent 2007: 151).

Given the differences in the nature of the violence generated by the Nationalists and Republicans, it is not surprising that the Nationalist side perpetrated the majority of the killings the Civil War. Jackson made this point explicitly in his 1965 study and it has been sustained by more recent research conducted during the democratic period. A widely publicized study organized by Juliá (1999b: 407–12) concludes that during the years of civil conflict the Republican side committed 37,843 killings and the Nationalist side 72,527. This is a partial account with 25 of the 50 Spanish provinces studied. An earlier study (Casanova 1992: 8–9), with 90 percent of all provinces studied, reached a somewhat similar conclusion with respect to the imbalance of the Civil War killings: 45,000 by the Republicans and 98,000 by the Nationalists. Most of the dead, regardless of side, were hurriedly buried in makeshift graves in remote parts of the country, and their fates after the end of the war pointedly reflect the terms of the Nationalist victory.

As the absolute winner of the Civil War, Franco proceeded to exhume and give proper burials to the remains of those who died defending the Nationalist side. The remains of those resting in Republican graves were forgotten as punishment for betrayal of their country. For the duration of the dictatorship, and at least several decades into the democratic period, thanks to the silence over the past provided by the Pact of Forgetting, the remains of those killed on the Republican side would rest undisturbed in so-called *fosas comunes* (mass graves).[7] This unequal treatment of the war dead left a daunting and gruesome future legacy. Once the excavation of the mass graves began in the mid-2000s, as part of the movement to "recover" the historical memory, one observer noted that "The dotted map of likely sites between the Basque Country and Andalusía, Castilla-León and Valencia makes the peninsula look like a child with chickenpox" (Treglown 2009: 18).

The number of people forced to leave Spain suggests further evidence of the brutality of the Civil War. Approximately 500,000 people fled the country between 1936 and 1939, the bulk of them repatriated to France and North Africa, in "the largest forced migration of people from Spain since the expulsion of the Moors from the Iberian Peninsula in the beginning of the 17th century" (Alted 2005: 52). How many of them never returned to Spain after the Civil War, making their permanent home abroad and comprising what is commonly referred to as the "Republican exile," remains in dispute. Estimates range from a third to a fourth (Rubio 1977: 207). What is clear is that the Republican exile triggered a tremendous brain drain that dealt a grave blow to the nation by depriving it of considerable professional and intellectual capital, including the leaders of the Republic, who set up a government in exile in France, and some of the most prominent Spanish thinkers of the day, including an estimated 12 percent of all university professors (223).

Exile for many Republicans turned out to be more horrendous than what they had escaped from in Spain, giving rise to the popular view of the exile experience created by the Civil War as a "second" civil war.[8] In this second war, the Civil War is extended beyond Spanish soil into Europe and transatlantic locations across the Americas, such as Mexico, Argentina, and Puerto Rico, where those detached from the homeland were engaged in a perpetual struggle with the memory of the conflict they left behind. Dehumanization, despair, and even death characterize the lives of Republican exiles (Stein 1979; Kamen 2007). An unknown number of Spaniards were interned in hastily created concentration camps along the Spanish-French border toward the end of the Civil War. Also unknown is the number of Republican "war children" evacuated from Spain by their parents once a Nationalist victory seemed imminent and sent to Russia, where they faced the hardships of World War II, including having to defend Russia against Hitler's invasion. Approximately 8,000 Republican exiles were imprisoned at Mauthausen, a Nazi concentration camp in upper Austria, and only about a quarter survived this harrowing experience.[9]

A second wave of Spanish exiles, estimated at more than 300,000, was triggered by the economic misery of the postwar years (Foweraker 1989: 64).

During the so-called *años de hambre* (the years of hunger), 1939 through the late 1940s, near abject poverty befell many parts of the Spanish territory, the result of the convergence of a multiplicity of factors, including agricultural stagnation (the consequence of a terrible drought, one of the worst in Spanish history), widespread unemployment and underemployment, the western economic boycott of the Franco regime intended to accelerate its demise (which kept food and medicine away from Spain), and an ill-advised policy of economic autarky designed by the government (led mainly by military officers) to free Spain of foreign economic influence and dependency.

The signs of misery were everywhere. Describing life in postwar Spain, British journalist John Hopper wrote (1986: 64): "Poor peasants lived off the grass and weeds, cigarettes were sold one at a time, the electricity in Barcelona was switched on for only three or four hours a day, and trolleybuses in Madrid stopped for an hour in the morning and an hour in the afternoon to conserve energy." Health indicators suggest that in the immediate postwar period (1940–1945) malnutrition, low infant birth weights, and disease led to at least 200,000 excess deaths over the 1935 mortality rate (Boyd (1999: 96). The overall standard of living was cut by half between 1936 and 1956, and not until the early 1960s were prewar levels of economic growth were restored (Foweraker 1989: 64). Broke and impoverished, Spain was forced to depend on foreign aid in the form of loans and foodstuffs (beef and grain) from Argentina's Peronist regime, which was sympathetic toward Franco, to deal with a desperate economic environment approaching mass starvation.

A Violent and Vengeful Regime

After the Civil War ended in 1939, Franco inaugurated a political regime that was diametrically opposed to the Second Republic. Reflecting the influence of the Falange, the nascent authoritarian regime defined itself as "a nationalist-syndicalist, totalitarian, one-party state" (Boyd 1999: 92). Accordingly, civil and political rights were circumscribed, including limits on expression and association; regional autonomy was abolished; and secularism, arguably the main trait of the Republican era, was all but destroyed with the restoration of Catholicism as the state's official religion. This new political order, christened with the fascist moniker Estado Nuevo (New State), was imposed without regard for its human cost. Its establishment meant that the bloodshed and suffering of the Civil War extended well past the end of the war. In fact, Spain was more deadly after the end of the Civil War than during the war itself. The estimated 200,000 "red" prisoners who died of execution, hunger, and disease in the concentration camps established by Franco in 1939–1943 far exceeds the number who died on the battlefield (Jackson 1965: 539; Preston 1995: 230).[10]

The violence of the postwar years was in keeping with the Franco regime's intentions of eradicating any vestige of Republican opposition and gaining the acquiescence of the population as a whole. As observed by Vincent (2007: 157), "The Francoist regime was born in violence and depended on violence. Killing was essential to its initial display of power." Violence was also central to the regime's sense of identity, which celebrated Franco's absolute military victory over the Republicans during the Civil War. Franco would remind the Spanish people: "We did not win the regime we have today hypocritically with some votes. We won it at the point of the bayonet and with the blood of our best people" (Rigby 2000: 73). Violence was also part of the Franco regime's early ideological framework of National Catholicism, which included a brew of traditional Spanish fare such as Catholicism, the view of the peasantry as the embodiment of national virtues, unification of Spanish territory under one homogeneous culture and a single hegemonic language (Castilian), and the use of violence as a "creative and purifying" force (Richards 1996: 152).

For Franco, an absolute military victory over the Republicans during the Civil War was not sufficient; it was imperative to cleanse the country of the foreign virus of liberalism that had infected the nation. This reflected Franco's regard for socialism as "a hereditary form of biological degeneracy," a claim that many on the Republican side regard as evidence that Franco's aim to eradicate the enemy was "tantamount to genocide" (Treglown 2009: 21).[11] Indeed, Franco was in the habit of using the metaphor of Spain as a sick patient in need of radical treatment, which he employed early during the regime in a speech to the nation on December 31, 1939, when he announced his intention to purify Spain of "wicked, deviant, politically and morally poisoned elements . . . those without possible redemption within the human order" (Richards 1996: 158). The prescription for such a condition, according to Franco, required nothing short of the creation of a quarantined society, one undergoing treatment in isolation and divorced from corruptive behaviors and practices such as those that had afflicted Spain under the Republican period and brought about the Civil War.

Among the most obvious targets of Franco's post-Civil War policy of purification were the *huídos* (fugitives), the Republicans who took to the hills rather than surrender to Franco, and subsequently the *maquis*, the Spanish exiles who joined the French resistance and began to reenter Spain after the end of World War II with the hope of toppling the Franco regime. After Franco's Nationalist army succeeded in eliminating not only the surviving cadres of the Republican political parties but also "the leaders, middle-rank functionaries, and rank-and-file members of the socialist and anarcho-syndicalist unions as well as members of the liberal intelligentsia," the *huídos* were the only source of internal resistance against the authoritarian state (Preston 1995: 230). The *maquis* began to appear in 1944, when signs of the collapse of the Nazi regime in Germany were becoming apparent, and at least until 1948 remained a considerable irritant to the Franco regime by staging attacks throughout the country, often taking over small localities. Neither group, however, in the end was a match for Franco's army, which succeeded in eradicating all guerrilla activity by the late 1940s.

The Francoist repression, however, was hardly limited to the *huídos*, *maquis*, Republican leaders, and members of the radical left such as the labor movement; the subjugation reached deep into the social fabric of Spanish society. Franco's ability to suppress the populace was greatly aided by the Western powers' preoccupation with the advent of World War II, and later with the geopolitical divisions created by the Cold War, which forced Britain, France, and the United States to turn a blind eye toward Spain. It was not until the mid-1950s with the signing of the Pact of Madrid (1953), which channeled American military and economic assistance to Franco in exchange for the right to establish American naval and air bases on Spanish soil, that the West began to reconnect with Spain in an effort to deter the global spread of communism. Such disregard for the fate of Spain and its people under Franco allowed the authoritarian regime to impose harsh policies of political purification without a care for its international reputation.

As with the number of Civil War casualties, the number of Spaniards imprisoned by the Franco regime for political reasons remains intensely debated, with some estimates as high as 400,000 (Preston 1995: 230). The regime's official numbers are dramatic enough: 270,000 in 1940 and 45,000 more by 1945 (Richards 1996: 158). This vast repression was facilitated by the 1939 Law of Political Responsibilities, a law that was applied retroactively and demanded "economic compensation not only from those who had actually opposed the regime in the Civil War, but also from anyone who had made the so-called 'National Movement'—or the military rising—necessary" (Ruiz 2005: 5). Such a sweeping legal mandate made virtually everyone who had sympathized with the Republican government—including liberals, teachers, masons, intellectuals, regionalists, labor leaders, and urban workers—a target for prosecution by the Franco regime.

Life as Franco's prisoner reveals the sinister nature of the Francoist repression. Many Republican prisoners were tortured by military psychiatrists determined to eradicate "the germ of anti-nation, a form of degeneracy that if not cleansed to the last trace would contaminate the healthy body of Spain" (Graham 2004a: 2). Other notable torturers were the nuns running the women's prisons, the reported site of "episodes of extreme atrocity, of mental and physical abuse" (Faber 2007: 142). Homosexuals became a target of the state after 1954 with the enactment of the Vagrancy and Villainy Act, a law replaced in 1970 by the more repressive Social and Menace Rehabilitation Act, "a fiercely anti-homosexual text that reified the conceptualisation of homosexuality as an anti-social, dangerous activity" (Calvo 2005: 96–98). An untold number of homosexuals (mostly male), or *invertidos* (inverted) were imprisoned, tortured, and locked in mental institutions as a consequence of these laws.

For many of Franco's prisoners, captivity turned into outright slavery. "Spain became an immense jail, in which the vanquished were put at the service of the victors," observes historian José Luis Gutiérrez.[12] Approximately 280,000 individuals convicted under the 1939 law were forced to work in the construction of their own jails (such as Carabanchel on the outskirts of Madrid) and concentration camps (such as Merinales in Andalusia) and massive public infrastructure projects (such as the Guadalquivir Canal, at the time the largest Spain had undertaken, built to provide irrigation to the region of Andalusia). Prisoners were also conscripted to work in the iron foundries of Bilbao and the mines of Asturias, and to erect monuments glorifying the authoritarian regime. According to historian Antonio Miguel Bernal, by 1941, approximately 10 percent of Spain's male labor force were in jail.[13] Many prisoners, grouped into twenty-four industries and 602 trades and professions, were parceled out to the private sector, especially to construction companies. Legitimizing this system of forced labor, from which the cash-strapped state benefited generously, was the Catholic notion of "expiation through suffering," which allowed prisoners to redeem their political sins by offering their labor to the nation for free. "Redemption, when it was offered, could only come through labor," remarked Franco in a December 31, 1938, speech (Richards 1996: 158).

Separating prisoners from their children was another common form of Francoist punishment. Auxilio Social (Social Aid), the largest social welfare agency in Franco's Spain, is directly responsible for taking many prisoners' children and placing them in state orphanages, where they were mistreated physically and mentally. According to one account (Faber 2007: 142), Auxilio Social officials separated some 30,000 children belonging to the "reds" based on the theory by military psychiatrist Antonio Vallejo Nájera that "these children should be saved from the degenerative environment of their leftist parents."[14] This "totalitarian scheme," according to one study (Cenarro 2008: 41–50), employed welfare programs to incorporate individuals into the state "not as social subjects entitled to social rights" but as "members of a hierarchically ordered state-controlled national community," and was grounded in a "mix of eugenicist theories and Catholic ideologies whereby pro-republican attitudes were seen as the result of the lower classes' polluted social and ideological background."

The Basque Repression

Also targeted by the Francoist repression were those opposed to Franco's myth of a culturally homogeneous Spain—key among them Basque nationalists. Until its very end, the Franco regime treated the Basque Country as occupied foreign territory or a colonial outpost. Underscoring this "occupation" were laws that applied exclusively to the Basque territory in an attempt to stamp out separatist sentiments. A case in point was the banning of the public use of Euskera, the Basque Country's ancient language. The regime also banned public display of the Basque flag and the very intrusive, seemingly incomprehensible policy of forbidding parents to give their children Basque names. These policies resulted in thousands of Basques being arrested, tortured, or forced into exile during the years leading to the democratic transition. In doing so, the Franco dictatorship succeeded in creating an environment of societal resistance and resentment toward the old regime across the Basque territory unique in Spain.

By far the most important manifestation of Basque resistance to the regime was the emergence of Euskadi Ta Askatasuna (ETA).[15] Middle-class university students founded ETA in 1959, frustrated with the perceived passivity of mainstream Basque nationalists toward the Franco regime—such as those heading the Partido Nacionalista Vasco (PNV), the historic advocate of Basque nationalism. For ETA's founders, the PNV was nothing short of "a collaborationist organization of Francoism" (Muro 2005: 579). ETA's political orientations have varied over the years, but they have consistently adhered to the thinking of Sabino Arana, founder of Basque nationalism, who espoused the superiority of the Basque race and the need to prevent cultural contamination from Spain. Since embracing armed struggle in 1968, ETA has been a thorn in the side of the Spanish state.[16] Its boldest act of terrorism was the 1973 assassination of Admiral Luis Carrero Blanco, Franco's alter ego and designated political heir, which unleashed a wave of state oppression of the Basque region unlike that experienced by any other part of the country.

At the infamous Burgos trial of 1970, the Franco regime court-martialed and sentenced to death sixteen ETA members, including two women and two priests. Widespread international outrage, including opposition to the executions from the Vatican, a long-time supporter of the Franco regime, spared their lives. Decidedly less fortunate were the two ETA members and three communist leaders executed in September 1975, the last official act of state violence of the old regime, just as the democratic transition was appearing on the horizon. No fewer than thirteen countries withdrew their ambassadors from Madrid in protest against the killings. In March 1976, in one of the more notable acts of state violance during the democratic transition, the state police opened fire on a demonstration by Basque workers in the city of Vitoria, resulting in five deaths.

Less known, at least until quite recently, were the extrajudicial strategies the state used to suppress Basque nationalism and eradicate ETA. From the inception of ETA terrorism in the early 1960s through the mid-1980s, the state conducted a "dirty war" against suspected ETA members, which ended up killing many ordinary citizens on both sides of the French-Spanish border who got caught in the crossfire. The war's architect was none other than Carrero Blanco, who believed that "only a specialized anti-terrorist force that would fight the terrorists with their own tactics could defeat the terrorists" (Encarnación 2007: 961). With that goal in mind, and well before his spectacular assassination by ETA in 1973, Carrero Blanco laid the groundwork for the creation in 1975 of Batallón Vasco Español (BVE), a right-wing antiterrorist paramilitary group. Managed by military officers and staffed by mercenaries, the BVE was active on both sides of the French-Spanish border between 1975 and 1981, and became the prototype for the Grupos Antiterroristas de Liberación (GAL), the state-sponsored death squads in operation between 1982, the year that marked Spain's return to left-wing rule since the Republican period, and 1986.

Francoist Political Socialization

A more subtle but no less insidious form of Francoist repression was the cynical manipulation of Spanish history. As the victor in the Civil War, Franco had ample opportunity to rewrite history for his own political purposes. His manipulation of Spanish history aimed to confuse and obscure the facts about the Civil War, with the intention of socializing the citizenry into accepting a state-sanctioned interpretation of the war that bore little connection to history and served to justify the authoritarian regime. Aiding Franco's manipulation of history was the public's high level of ignorance about the events leading to the Civil War, a development greatly facilitated by the reluctance of ordinary Spaniards to talk candidly about the Civil War as part of their daily lives. According to one survey (CIS 2008), 43 percent of respondents claimed that during their childhood and adolescence their families spoke "little about the war," while 30 percent claimed there was no discussion of the war at all. But ignorance about the Civil War was also cultivated by a dearth of objective attention to the war on the part of education authorities.

An exhaustive study of Spanish textbooks of the Francoist era by historian Rafael Valls (2007: 157) notes: "History textbooks of this period scarcely ever present detailed historical information about the Second Republic and the Civil War. Instead, they reduce their presentation to negative moral judgment of the Republican period, in which the names of major protagonists are omitted, together with their reformist efforts. The result is that textbooks avoid presenting even minimal historical context for this period, which could facilitate the students' ability to understand its development." Valls adds that treatment of the Civil War is not "well-developed" in the textbooks of the Francoist era.[17] Indeed, the textbooks emphasize that during the 1930s Spain experienced not a war per se but rather an epic rescue by Franco's Nationalist army. Thus, El Alzamiento (The Uprising), Franco's rebellion against the Second Republic, is described in "near mythical terms," presenting those who staged this insurgency as "representing everything of sanity that remained in society." By contrast, particular scorn is reserved for the Republicans and the Republican period. Valls notes that the need to legitimize the illegal military intervention staged by Franco in 1936 led unavoidably to the "demonization of all reformist projects of the Second Republic and those who had been involved in carrying them out." All Republican efforts are described as "anti-national, anti-Catholic, manipulated by foreigners, separatist, Marxist, Bolshevik and causing disasters, disorder, and crimes." The deliberate point is to associate the history of the Republic with partisan squabbling and endemic anti-clericalism.

Whenever the actual conflict among the Spaniards is discussed in Francoist textbooks, it is euphemistically referred to as "The Crusade," "The War of Liberation," or "The War of Salvation," and generally characterized as a clash of patriots against hostile foreigners, communists, and anarchists in particular. The intention of state authorities was to portray the Nationalist victors as saviors and the defeated Republicans as foreign-influenced traitors. Only after Franco's death in 1975 did official education materials accept terms such as "The Spanish War" or "The War of Spain" to refer to the Civil War. It was also during the late Franco period that "acts of heroism on both sides" of the Civil War began to be noted. This period also began to see descriptions of the early Franco period as having entailed "a difficult period of domestic conciliation." The textbooks, however, "say nothing about the repression and violence carried out during the Civil War by the rebels, or the repression of the first years under Franco, of the large population of exiles caused by the war, nor of the severe poverty that the majority of the population suffered during the twenty years from 1940 to 1960."

Glorifying the Nationalist Cause

State policy under Franco reinforced what was being taught in the classroom by emphasizing the theme of national salvation from the chaos and destruction of the Civil War together with a determination never again to experience this kind of travail. It was routine for Franco to exaggerate the number of people who died in the Civil War, a conflict he himself provoked. *Un millón de muertos* (one million dead) was the phrase commonly used by Francoist authorities when accounting for the number of Spaniards who perished in the Civil War, a figure that, as seen already, does not correspond with historical research. More disturbing still, the mythical figure of one million was employed by the regime to suggest "ownership of the victims by the Nationalist side," as if "the only deaths had been those of the winning side; as if no Republicans had died on the fronts and in the rearguard, or had been shot in the subsequent period of repression" (Aguilar 2002: 75). In any case, the main intention of exaggerating the number of casualties was a calculated one: "to impress upon the people the extraordinarily high cost of the war (Jackson 1965: 526). This mission was boosted by conceptions of the Civil War in the popular culture. The phrase "one million dead" became engraved in the minds of the Spanish, especially after it became the title of one of the better-known fictionalized accounts of the Civil War by the novelist José María Gironella.

Key events of the Civil War were reconstructed in a way that bore virtually no connection to the historical record. A case in point is the bombing of Guernica, arguably the most iconic battleground of the Civil War, by German planes in April 1937, at Franco's request. According to official documents from the Basque government, the bombing reduced this historic Basque village to rubble and killed 1,654 people (about a third of the village's population). Such devastation inspired Picasso's iconic *Guernica*, a painting intended by the artist to depict the horrors of right-wing violence in his native Spain and credited with helping change world opinion about the Spanish Civil War in favor of the Republicans. Incredibly, the Franco regime turned this episode into evidence of the cruelty of the Basque people.[18] According to the Franco regime's official story, "the villagers torched their own city"; no German participation in the bombing is even acknowledged (Aguilar 2008: 163).

Public monuments glorifying the 1936 Nationalist uprising against the Republican government were designed to shape public perception about the Civil War and the dictatorship. The town of Belchite, in the province of Zaragoza, site of the Battle of Belchite (1937), was subjected to a bizarre form of memorializing by being preserved in its complete destruction as a "vivid testament of the catastrophe that occurred in Spain and of the supposed viciousness of the Republicans" (Aguilar 2008: 163)."[19] Franco rebuilt the city in 1939, next to the ruins of the old one, as an example of his regime's capacity to bring peace and order back to Spain. The ultimate (and most controversial) act of consecration of the memory of "the Spirit of 1936" and its protagonists, however, was the construction of El Valle de los Caídos, Franco's monumental edifice to the "heroes" of the Civil War, roughly 30 miles from Madrid. The monument owes its notoriety, among other reasons, to its imposing architecture, widely derided as a prime example of fascist theatricality. As such, El Valle seems to have failed to live up to the expectations of its main architect, Diego Méndez, who envisioned homage to traditional Spanish neoclassical architecture, along the lines of the neighboring royal monastery El Escorial, distinguished by its austere design. El Valle houses the Basílica de la Santa Cruz del Valle de los Caídos, only slightly smaller than St. Peter's Basilica at the Vatican (its original size was actually larger than St. Peter's but it was later modified out of respect to the pope), topped by a 500-foot cross, the tallest in the world, visible from miles away.[20]

Franco intended El Valle—commenced in 1940, just months after the end of the Civil War—to be built in just one year to memorialize "the Christian struggle against the ardently anti-clerical Republic," in keeping with the notion of Spain as "God's chosen nation" (Hite 2008: 5). However, due to the economic hardship of the postwar years and the difficulties posed by the complexity of its design, the monument took nearly two decades to complete. Trying to lower construction costs during a time of great economic stress, Franco resorted to using Republican prisoners to help build the monument, thereby surrounding it with even greater controversy and infamy.[21] The workers were forced to quarry a cavern 250 meters deep into the rocks of the Sierra de Guadarrama, which houses the monument's main basilica.

By the time El Valle was inaugurated in 1959, its purpose had shifted dramatically by seeking to advance two seemingly contradictory goals: honoring Franco's victory over the Republicans during the Civil War (the original intent) and serving as a new symbol of national reconciliation. The latter is hardly a match for the former. The more than half a million people who visit El Valle annually, the vast majority foreign tourists, cannot escape the overwhelming sentiment of witnessing a shrine to Francoism.[22] Almost every feature of the monument seeks to link Franco's triumph over the Republicans to Spain's religious tradition of epic evangelizing crusades: from the reconquest of Spain in the fifteenth century over the Arabs, to the expulsion of the Jews from the Iberian Peninsula, to the "discovery" of the Americas. In this sense, El Valle serves as a powerful symbol of the symbiotic relationship between church and state that was consolidated under Franco.

El Valle's awkward nod to national reconciliation is suggested in the few hundred Republicans buried at the monument alongside some 50,000 Francoist supporters. How the remains of the defeated Republicans ended up buried beside those of the Nationalists at El Valle remains the source of some dispute. Some reports propose that this was a last-minute development suggested by the Catholic Church to underscore the monument's new mission of closing the wounds of the Civil War. According to this narrative, relatives of Republican casualties could have the remains of their loved ones buried at El Valle provided they had documentation proving their relatives were Catholics. Most likely, however, the Franco regime exhumed some of the unmarked Republican graves found throughout the country and reburied the remains at El Valle without anyone's consent, or simply buried Republican workers who helped build the monument. In any case, the existence of Republican remains at El Valle did not deter Franco himself from offending their memory in a speech to mark the dedication of the monument:

> The anti-Spanish forces have been defeated and destroyed but they have not died. Periodically, we see how they raise their heads, and, in their arrogant blindness, seek to poison and stimulate once again the innate curiosity and ambition of the young. For that reason it is necessary to silence the advice of the bad teachers over the new generations.[23]

After 1959, promoting national reconciliation was dictated by the political realities of the day. For starters, two decades into the Francoist era, the myth of salvation from war and destruction—the founding myth of the Franco regime—was wearing thin, if only because memories of the Civil War among ordinary Spaniards were becoming increasingly distant. After 1959, the regime was also quite keen on improving its image abroad, having found itself internationally isolated after the end of World War II and the defeat of fascism in Germany and Italy. The effort at promoting national reconciliation culminated in 1964 with the extravagant "Campaign of 25 Years of Peace," a series of commemorative events marking the twenty-fifth anniversary of the end of the Civil War. This grand commemoration included films, publications, and even a "peace parade" (highlighted, ironically enough, by a strong military presence) and was intended by the Franco regime to relegitimize its authority by highlighting its accomplishments rather than its origins (Aguilar 2002: 118–19).

Franco's vast propaganda machine, organized around a national news and documentary service, Noticiarios y Documentales Cinematográficos (NODO), played a prominent role in promoting the authoritarian regime's new emphasis on national reconciliation. Created in 1943 to facilitate dissemination of state cultural and information policy and to distill both domestic and international news for the public, NODO served the state with the dual purpose of consolidating control over information and using information as a propaganda tool. Its main products were newsreels, shown in the nation's cinema houses alongside feature films, the primary form of popular entertainment prior to the advent of television in the late 1960s.[24]

As a propaganda tool, NODO's primary mission was to promote the Franco regime and its accomplishments. The typical NODO newsreel highlighted the progress of the dictatorship, as suggested by the building of a new public work, such as a dam or a highway, as well as the purported benevolence of the dictator, as seen through the expansion of housing and recreational opportunities for the workers. Franco himself was a frequent subject of NODO documentaries. From 1943 to 1959, NODO's coverage of Franco emphasized crediting the dictator with keeping the nation from falling back into civil war; after 1959, coverage aimed to tie the dictator to the advent of "peace and progress." According to Ellwood (1995: 202), between 1943 and 1975, Franco appeared in over nine hundred NODO reports, which was equivalent to 4 percent of NODO's total production. Franco's appearances dwindled over the years from a record forty-five in 1965 to a mere nine in 1974, and two in 1975. This decline largely reflects NODO's skilled manipulation of the image of the dictator. Franco was most likely to appear on the screen during periods of economic growth and relative stability, and to fade away during times of economic crisis and domestic turbulence. Conspicuously absent were references to the economic misery of the immediate postwar years and the repression of political dissidents.

NODO was also in the business of producing documentaries that provided an in-depth look at historical events. The agency's most famous documentary, *El Camino de la paz* (The Path to Peace), dealt with the Civil War. Released in 1959, after memories of the war were no longer so vivid, the film conveyed the false impression that Franco's Nationalist uprising had been necessary to restore peace and order following the Second Republic's attacks on Spanish culture and institutions. Yet, as explained by Aguilar (2008: 128), *El Camino de la paz* also marked an important departure from the traditional depiction of the Civil War by suggesting a more realistic treatment than previous propaganda products from the regime. For one thing, an actual war was acknowledged, in contrast to previous interpretations of the Civil War as a crusade or liberation, and "reds" and "nationalists" were even mentioned as warring parties. The overall treatment, Aguilar wrote, is "more tragic than heroic," a point underscored by use of actual war footage.

The larger message—that no one should forget the bloodshed of the Civil War and the sacrifices that this fratricidal conflict entailed, was emphasized in the film's closing words: a plea to God "to never again allow Spanish blood to be spilled in civil wars."[25]

A Paradox of Forgetting

Although the Pact of Forgetting was intended to set the past aside, it had the paradoxical consequence of allowing for the persistence of plenty of reminders of the very things Spaniards were trying to forget. In keeping with the desire to avoid anything that could arouse political passions, those in charge of the democratic transition took no official position on the hundreds of monuments and memorials honoring either the Nationalist side in the Civil War or the Franco regime itself. Without national policy from the central government in Madrid dictating how to dispose of Francoist monuments and memorials, Spanish regional governments—created after 1977 when Spain undertook a massive process of state decentralization leading to the establishment of seventeen "autonomous" communities—adopted separate approaches. In Republican strongholds like Catalonia and Valencia, and in fiercely independent regions such as the Basque Country, symbols of the old dictatorship, like street names, were quickly replaced with Republican symbols and names of local significance. In parts of the country where Spanish nationalism was not controversial or Franco's Nationalist crusade enjoyed popular support, such as parts of Andalusia and Navarra, there has been little incentive to purge public spaces of the material legacy of the old regime.

More generally, the unwillingness of the political class to deal with the complexity of Franco's material legacy has resulted in a "syncretic process whereby the symbols of the old and new Spain coexist alongside each other" (Rigby 2003: 77). The most important material reminder of the dictatorship is the infamous Valle de los Caídos, but it is hardly the only one. Spanish currency bearing Franco's image remained in circulation until the disappearance of the peseta in the late 1990s with the introduction of the euro. The Francoist coat of arms was displayed in churches, convents, and monasteries for decades after the fall of the regime. As of 2004, Madrid was home to some 360 streets bearing the names of people or acts associated with the Franco regime, and until 2005 a statue of Franco in full equestrian attire adorned the Plaza de San Juan de la Cruz in Nuevos Ministerios, a central area of downtown Madrid that is home to embassies, government offices, and multinationals.[26] Remarkably, the statue, erected in 1959 by the Franco regime to mark twenty years of peace since the end of the Civil War, managed to survive the transition to democracy by nearly thirty years, until it was removed from public view on April 17, 2005, in an operation conducted under cover of night by officials from the city of Madrid and without authorization by the central government, with the pretext of renovating the plaza in which the statue stood. The sensitivity of the operation reflected a heated debate between those who argued that removing the statue amounted to "erasing history" and those who felt the public display of the statue suggested a callous disregard for the memory of Franco's victims.[27] This debate intensified as developments in Madrid triggered a flurry of efforts by officials in other Spanish cities to "rid the country of its fascist debris," as put to this author by a Spanish human rights activist.[28]

The Pact of Forgetting also left in place the very uneven fashion in which Franco had memorialized the victims of the Spanish Civil War. As observed by Faber (2006: 211), "by the time Franco died in 1975 his followers had had almost forty years to mourn their victims, exalt their heroes, and distort the historical record to their benefit while the opposition had been largely maimed and muted by censorship and repression." Ironically, the transition to a democratic regime would serve to perpetuate rather than address this imbalance in how the past was memorialized.

CHAPTER 2

Regime Transition and the Rise of Forgetting, 1977–1981

"The transition to democracy demanded that we overlook thousands of memories and claims that weren't convenient to bring up because they could endanger the pact of the transition."[1] This statement, made during the parliamentary debate over the 2007 Law of Historical Memory by Ramón Jáuregui, an influential socialist official, is pregnant with insights about why Spain willed itself into political amnesia on embracing democracy. At first glance, Jáuregui's statement reveals the striking pragmatism of left-wing leaders, who bore the moral responsibility of raising the issue of justice against the Franco regime and mobilizing civil society around the issue during the transition, if only because the left suffered the brunt of the Civil War killings and Francoist repression. But in the wake of Franco's death, the left's chief concern was not to punish the old regime but to get democracy off the ground in as swift and nonconfrontational a manner as possible.

Such a pragmatic stance for the left was rooted in a multiplicity of factors, beginning with the trauma of democracy's collapse during the interwar years and the ensuing decades spent in the political wilderness due to the ban on political parties imposed by the Franco dictatorship. The left's pragmatism was also anchored in the realization by the early 1970s that the kind of regime change that it had prepared for or had wanted for Spain—the toppling of the dictatorship—was unlikely to come into fruition due to the remarkable resilience of the authoritarian regime; this in turn deepened the desire for a swift transition. Left-wing leaders were also cognizant of the political environment in which the transition unfolded, especially rising political violence, and did not wish to pursue any policy that would make a delicate situation even more so. All of this made the left-wing parties extraordinarily cautious throughout the transition and its aftermath.

Decidedly less apparent in Jáuregui's statement is the connection to the nature of the change in political regimes. As seen in this chapter, the impact of the democratic transition on how the issue of the past was handled in Spain was at least twofold. On the one hand were the limitations on the pursuit of justice against the old regime occasioned by a process of political reform that was anchored upon the legal mechanisms of the authoritarian state. The self-reinvention of the Franco regime intended to accomplish the paradoxical goal of change within continuity by satisfying both the old regime's insistence that the transition to democracy be "legal" within Francoist law and the democratic opposition's desire for the expedient return of civil and political freedoms. On the other hand was the ethos of political consensus that permeated the democratic transition. Such consensus was made official policy by the first post-transition government as a means to cope with the multiplicity of problems involved in building a new democracy in the midst of a full-blown eruption of ethnopolitical violence.

Democratic Change Within Regime Continuity

Spain's transition to democracy began in earnest with King Juan Carlos' stunning betrayal of his pledge to a dying Franco to uphold the principles of Francoism.[2] Franco had handpicked the young king as his successor and had made the Spanish monarchy the linchpin of the strategy of "continuismo," or Francoism without Franco. But the king chose instead to put the nation on the path to democracy, as demanded by the public even before Franco's death. A highlight of the anti-Franco protest movement was a 1967 demonstration that drew some 100,000 workers to the streets of Madrid demanding "Franco no, democracy yes" (Gilmore 1985: 105). These mobilizations provided a counterbalancing effect to the rising elite-led transition. As contended by Maravall (1981: 15), the early days of the transition encapsulated "two counteracting dynamics; the dynamic of reform, negotiation, and pacts from above, promoted by regime reformists, and on the other, the dynamic of pressure and protest from below."

On the advice of his closest political mentors, the king's democratizing agenda called for a process of regime change that "did not violate the essential spirit of *franquismo*" (Podolny 1992: 90). For all intents and purposes, this meant a process of democratization that, born out of the very structures of the Franco regime, was free of any reprisal against the representatives of the authoritarian state. At the helm of this process was Adolfo Suárez, a Francoist official (head of the Movimiento Nacional, the closest thing to a political party in the Franco regime, and former director of the national television services), and generally presumed to be a member of the *renovadores*, a group of Francoist insiders committed to the reformation of the regime from the inside out. Indeed, Suárez's commitment to reforming the authoritarian state proved decisive in his selection by the king to head the transition to democracy.

Suárez replaced Carlos Arias Navarro, the last prime minister under Franco, who was dismissed from his post in July 1976 after proving a weak and indecisive leader in executing the king's demands for a speedy but orderly transition to democracy. Just before Franco's death in 1975, Arias Navarro proposed a set of political reforms, including the legalization of political "associations" (which avoided the much-dreaded "parties" label). But these reforms never made it out of the Francoist parliament. Such policy failures generated massive mobilizations by the general public in favor of the country's return to democracy. Arias Navarro's inept response to popular demands for political reform was to ratchet up political repression, a move that generated international condemnation of the Franco regime, including threats of an economic boycott by Western European trading partners.[3]

Given his intimate association with the Franco regime, Suárez's appointment came as a big disappointment for those hoping for a swift exit from nearly four decades of Francoism. "An historic error," was the characterization of communist leader Ramón Tamanes.[4] Yet Suárez was ideally suited for reforming the Franco regime from the inside out, a political transformation that had "no clear parallel or analogy in twentieth-century political systems" (Payne 1985: 25). Besides possessing a deep familiarity with the structures of the Franco regime, Suárez was young (forty-three), photogenic, and a master diplomat. The last trait allowed him to develop close ties and considerable trust with the democratic opposition in a remarkably short period of time. Soon after his appointment as prime minister in July 1976, Suárez began to organize secret talks, often late at night in Madrid restaurants, with the leaders of the still-illegal socialist and communist parties to convince them he had every intention of establishing a Western-style democracy.

To prove that his democratizing intentions were real, Suárez ordered an amnesty policy on June 30, 1976, that freed some political prisoners jailed by Franco and ended the harassment of left-wing leaders by the police, many of whom were returning to Spain for the first time after decades of exile abroad. Although criticized by some quarters on the left as insufficient, Suárez's amnesty was widely praised by others, such as the left-leaning *El País*, a new liberal newspaper that quickly established itself as Spain's paper of record, which termed it "the best possible of amnesties, although not the most comprehensive or the most desirable of amnesties" (Aguilar 2002: 193). The 1976 amnesty law, enacted as a royal decree, was also intended to plant the seeds for a central theme of the eventual democratic transition: the usefulness of forgetting as a way to overcome the divisions of the past and embark on a peaceful democratic future. The preamble to the law explicitly advocates forgetting the past as a precondition for peaceful democratic coexistence: "As Spain is now heading toward a fully normal democratic state, the moment has come to complete this process by forgetting any discriminatory legacy of the past in the full fraternal harmony of all Spaniards" (quoted in Aguilar 2002: 193).

In keeping with the king's wishes for democratization, Suárez wisely remained deferential toward the Franco regime by insisting that its very institutions were being employed as democracy's midwife. In this way, the transition to democracy was made legitimate under Francoist law. This explains common characterizations of the political reforms instituted in 1976 as "cross-eyed" since the reforms managed to accomplish two seemingly incompatible demands: full democracy for the historic opposition to the Franco regime led by the communist and socialist parties and constitutional continuity for Francoist authoritarians. On November 18, 1976, working in consultation with speaker of the Francoist Assembly Torcuato Fernández Miranda, the "Fundamental Laws," the guiding legal framework of the Franco regime, were amended with the passage of the Law of Political Reform. This was an enormous victory for Suárez; only 15 percent of the deputies refused to endorse the law.

Suárez's reform package called for the legalization of political parties and independent unions, freedom of association, the right to strike, dissolution of the Francoist parliament and the Organización Sindical Española

(OSE), a corporatist syndicate that incorporated both employers and workers, and scheduling of democratic elections.[5] No reference of any kind to the issue of justice against the old regime or reparations to its victims was incorporated into the text. On December 15, 1976, the Law of Political Reform was put to a national referendum, garnering 94.1 percent approval from the electorate on a turnout of about 80 percent of eligible voters. In essence, Suárez succeeded in forcing the Franco regime to self-liquidate while allowing the old regime to dictate the terms of the transition and accrue considerable power to shape the politics and institutions of the emerging democracy.

In no small part due to his skillful and expedient management of the transition, Suárez emerged the undisputed winner of the national elections on June 15, 1977. He was "the best-known politician in Spain, and the one perceived as the most capable of solving a whole series of problems—prices, public order, unemployment, strikes and the inauguration of democracy" (Tusell Gómez 1985: 95). Suárez's Unión de Centro Democrático (UCD), a coalition of fourteen small parties of a center-right orientation, won 34.6 percent of all votes and 47.4 percent of parliamentary seats. The Partido Socialista Obrero Español (PSOE) came in second, with 29.4 percent of all votes and 33.7 percent of parliamentary seats. The Partido Comunista Español (PCE) tallied an embarrassing third place finish, with 9.3 percent of all votes and 5.7 percent of parliamentary seats, barely ahead of the neo-Francoist Alianza Popular (AP), which managed to get 8.8 percent of all votes and 4.6 percent of parliamentary seats. With this victory, Suárez was

Table 2. Spain's First Post-Transition Elections (1977 and 1979)

	1977			*1979*		
Party	*% of votes*	*No. of seats*	*% of seats*	*% of votes*	*No. of seats*	*% of seats*
PCE	9.3	20	5.7	10.8	23	6.6
PSOE	29.4	118	33.7	30.5	121	34.6
UCD	34.6	166	47.4	35.9	168	48.0
AP/PP	8.8	16	4.6	6.1	9	2.6
CiU	2.8	11	3.1	2.7	1	0.3
PNV	1.7	8	2.3	1.5	7	2.0

Source: Spanish Interior Ministry.

entrusted with governing the nation through the "Constituent" period, which concluded with another national election in 1979, which Suárez also won with 35 percent of all votes. Table 2 shows the configuration of political forces in Spain between 1977 and 1979.

The Left and the Missing Past During the Transition

Remarkably, Spain underwent the transition to democracy without calls for justice against the old regime from the democratic opposition—not even a formal condemnation of its evils was demanded. During the 1977 elections the issue of justice against the Franco regime generated virtually no attention. Curiously, the PCE, the last party to be legalized in anticipation of the elections, was the most decisive in making public its desire not to delve into discussions about the past and advocating for outright forgetting. The PCE, according to Aguilar (2002: 244), "did everything in its power not to stir up the old and difficult memories of its role during the Civil War." Nowhere in the position papers of PCE party leaders during the transition can one find even passing reference to the issue of retribution toward the Franco regime (Carrillo 1965, 1967).

Instead of pushing for transitional justice, the PCE focused its demands on the creation of a provisional government of national unity that excluded members of the old regime and a referendum on whether Spain should adopt a monarchical or republican form of government.[6] After the 1977 Law of Political Reform was enacted, the PCE proposal for a provisional government and a referendum on the monarchy was rendered moot since the law was widely interpreted as "a vote in favor of the monarchy" (Aguilar 2002: 170) and the communists began to press for a broad amnesty accord as their biggest objective.[7] In his speeches during the 1977 electoral campaign, PCE general secretary Santiago Carrillo announced that in the first parliamentary session the main objective of the communists would be "an amnesty law for prisoners and exiles."[8]

The socialists also skirted the issue of justice for the old regime. After the return of the PSOE leadership from exile in France in 1974, the party began to mobilize the general public with calls for dissolution of all repressive institutions and extension of rights to all persons deprived of them for political or trade union activity (see González 1976; González and Guerra 1977).

But these calls were intended to demand "the introduction of democratic reforms and not the expulsion or trials of those guilty of repression" (Aguilar 2001: 100). By the 1977 elections, PSOE legislative priorities were listed as: (1) amnesty law; (2) law of political parties; and (3) dissolution of repressive laws.[9]

Even radical left-wing groups that did not support the establishment of democracy in Spain chose not to raise the possibility of military trials, bureaucratic purges, or any other type of retribution toward the old regime. Far-left groups such as the Revolutionary Communist League limited their demands to dismantling the Franco regime and its repressive apparatus. Not even ETA, by far the most radical force outside the mainstream political establishment during the democratic transition, had anything to say about transitional justice. Instead, like other revolutionary movements of the period, ETA members chose to distance themselves from the democratization process in Madrid in protest against what they perceived as an illegitimate transition to democracy, since neither the right nor the left approved of the principle of regional self-determination. Herri Batasuna, ETA's political branch, branded the democratic transition "the pure continuity of Francoism" (Laiz 1995: 256).

For the entire duration of the democratic transition, the only significant breach of the silence over the past came from the leaders of the PSP, a small socialist party that eventually merged with the PSOE. During the parliamentary deliberations over the draft of a new constitution enacted by popular referendum in 1978, PSP president Enrique Tierno Galván, a former university professor turned politician (he was elected to the Congress of Deputies from the province of Madrid in 1977 and subsequently elected mayor of Madrid in the first provincial elections of 1979), proposed that the preamble of the constitution include a brief statement referring to "a long period without a constitutional regime, of negation of public freedoms, and lack of recognition of the rights of nationalities and regions that make up the unity of Spain" (Balfour and Quiroga 2007: 45). He argued that "forgetting the past completely is forgetting those who have suffered the consequences of the past. There is a large sector of the Spanish people who cannot be forgotten; those who have suffered, and the least they deserve is that reference be made to this past, because thanks to their suffering we are winning today." Tierno Galván's eloquent pleas failed to garner support from either Santiago Carrillo of the PCE or Felipe González of the PSOE, and in the end these pleas were drowned by the right-wing opposition led by AP, which contended that the constitution's preamble "should leave history in peace" (Balfour and Quiroga 2007: 46).

The Traumas and Lessons from the Past

The PSOE and PCE decision not to make an issue of the past during the transition reflected how deeply traumatized the left was by the Civil War and its aftermath, a point broadly displayed at the 1962 Munich Congress, a gathering in which prominent figures of the Republican exile, including many old socialist hands, declared their desire for "political prudence" in any process of political change in Spain and renounced all active and passive violence before, during, and after the transition to democracy (Aguilar 2002: 103).[10] Numerous position papers presented at the Munich conference made reference to the Civil War as a fratricidal war, and discussed the need to overcome this conflict through reconciliation rather than recrimination, together with a desire to avoid any repetition of the tragedy at all cost. These commitments, according to Aguilar (2002: 103), were greatly influenced by the "ghosts" of the Civil War, since what brought together the representatives of the Republican exile to Munich was having lost the war and being forced to live their lives outside of Spain. The conference concluded with a speech by Salvador de Madariaga, former ambassador to France during the Republican period, who noted to great applause that "The Civil War that began in Spain on 18 July 1936 and that the Franco regime has maintained artificially through censorship, the monopoly of the press and radio and victory parades ended in Munich the day before yesterday, 6 July 1962" (Aguilar 2002: 104–5).

As left-wing leaders began to assert themselves in domestic politics during the early 1970s, they displayed a keen desire to set aside the ideological battles of the past. This was in keeping with the view that heightened political polarization had caused the collapse of the Republic and the Civil War. Socialist elder Enrique Múgica in an interview with *El País* during the opening of the PSOE's first party congress held in Spain in 1976 noted that "This country has to leave behind the many decades of conflict, translated into bloody antagonism, and it has to formulate a dialectic of class in terms of peaceful co-existence."[11] PCE leaders made analogous statements. Perhaps the most eloquent words were those of Santiago Álvarez, a communist leader tortured and sentenced to death by Franco. In exhorting his fellow communists, the most important source of domestic opposition to Franco's regime since the end of the Civil War, to moderate their political demands, he noted:[12]

> This memory of the past obliges us to take these circumstances into account, that is, to follow a policy of moderation. We feel responsibility for this process of democratization and the need to make a superhuman effort so that this process is not truncated. This is a unique moment in Spanish history. After more than a century of civil wars and a vicious cycle of massacres among Spaniards, which began after the War of Independence and ended in June 1977 with the first elections based on universal suffrage, this is the moment when it is possible to end this cycle and to open a period of civilized life, politically speaking. In this sense we cannot allow ourselves the luxury of expressing opinions that might be misunderstood, which could be, or appear to be, extremist.

Certainly, much of the introspection about the past that the left engaged in during the transition reflected deeply on its own political behavior during the interwar years. That history made its leaders embarrassed and apprehensive about the prospect of revisiting the past. By almost any account, the pact to forget helped conceal a painful and difficult history of left-wing politics. Although the bulk of the violence, human rights abuses, and political excesses of the interwar years belonged squarely to the right (see Chapter 1), the political sins of the left during the Second Republic and the Civil War were not insignificant; quite the contrary. During the early years of the Republic (1931–1933), dominated by an alliance of Republican and socialist forces, the government engaged in a host of controversial and illicit activities, including active repression of anarchist groups, a dominant force in the labor movement that rapidly became a thorn in the side of the government.

The most emblematic example of the Republican repression of the anarchists was the Casas Viejas affair, in which the Assault Guards, a paramilitary unit in charge of maintaining social order, stormed into a small and impoverished Andalusian village in an attempt to put down a rebellion. Several villagers were killed as the Guards made their way into town, and a reported fourteen prisoners were executed in cold blood. News of the killings shook the liberal Republican government to its core. As analyzed in one account, "The image of heavily armed Civil Guards and contingents of the newly formed Assault Guards—the latter ostensibly paragons of Republican legality—wantonly murdering simple, impoverished peasants in a grossly unequal struggle aroused indignation in almost every sector of Spanish society" (Bookchin 1977: 247).

During the Civil War, the left also committed its fair share of political killings, usually reprisals against the Nationalists. One of the most egregious episodes of reprisal by either side is generally attributed to the communists: the 1936 massacre of Paracuellos del Jarama, a killing rampage in a small town in the province of Madrid, in which an estimated 3,000–5,000 Nationalist prisoners (mainly Falangists and military officers who participated in the 1936 uprising against the Republic, and those who refused to defend the Republic) were executed by left-wing militias while being transferred among several of Madrid's prisons. Historians have pinned this episode on the PCE and on General Secretary Carrillo in particular, to whom the actual authorization for the killing of the prisoners has been attributed.[13]

After the Civil War ended, the PCE strengthened its ties to Moscow, another troublesome aspect of that party's history that its leaders were more than willing to forget during the transition. As noted by Mujal-León (1985: 165), after the Civil War there was "no self-criticism, no public apology" on the part of the communists for, among other political offenses, "the slavish adherence to Stalinist directives, which led to the deaths of anarchists at the hands of party members in Catalonia in 1937 and 1939." Among the notable "crimes" of the PCE was its ostensible complicity in the assassination of Andreu Nín, co-founder of the Workers' Party of Marxist Unification (POUM), a communist alternative to the Moscow-loyalist PCE, by the Soviet secret police and of Leon Trotsky by a Catalan communist in Mexico. Surely, any revisiting of this history would have resulted in bringing back "unwelcome memories" (166).

The PSOE had its own difficult history to contend with. As Faber (2006: 211) has noted, its past was "a source of embarrassment not pride and for a long time it seemed in bad taste even to bring it up." The most obvious part of this "embarrassing" past was the polarizing role the party played during the interwar years, including radicalizing the working class by encouraging the kidnapping and killing of prominent members of the business community, and seizure of private property. Workers' groups linked to the PSOE, such as the UGT, were responsible for many of these actions. During the years leading to the Civil War, the UGT joined the anarchist CNT, which was especially powerful in Barcelona, Spain's traditional business center, in burning churches, terrorizing clergy, murdering high-profile industrialists, and collectivizing industry and farmland. As noted by Bookchin (1977: xiv), "Socialist workers in Madrid often acted as radically as anarcho-syndicalist workers in Barcelona. They established their own militias, formed street patrols, and expropriated a number of strategic factories, placing them under the control of workers' committees."

The behavior of the PSOE leadership while in exile in France was another source of embarrassment for the socialists as democracy was approaching. As Balfour and Quiroga (2007: 85) have argued, the PSOE acceptance of the pact of silence helped transform Spain from dictatorship to democracy without creating a major rift with Francoist elites, but collective amnesia about the past had the added value of hiding the PSOE's "serious lack of involvement as an opposition force during Francoism." In this respect, the contrast with the communists is telling. After the end of the Civil War, the PCE stayed underground in Spain and fought the old regime from within by organizing civil society (especially workers and students) and infiltrating state institutions. Especially notable was the penetration of the OSE by the Comisiones Obreras (CCOO), a semi-autonomous union the PCE successfully infiltrated and employed to get a foothold inside a resurgent labor movement.

When the PSOE went into exile, by contrast, its leaders engaged in intense and pointless ideological debates, such as whether the party should collaborate with the communists in the struggle against Franco, and later over whether the party should remain faithful to its Marxist, revolutionary origins or embrace a more moderate model suggested by social democracy. The consequence of this prolonged intraparty fighting was to neglect the underground struggle against Francoism within Spain. The socialist leadership also grossly miscalculated the most effective mode of fighting Franco, choosing in the end a strategy that favored enticing the Western powers to boycott the regime in the hope that this would trigger its demise. With the rise of the Cold War and the Western struggle against communism, the Franco regime proved very adept at playing its anticommunist credentials to gain recognition by the international community, which was eager to embrace Franco as an anticommunist stalwart. To the great benefit of the PSOE, all these embarrassments were conveniently swept aside by the Pact of Forgetting. In the new democracy, lack of knowledge about the past allowed the PSOE to reintroduce itself to the Spanish public as a fresh political alternative to the reinvented Francoists that comprised the center-right UCD and the history-weary PCE.

Tactical Shifts and Political Restraint

Further dissuading the left from pursuing justice toward the Franco regime was the desire for a swift and peaceful return to democracy instilled by the failure of attempts to uproot the Franco regime. For Carrillo and other communist leaders, the political bargain for the left implicit in Suárez's reform process—a swift return to democracy in exchange for no reprisals against the old regime—was one they were willing to embrace once the prospect of a revolutionary take-over seemed all but impossible. In essence, the left was willing to trade justice and accountability for democracy and legality. As Carrillo explained in justifying his own political behavior during the transition, "the right's willingness to relinquish power and share it under democracy was the left's compensation for giving up claims of retribution for the Francoist repression."[14] Surely, not everyone in the PCE and the left at large agreed with the pragmatism shown by Carrillo on transitional justice, but few were willing to openly contradict him on the issue, especially after other options for returning Spain to democracy had proved futile.[15]

By the early 1970s, the PCE had begun to move away from a strictly oppositional stance toward the Franco regime, even though this position was not self-evident in the official party platform. A 1973 political manifesto noted that "the transition from dictatorship to democracy has to occur through a real political revolution; through the struggle of our people; a struggle articulated by the forces of democracy, triggered by a peaceful general strike."[16] This remained the PCE's official stance through 1976, with the party believing "that the Franco regime could not be reformed but had to be brought down" (Mujal-León 1985: 165). The party's actions, however, suggested a different reality. In 1970, the PCE signed the Pacto por la Libertad, an agreement that declared the "willingness to reach agreements with virtually all parties, including those on the right," and committed the leadership of the party "to reconciliation with the army and the church and to the ultimate construction of Socialism gradually through democratic means" (Gunther et al. 2004: 93).

Dictating this important shift in political tactics within the PCE was the realization that after decades of attempts to rally the masses against the Franco regime, a revolutionary take-over seemed all but unattainable. This was especially so after the dramatic economic takeoff of the late 1960s, which left ordinary Spaniards uncertain about radical political change and quite supportive of the idea of a peaceful and gradual change to democratic government. Survey data from the mid-1970s show that a once radical working class was no longer so radical. By the mid-1970s, only 37 percent of the workers identified themselves as belonging to the working class (Pérez-Díaz 1980: 3).

Also pushing the PCE toward more moderate and conciliatory political stances were the ideological changes afoot in the party's leadership. Unlike the hierarchy of the communist Party in Portugal, which remained wedded to Moscow during that country's transition to democracy, and the South American left, which developed during the Cold War, under the spell of Castro's Cuba and against the imperialistic policies of the American government, by the early 1970s the Spanish communists had effectively divorced themselves from the orthodoxy of Marxism-Leninism by embracing "Eurocommunism," a political movement that "questioned the socialist nature of the Soviet system" (Mujal-León 1985: 167). Surely not everyone in the PCE leadership agreed with this "moderating" of orthodox left-wing thinking. As late as 1978, Dolores Ibárruri, known as La Pasionaria, the PCE matriarch and president, who spent the bulk of the Francoist era in exile in the Soviet Union, could be heard making such controversial statements in the media as "we have not renounced the dictatorship of the proletariat" (Gunther 1986b: 94). Unsurprisingly, on her return to Spain from the Soviet Union Ibárruri proved such an embarrassment to the PCE "that she was subjected to something approaching house arrest" (Hopper 1986: 273).

The final nail in the coffin of the PCE plan for a revolutionary overthrow of the Franco regime was, ironically, the popular revolt that brought down the Salazar-Caetano dictatorship in neighboring Portugal. For much of the time the PCE spent battling the Franco regime, the revolution that began in Portugal in April 1974 must have represented everything the Spanish communists had ever desired for themselves and for Spain. The Portuguese state went into complete crisis after military rebels opposed to the colonial wars (which Portugal fought in various African spots, hoping to hang on to its overseas possessions after most other European colonial powers had begun a process of decolonization) staged a successful coup against the authoritarian state (Costa Pinto 2001). This allowed the Portuguese Communist Party to assume control of parts of the state like the Vertical Syndicate, which controlled the state-created labor movement and state-owned media. These resources allowed communist leaders to influence the imposition of a sweeping policy of nationalization of private businesses that created state monopolies in the main sectors of the economy, and to pursue an aggressive policy of purges (the so-called process of *saneamento*) intended to cleanse the state of its authoritarian heritage (Costa Pinto 2006).

By the mid-1970s, however, a Portuguese-style revolutionary takeover of the state was hardly in sync with the PCE political program. The party had already embarked on a process of reinvention designed to make itself acceptable to the general public and be seen as such by other actors in politics. Such a change in image made the party react with a great sense of trepidation about developments in Portugal. Soon after the toppling of the Salazar-Caetano regime, the Portuguese revolution, despite its generally bloodless nature, began to look and feel too close for comfort as Portugal's mass mobilizations, land seizures, and business expropriations eerily echoed Spain's own revolutionary past during the years leading to the Civil War. Thus, avoiding a Portuguese-style transition out of authoritarian rule became an explicit desire of many Spanish political leaders. "To me Portugal is full of danger," Carrillo wrote in April 1975 in *Mundo Obrero*, the PCE official paper, on the first anniversary of the revolution in Portugal, adding that the policies of the Portuguese Communist Party were "leading to something similar to Maoism."[17]

The PCE's shift in political tactics brought the communists in line with their historic nemesis: the French-based PSOE, already on record as espousing a nonviolent form of regime transition in Spain. Although the PSOE leadership, as recently as its 1974 congress in Suresnes, France, had opposed "any reform, continuation or transformation of the [Franco] regime," prominent socialist figures had come to terms with the possibility of having to negotiate the transformation of the Franco regime (Gunther 1986: 13) well before the transition to democracy. As with the PCE, this decision largely reflected a realization that the PSOE's own strategy for an outright rupture with Francoism was unlikely to come to fruition. The PSOE's plan for uprooting the Franco regime rested not on an internal revolution, but rather, as noted previously, on convincing the West to isolate Franco in the hope this would eventually bring the regime to its knees. This strategy could have worked were it not for the Cold War, which forced much of the West, including the United States, into an alliance of convenience with Franco. By time the 1953 Pact of Madrid was signed, which allowed American military bases in Spain in exchange for economic aid, the PSOE strategy for external liberalization of Spain was all but dead, forcing the party to consider other alternatives.

As with the PCE, the PSOE embrace of reform over rupture in the transition to democracy also reflected ideological changes afoot in the party's leadership. While in exile in France, the socialist leadership became "unabashedly pro-European" (Mujal-León 1985: 166). Moderate left-wing leaders like Willy Brandt, François Mitterrand, Pietro Nenni, and Olaf Palme, who dominated socialist politics in Western Europe during the 1970s, became the model for Felipe González, the young and charismatic socialist leader who in 1974 wrestled control of the PSOE from the generation of exiled socialist leaders who fought Franco during the Civil War. González also kept at bay avowed old hand Marxists in order to reinvent the party into a Spanish version of the modern European left.

A Violent Political Environment

Yet another factor forcing the hands of the left on the issue of justice against the old regime was the violent political environment in which democratization unfolded in Spain, which vividly recalled the violence that engulfed the country during the interwar-years. As shown in Table 3, between 1968 and 1980 almost 500 people perished in Spain as a consequence of politically motivated killings, with the largest number of deaths committed by ETA, followed by the state, police, extreme left, and extreme right. Between 1979 and 1980, a period that coincided with the negotiation and ratification of the Basque autonomy statute, ETA killed 242 persons—one third of all those killed since the beginning of the transition (Llera 1993: 172). In 1980 alone, ETA perpetrated 100 killings, a record to date for the organization, which according to a headline from *El País*, amounted to "one dead every sixty hours."[18]

ETA entered the national consciousness on December 20, 1973, with the spectacular assassination of Admiral Carrero Blanco (his vehicle was blown to pieces by 100 kilos of explosives buried under the street), Franco's alter ego and designated political heir. This killing signaled a radical change in ETA's political tactics—away from bombing public monuments and military installations to targeting politicians for assassination. Carrero Blanco's assas-

Table 3. Political Violence During the Democratic Transition

Year	*ETA*	*GRAPO*	*Extreme right*	*Police/ Guardia Civil*	*Total*
1968	2	–	–	–	2
1969	1	–	–	–	1
1971	–	–	–	1	1
1972	1	–	–	2	3
1973	6	–	–	1	7
1974	18	–	–	-	18
1975	14	7	–	2	23
1976	18	2	1	22	43
1977	11	8	8	23	50
1978	64	6	4	15	89
1979	67	29	10	20	126
1980	96	6	20	n/a	122
Total	298	58	43	86	485

Source: Data for 1968–1978, López-Pintor (1980: 17); data for 1980, Muro (2008: 122).

sination was supposed to be the catalyst of a strategy of "action-repression-action," a cycle of violence in which one provocation by ETA would unleash a wave of indiscriminate brutality on the part of the state, which would then trigger another daring action by ETA (Muro 2008: 15). The end result would be wholesale state repression, initiated by a military coup, with the goal of eradicating ETA. This oppression would create revolutionary chaos by provoking the masses to revolt against the military, thereby creating the political conditions that would allow the Basque region to declare its independence from Spain.

Although ETA's grand scheme did not materialize, the organization succeeded in triggering a violent cycle of provocation and retaliation reminiscent of the rash of political assassinations that started the Civil War. The assassination of Carrero Blanco prompted the state to execute two ETA members and three members of the PCE on September 27, 1975. In retaliation, on August 2, 1975, the extreme left organization Grupos de Resistencia Anti-fascista Primero de Octubre (GRAPO), a Maoist group that targeted what it referred to as "the oligarchy," killed two policemen in the center of Madrid, and a few months later (on October 1, 1975), the organization executed four more policemen and seriously injured a fifth. On January 24, 1977, just months before the first general elections of the post-Franco era, neo-fascist groups murdered five labor lawyers affiliated with the PCE, in what came to be known as the "Atocha Massacre" since the killings took place in the vicinity of Madrid's Atocha railway station. On March 22, 1978, GRAPO members shot dead the general manager of prisons for the killing of an incarcerated anarchist at Carabanchel Prison in Madrid, a prison built by Franco's political prisoners, beaten to death by prison guards.

This mayhem contributed to "an atmosphere of fear and uncertainty within both the state and civil society" that threatened to derail the process of democratization, most likely by inviting a military coup (Muro 2008: 122). It also put considerable pressure on politicians to avoid anything that would aggravate an already delicate situation, something the left took to heart. Convinced that ETA's goal in assassinating Franco's successor was not democratization but rather political de-stabilization, the left committed itself to peace and order. In the immediate aftermath of the attack on the head of the government, PSOE and PCE leaders reiterated their unequivocal rejection of violence and renewed calls for negotiations with the Franco regime. Paradoxically, Carrero Blanco's assassination ended up helping rather than hurting a negotiated approach to the democratic transition. According to Mujal-León (1985: 278), Carrerro Blanco's assassination removed from the political scene "the grey eminence of the regime, the man upon whom Franco relied to ensure an orderly transition and to control the soon-to be-crowned king."

The Transition and Its Legacies

In the end, however, it was the political dynamics set into motion by the authoritarian regime after Franco's death that proved most decisive in shaping the behavior of the left with respect to the past during the transition. There is little doubt that Suárez outsmarted his opposition. In essence, Suárez handed the democratic opposition nothing short of a fait accompli. Left-wing leaders never expected in their wildest dreams that the Franco regime would commit to full liberalization, as false attempts at reform under the Arias Navarro government had proved. Indeed, Suárez's political gamble accomplished something many doubted would ever be possible in Spain: a regime change to democracy that pleased both Francoist insiders and advocates of democracy. The political observer Pablo Lucas Verdú has noted that Suárez played "a clever and efficacious game" that earned him "the hatred of the far right, the support of the real players, and the tolerance of the opposition."[19]

To be sure, exclusion from the process of political reform did not sit well with either the PCE or PSOE. Being on the outside put the leadership of both parties in the awkward position of having to criticize a reform package intended to bring about instant democracy since its legitimacy was compromised by being "the product of the institutions of the dictatorship," as expressed by the communist trade union leader Marcelino Camacho.[20] However, the left's opposition to the 1976 Law of Political Reform was purely symbolic, especially after Suárez had the good sense to put the new law to a national referendum to add democratic legitimacy to the actions taken by an authoritarian parliament. The left organized an abstention campaign against the referendum, which largely fell on deaf ears since the public was eager to move ahead with democratization through the existing mechanisms of the authoritarian regime. A May 1975 poll published in the magazine *Cambio 16* showed that the majority of the public (60 percent) believed the country could not evolve toward democracy without reforming the Fundamental Laws.[21]

Employment of the mechanisms of the old regime to democratize the state also left little if any room for the left to affect the scope of political reform by extending it beyond that dictated by the Francoist reformers. Around the time of the enactment of the 1976 Law of Political Reform both the PSOE and the PCE were still illegal and hence had no say or representation in the parliament. In fact, both organizations were barely viable at the time when the nation was readying itself for the first democratic elections in four decades. The PSOE was a ghost of its former self, with barely 50,000 registered members just months before the 1977 elections (Gunther 1986a: 11). As a result of its early infiltration of civil society, especially the trade union movement and student associations, and financial assistance from Moscow, the PCE was in better organizational shape, but its membership was quite low, and estimated to have peaked at 200,000 around the time of the 1977 elections (Gunther 1986b: 103).

After the 1977 elections, the main obstacle for the pursuit of justice toward the old regime was posed by the reservoirs of authoritarian power left in place by the transition. As observed by Malefakis (1982: 216), in post-transition Spain, "state power remained completely in the hands of persons intimately involved with Francoism. Its legacy was liquidated not by outsiders but by some of the very persons entrusted with its preservation." This situation, Malefakis contends, meant that in Spain "leading figures of the antecedent regime would play a greater—indeed the dominant—part in the shaping of the political regime" (215), a striking contrast to all post-World War II successor democracies except for Italy. Thus, while the democratic reforms instituted after 1976 transformed the political nature of the regime, they left the institutional-bureaucratic structures of the state virtually unchanged. There was, in fact, no significant rupture during the transition with the administrative apparatus of the state, from the top echelons of government, to the national civil service, to the provincial level.

According to one extensive study of ministers and regimes in twentieth-century Spain, "the overwhelming majority of the fifty-one UCD ministers had previously occupied second- or third-level executive positions during the last years of Franco's regime and the democratic transition, and almost one-third of them had been members of the corporatist Cortes, the Francoist parliament" (Linz, Jerez, and Corzo 2001: 29). Francoist influence over local government was even more pronounced, since local officials appointed under Franco remained in office until March 1979, and many managed to get re-elected after 1979 elections (Malefakis 1982: 216). More notable and consequential was the complete lack of rupture with the old regime in the judicial apparatus, a branch of the government that since the end of the Civil War in 1939 had been pivotal in legitimizing the repression of the regime through its last days.

Because of the nature of the transition in Spain, there was no need to purify judicial institutions by purging individuals affiliated with the old regime. As might be expected, this had important implications for any kind of justice for the old regime. The survival, virtually intact, of the Francoist judicial apparatus, meant the transfer into the new democracy of a corporate judicial culture steeped in Francoism and reproduced through recruitment practices noted by a high degree of nepotism and political patronage (Gil 2009). This meant, in turn, a stiff resistance by the judicial apparatus to implement the laws enacted by the new democratic regime, to say nothing of embracing judicial innovations such as transitional justice, especially in the highest echelons of the judicial system. As reported by Aguilar (2013: 14), "The judges who publicly expressed their Francoist ideology were few and far between, but they occupied the highest positions on the judicial ladder." Meaningful reforms to the judicial system did not arrive until the mid-1980s, when the new socialist government lowered the retirement age of judges with the aim of removing those most closely associated with the Franco regime (see Magalhães, Guarnieri, and Kaminis 2006).

Yet it was the military that represented the very embodiment of authoritarian power in the new democracy. Any attempt by the government and/or the opposition to pursue justice against the old regime would have put the nascent democracy "in mortal danger" by antagonizing the one actor with the means to derail the democratization process.[22] Although by no means a monolithic institution, throughout the transition the military was "the main bastion of ultra-rightist political reaction" (Rigby 2000: 76). As such, throughout the transition and its aftermath civilian leaders were keenly aware of the dangers posed by the military. According to Payne (1986: 184), during the twenty months that followed the attempted military coup (discussed below), Spain operated as a *democracia vigilada* (guarded democracy), requiring civilian leaders to "negotiate each new step in policy or major personnel change with the senior military commanders." Thus by choosing not to confront the military on the issue of the political excesses of the authoritarian state past, the left hoped to ensure that the right (and this included the military) was in the fold of the transition process and hence less of a threat to the emerging democratic regime and the left itself. In a revealing 2002 interview, Alfonso Guerra, second in command of the PSOE during the transition, and González's deputy prime minister in 1982–1992, remarked: "In the transition, we forgot about what the right wing had done on the condition that it did not repeat the same behavior" (Humlebaek 2007: 7).

Not surprisingly, fears about the military made both the PCE and PSOE leery of pressing for any policy that could be interpreted as retaliatory toward the old regime, a position that intensified as the military threat to the new democracy increased. A coup planned for November 17, 1978, the so-called Operation Galaxia, designed to prevent the constitutional referendum from taking place, was discovered just weeks beforehand. The threat the military posed to democracy materialized on February 23, 1981. On that date, lieutenant colonel Antonio Tejero staged a military rebellion against the new democracy (the so-called Tejerazo) by holding hostage the members of the Congress of Deputies. The proverbial straw that broke the camel's back was the granting of limited autonomy to Catalans, Basques, and Galicians, which the military, fully inculcated by Franco into the idea of an indivisible Spain, read as a sign the nation was coming apart. Although the coup failed, it reminded the government and its opposition of the capacity of the armed forces to disrupt the new political order, and this in turn gave civilian leaders a renewed sensitivity to how far they could push the military. But it was the opposition, led by the PSOE, which was most affected by the aborted coup. The failed coup awakened the "memory of the terror imposed by the winners of the Civil War and pushed the left into submission and to reaffirm its support for the limits of the reformist process."[23]

The Politics of Consensus and the Rise of Forgetting

Alongside the restoration of democracy in Spain rose "the politics of consensus," the Suárez administration's grand strategy for institutionalizing democratic institutions. It called for avoiding any policy or political stance that could bring the nation's leading political forces into direct conflict, and for extensive collaboration between the government and its opposition in crafting new democratic institutions. Undergirding the politics of consensus was the distribution of political power that emerged from the 1977 elections. Despite consecutive electoral victories in 1977 and 1979, the UCD never enjoyed control of an absolute majority of parliamentary seats. This meant that the Suárez administration required cooperation from the opposition parties in the parliament to see its policies executed, especially the drafting of a new democratic constitution. Thus, bringing the left into the policy-making fold became a priority for UCD governments in 1977–1981, often to the consternation of the far right, the military, and even the business community (see Bermeo with García-Durán 1994; Encarnación 1997).

For the left, participation in the politics of consensus had many advantages, from having a say in the design of the new democratic regime, to gaining full admission into the political establishment, to moderating its political image in the hopes of increasing its electoral appeal. Arguably, the most important lesson the PSOE took from its electoral defeats in 1977 and 1979 was that the party was not entirely free of the reputation for political extremism that it earned during the Republican period. Indeed, the 1979 elections were regarded by PSOE leaders as "a failure" since there was virtually no improvement over the 1977 elections (Méndez-Lago 2006: 174). Embracing an image of political moderation thus became the PSOE's core strategy for increasing its electorate. In practical terms this meant moving the party to the center-right, the position occupied by the ruling UCD. A survey by the party confirmed this: "The PSOE has chances to improve its vote both to its left and to its right, but quantitatively speaking the latter yields by far a greater probability of growth" (174).

Amnesty and Amnesia

The linchpin of the politics of consensus was a comprehensive amnesty law, approved by the Congress of Deputies on October 14, 1977, the first order of business for the new political administration. This new law diverged significantly from the 1976 amnesty law announced by the king. Unlike the 1976 decree, the 1977 law was the product of a democratically elected body that incorporated considerable political diversity. The second law also called for a comprehensive amnesty, and left in its wake very little ambiguity that the intention was anything short of political amnesia, since the law was framed by the government, with the support of the opposition, "to make it possible for the new generations to forget Franco . . . to erase any traces of the dictatorship" (Jáuregui y Menéndez 1995: 29–30). The so-called *punto final* (full-stop) provision explicitly absolves from prosecution "crimes and misdemeanors that may have been committed by state authorities against the rights of others." While the 1976 law excluded crimes that "may have endangered or harmed the life or integrity of any person," the 1977 law provided immunity for "all acts of political intentionality . . . regardless of whatever outcomes that they may have generated."[24] The new amnesty law also extended the deadline for immunity from prosecution from December 15, 1976, to October 6, 1977.

The conflation of amnesty and amnesia encapsulated in the 1977 amnesty law can be appreciated in the calls for mutual forgiving and forgetting that dominated the debate of the amnesty bill in both houses of the Spanish Congress. As noted by Aguilar (2001: 103), "during the parliamentary debates, almost all groups praised the law precisely because it was an instrument of 'national reconciliation,' intended to 'close the past,' 'forget,' and start a new phase.'" "Amnesty is a process to reach national reconciliation," Suárez remarked in an interview with *El País* around the time the amnesty law was being debated in the national parliament.[25] In speeches to the Congress of Deputies Suárez posited amnesty as "a new horizon" for Spain, something that would allow the country to "empty its jails," "generate good will," "eliminate any desire for revenge from anybody toward anybody," and "move the country forward toward full democracy."[26] Suárez's political opposition also broadly praised the amnesty law, creating one of the purest moments of national reconciliation in the democratic transition.

Felipe González declared the law "enormously positive," while Santiago Carrillo noted: "I hope the law will close a long and tragic period of Spanish history."[27] Perhaps the most reflective words belong to CCOO leader Marcelino Camacho, who expressed his joy at the "exceptional day that would allow me, an old communist of very humble origins, to speak and defend a project of amnesty with the very people who fired me from multiple jobs." Praise for the new law also came from regional nationalists in the Basque Country, whose relations with Madrid have historically been tense. In the expressive words of Xabier Arzalluz Antia, a leader of the Basque Nationalist Party, the amnesty law offered "forgiveness from everybody to everybody."[28]

The politicians' support for amnesty, and more generally for forgetting the past, was echoed in the media. As the parliamentary debate over amnesty got under way, *El País*, whose views during the transition are generally thought to reflect those of the PSOE, perhaps even more forcefully than the political class itself, made the argument for why Spain should embrace amnesty and forgetfulness as a means to facilitate democratic co-existence. Indeed, the paper could not have been more explicit in justifying amnesty as a means to introduce a wholesale approach to forgetting. An editorial urging passage of a comprehensive amnesty law argued that

> Amnesty is an exceptional act, justified by the reasoning of the State and the necessity to erase the memory of acts as bloody and painful as a civil war—a war between brothers—and a long dictatorship. Democratic Spain should, from this point forward, forget the responsibilities and the events of the Civil War and make an abstraction of the forty years of dictatorship. Looking backwards should only have the purpose of reflecting about the causes of the catastrophe and ways to prevent its repetition. A people cannot and should not lack historical memory; but this should only serve to promote projects of peace and cohabitation toward the future and not to feed old hatreds.[29]

Support for the amnesty bill in the final vote was overwhelming: 93.3 percent of parliamentarians voted in favor of the measure, 5.6 percent abstained, and 0.6 percent opposed it. Not everyone was enamored with the law, however. Donato Fuejo Lago, speaking for the PSP, noted he and others on the left would have liked to see a more generous law—one that would have combined political amnesty with some reparations for or acknowledgment of the victims of the Civil War and the Franco dictatorship.[30] In his testimony following the vote he noted: "It would have been necessary for this proposed bill to have included a form of moral reparation which might bridge the gulf which broke our society in two." Such a nod toward reparation and reconciliation was needed; since "justice had not been done with regards to those who had fought for democracy over so many years, a feeling of frustration might build up that would be detrimental." Yet Fuejo Lago joined other left-wing leaders in supporting the amnesty law because "it was a result of a compromise between the various groups that had taken part in drafting the law, a compromise that had been necessary in order not to endanger the existing freedoms."

Ironically, the strongest dissenting voice came from the far right, which benefited most generously from a blanket amnesty. Congress deputy Antonio Carro Martínez of the neo-Francoist AP, which opposed the law, called amnesty "bad medicine; instead, we should have the strict application of the law."[31] He added that while he recognized the legitimacy of the amnesty law, he warned that it would set "a very poor precedent for the rule of law: it takes us on a slippery slope toward debasing the law, the government; the end is anarchy."[32] Underlying such opposition to amnesty was the authoritarian regime's historic resistance to dealing with its opposition with any kind of humanity. According to Aguilar (1996: 9), "Franco consistently refused to accept any measure which would have signified the rehabilitation of the vanquished or the recognition of the justice of their cause. Much of the legitimacy of the regime, which might be called its source of legitimacy, came from its victory in the war." Such convictions led the Franco regime to repeatedly ignore calls for amnesty for political prisoners, especially by the still-illegal trade union movement, whose strikes by the early 1970s had acquired a decidedly political coloring (Castells 1977: 158). Indeed, as seen already, only after Franco's death in 1975 did the state, now under the command of the King, begin to take the initial steps toward emptying the state's prisons of political prisoners.

Democratizing with Consensus

Amnesty was followed by a period of intense cooperation between the government and the opposition in crafting democratic institutions, launched by the epoch-making Pacts of Moncloa, a set of political accords signed by all the major political parties represented in the Congress of Deputies. Although designed to help the Spanish economy cope with the domestic difficulties brought about by the international energy crisis of the late 1970s, which sent inflation and unemployment soaring while driving industrial productivity down, the real purpose of the Moncloa accords (named after the prime minister's residence) was to create a political climate that would lead to acceptance of a new democratic constitution by all the key political forces (Encarnación 1997).[33] The text of the pacts contained the entire political program of the incoming government, from inflation and wage policy, to military reforms, to the initial framework for dealing with demands for autonomy from the regions (CCOO 1989: 41–66). Signed to great fanfare at the Moncloa Palace on October, 27, 1977, and translated into law soon thereafter, the Moncloa accords are commonly referred to as the symbolic end of the Spanish Civil War for the spirit of national consensus that they encapsulated.

With the past conveniently tucked away with a commitment to forget, Spanish politicians were able to secure compromises on all the pivotal issues affecting the new constitution in a political environment that was essentially free of recriminations and political grandstanding. According to one media report, during the first day of deliberations over the draft of the new constitution, "not a single act of ire, political infantilism, or demagoguery was observed."[34] Immediately following the 1977 elections, seven political notables—drawn from the major political parties—sequestered themselves in a secret location, away from the prying eyes of the public and the media. The secrecy was intended to shelter politicians from taking public positions that their particular constituencies might object to, to say nothing of avoiding the public image of bickering politicians. Two major political settlements were incorporated into the new constitution. The first one, widely regarded as a major concession on the part of the left, created a parliamentary monarchy. For many liberals, this meant accepting the legitimacy of the monarchy, a historic symbol of political absolutism, and giving up on the cherished dream of restoring Spain's republican tradition with the creation of a third republic. "Democracy is synonymous with Republicanism," Carrillo (1965: 11) contended prior to Franco's death. But the monarchy had earned a place in the evolving democratic regime by King Juan Carlos's bold leadership, which accounts for the very high esteem among the public the monarchy has held in the post-Franco era.

In the second compromise, the political class sought to solve the conundrum posed by the demands for self-governance by Spain's separatist-nationalist communities. The failure to deal successfully with these demands in the 1931 constitution was widely seen in 1977 as having contributed to the failure of the Second Republic. Yet getting to a solution seemed on the surface close to impossible: the right had historically opposed any degree of regional autonomy fearing that this would eventually lead to the dissolution of the nation; the left for its part had historically supported federalism and even self-determination. In 1975, the PCE manifesto defined the right of self-determination of Catalonia, the Basque Country, and Galicia as "inalienable," while the PSOE, a year later, declared that "all regions had the right to break away from the Spanish state" (Quiroga 2011: 138). The solution arrived in the form of a highly contradictory constitutional compromise that stresses the "indissoluble unity of the Spanish nation," effectively eliminating the possibility for self-determination, alongside the recognition of a variety of "nationalities" in the Spanish territory and the right of any region to self-governance. This compromise opened the way for the creation of *las autonomías*, a system of regional self-governance distinguished by its asymmetry, with the "historic" autonomous regions (Catalonia, the Basque Country, and Galicia) enjoying more autonomy than the rest. As such, the system remains closer to "regionalism" than to "federalism," a term studiously avoided in the 1978 constitution (Encarnación 2008b).

Another thorny issue negotiated by the constitutional committee was church-state relations. There was a desire in the committee that the new constitution strike a compromise between the shrill anti-clericalism of the 1931 Republican constitution, which bluntly stated that the Spanish State "has no official religion," and Franco's confessional Catholic state, which made Catholicism the official religion. The final church-state settlement guaranteed freedom of religion and worship, absence of an official state religion, and state neutrality on religious issues; nonetheless, it managed to recognize the historic importance of the Catholic Church in the public life of the Spanish people. Article 16 states that "public authorities shall maintain the consequent relations of cooperation with the Catholic Church and other confessions." This stipulation has allowed the Church to retain extensive public financing for educational, cultural and ecclesiastical activities. Among the strongest defenders of the compromise was the PCE, which argued for the need to avoid the social polarization of the 1930s by respecting the views of church leaders, especially Cardinal Tarancón of Madrid. During the constitutional debate, Tarancón warned the parliamentarians that "The Church is a social reality . . . and politics has to bear in mind and respect the real life of the people; it cannot ignore the fact that the majority of the Spanish people belong to the Catholic Church" (Brasslof 1998: 95).

After Consensus: The Political Uses of Forgetting

Although the formal period of consensus ended with the enactment of the constitution in 1978, a commitment to forgetting the past remained firmly in place. For one thing, continuing fears about the military made the government and the opposition leery of any digging into the past. Forgetting also afforded particular political advantages for both right and left. Given its Francoist background, the Suárez administration clearly benefited from a policy of forgetting and moving on. The left's willingness to keep a lid on the past through the end of the UCD government in 1981 can be seen in the policies pursued by the PSOE and PCE. Between 1978 and 1981, the left's attention to the past concerned matters not deemed especially controversial, such as the inadequacy of reparations in the 1977 amnesty, which led to several new laws to compensate those victimized by Franco's repression. These actions included restoring pensions to Republican Civil War veterans and teachers purged during the Civil War, reinstating civil servants dismissed from their jobs during the dictatorship, and allowing financial compensation to those who suffered injury or mutilation during the Civil War and restitution of confiscated property to the trade unions.[35] Because of the budgetary pressures exerted by the economic crisis that accompanied the transition, full implementation of this initial attempt at restitution did not materialize until the mid-1980s with the PSOE ascent to power.

A driving factor behind the left's continued neglect of the past was the PSOE's political transformation that preceded the 1982 national elections. After 1979, "the socialists began to use a new language in which the key words were no longer 'working class,' 'democratic socialism,' or 'Federal Republic,' but 'modernization,' 'Europeanization,' 'democratic consolidation,' and the 'strong internal unity of Spain" (Juliá 2003: 113). More specifically, after the 1979 elections, the PSOE redefined itself from "a class party, Marxist and democratic" to "a class party, of the masses, democratic and federal"; it also abandoned "mass mobilization rhetoric and radical ideological commitments" (Gunther 1986a: 15). Such a political makeover benefited (indeed, probably depended on) the capacity of left-wing leaders to keep their history of political radicalism out of view. "Surely, the last thing the PSOE wanted as it began to make the case to the public why it had to remove the UCD from power was to remind the public of the party's participation in the mayhem of the inter-war years, including political assassinations, attacks on the Catholic Church and the business class," observed José María Zufiaur, a socialist trade union leader.[36]

The biggest incentive for the left, especially the PSOE, to carry on with politics as usual with respect to the past, however, was that forgetting came to be seen as an essential ingredient of the project of modernizing Spain, especially incorporation into Europe. With the enactment of a new democratic constitution in 1978, the left's long-deferred dream of joining Europe was finally within reach, and this time the left was determined not to squander this dream with a fight over the past. As observed by William Chislett, a journalist who covered the Spanish transition to democracy for the *Times* of London and presently a columnist for the Spanish paper *El Imparcial*, "For Spanish politicians the decision to forget their recent bloody history instead of tearing at each other's throats as soon as Franco died showed that they wanted to move ahead and modernize." This was especially the case for the left's leaders, adds Chislett, "many of whom were ashamed of their pasts and Spain's long history of being regarded as backward."[37] On the contrary, the left was determined to put the policy of forgetting to the service of its own political goals. As seen next, once it reached power in 1982, forgetting provided a useful political framework for the PSOE to obscure its own history of political radicalism and to re-imagine Spain as a modern, European society.

CHAPTER 3

Socialist Rule and the Years of "Disremembering," 1982–1996

It is ironic that the heyday of the Pact of Forgetting arrived during the 1980s and 1990s, a period when politics was dominated by the PSOE, one of the governing parties of the Republican period, a primary target of Franco's repression, and an organization with a long history of political progressivism. Yet at no point during the four legislative sessions controlled by the PSOE (1982–1996), often with huge parliamentary majorities, did the party undertake any meaningful steps to confront the past that was so conveniently swept under the rug during the transition, including exposing the repression of the left at the hands of Franco during the Civil War and his long dictatorial regime. Quite the contrary; following its overwhelming electoral victory of 1982, the PSOE ushered in *la desmemoria* (the disremembering), a policy that stressed "liberation from past traumas as well as a refusal to face them" (Graham and Labanyi 1995: 313). Unsurprisingly, socialist rule during the 1980s and 1990s has been characterized by some as "the years of great silence and of no memory" (Gálvez Biesca 2006: 3).

Among the obvious reasons for the PSOE's wanting to prolong the Pact of Forgetting was the party's desire to convey the message, especially to the military, that the advent of a left-wing government did not pose a threat to the political status quo that consolidated after Franco. Although democracy no longer seemed at risk in 1982, the capacity of the military to derail democracy could not be discounted, as the aborted 1981 coup had effectively shown. The PSOE also faced an overload of political and economic problems inherited from the previous ruling party (the UCD), including restricting the prerogatives of the Catholic Church on issues like abortion and education, normalizing relations with newly created regional governments in Catalonia, the Basque Country and fifteen other regions, reforming Franco's outmoded economic structures, modernizing the military, and incorporating the country into the European Economic Community (EEC), the precursor to the European Union (EU). By sticking to a policy of letting bygones be bygones, the PSOE ensured it had sufficient political capital to fight other battles. However, as shown in this chapter, less self-evident political advantages in the end proved more convincing in driving PSOE commitment to the Pact of Forgetting.

The PSOE returned to power strongly believing that Spain's national interest rested firmly in its capacity to approximate its own identity to that of Europe. Thus, after 1982 the Pact of Forgetting became a foundation for propelling and sustaining an ambitious project of reimagining Spain's national identity as a modern, forward-looking, European state; a longtime dream of the Spanish left, especially for the PSOE, the most European of Spanish left-wing organizations. This image makeover, capped with Spain's incorporation into the EEC in 1986, benefited tremendously from the Pact of Forgetting since the pact repressed the very things that made Spain look anachronistic, backward, and positively un-European. The pact also obscured (if not obliterated altogether) earlier markers of Spanish national identity, such as imperialism, state centralization, and Christian-Catholic civilization, which the PSOE's leadership on the whole found distasteful. Under the PSOE's cultural and educational policies, these traditional aspects of Spanish identity were recast as idiosyncrasies of the like that any European state might have, rather than as defining national characteristics.

The Return of the Left

Spain's first left-wing government since the interwar Second Republic is widely regarded as a major marker in the country's democratization (see Gunther 1986a; Maravall 1985; Linz and Stepan 1996; Royo 2000; Méndez-Lago 2006). Above all, the 1982 elections that brought the PSOE to power for the first time since the 1930s are seen as signaling "the end of the transition to democracy" by demonstrating the nation's capacity to organize a peaceful handover of power (Vincent 2007: 224). But the victory itself was significant. On the one hand, it highlighted the dramatic rehabilitation and mainstreaming of the left. As seen in Table 4, the PSOE's performance in

Table 4. Socialist Electoral Dominance, 1982–1996 (percent of seats in Congress of Deputies)

Party	*1982*	*1986*	*1989*	*1993*	*1996*
PSOE	57.7	52.6	50.0	45.4	40.3
AP/PP	30.3	26.0	30.6	40.3	44.6
PCE/IU	1.1	2.0	4.9	5.1	6.0

Source: Spanish Interior Ministry.

1982 exceeded all expectations: 48.4 percent of all votes, translated into 202 seats in the Congress of Deputies or 57.1 percent of all seats. The elections also underscored the arc of the PSOE's remarkable metamorphosis, from a Marxist working-class organization at its inception in 1879 through at least the 1979 elections to a "catch-all" political party by the early 1980s. Only 19.1 percent of the PSOE vote in 1982 came from manual workers, and over 50 percent came from practicing Catholics, confirming that the PSOE victory "did not rest on any one particular class, regional, or even ideological base (Vincent 2007: 224). Clearly, the party's strategy, unveiled after the 1979 elections to increase its electoral appeal by cultivating support outside traditional PSOE constituencies—workers, intellectuals, and Republicans—had paid off handsomely.

On the other hand, the 1982 PSOE victory dramatically transformed Spain's political map, given the nearly complete collapse of the opposition. The UCD share of the popular vote went from 38 percent in 1979 to 6 percent in 1982. After this meltdown, characterized by López Pintor (1985: 305) as "an electoral defeat without precedent in contemporary European politics," the UCD largely disappeared from national politics, clearing the way for the PSOE's dramatic ascent to political power during the 1980s and 1990s. Between 1982 and 1996, the PSOE won national election after election, dominating Spanish politics like no other party in the history of electoral politics in Spain.[1] Indeed, fears of "pri-ismo," a reference to the Partido Revolucionario Institutional (PRI), the party that institutionalized one-party authoritarian rule in Mexico after its revolution, were widespread during the 1980s and early 1990s. It was not until 1989 that the PSOE lost its parliamentary majority, when a viable alternative finally arrived on the national political scene with the emergence of the Partido Popular (PP), a reincarnated Alianza Popular, the neo-Francoist party formed after Franco's death.

As might be expected, the PSOE's post-1982 electoral hegemony occasioned calls from some socialist quarters for action on the issue of the past. Those making these calls, perhaps sensitive to the charge that they wanted to open old wounds that could destabilize democracy, couched their arguments not in terms of retribution against the old regime but rather as a deferred ethical obligation. The most thoughtful arguments came in the form of an unsigned petition to the government published in the magazine *Diario 16*, which appeared just after the inauguration of the new government.[2] In it, a group of socialist activists urged the González administration not to let the nation's serious social and economic ills, "such as rising unemployment and escalating food prices," diminish the importance of ethical problems left unattended by the previous government, especially the issue of "moral reparation" for those victimized by the past.

The petitioners anchored their arguments for moral reparation on the unequal consequences of the 1977 amnesty accord. They observed that the legal and practical effect of amnesty for the forces that destroyed democracy and supported the Franco regime for decades allowed them to retain their "ideological, political and economic positions without any fear of retribution or revenge." By contrast, the "old Democrats" were forced to make do "with being released from the harassment of the law." The statement also made note of reports that the modest compensations designed to accompany the amnesty law (such as reinstatement of jobs and restoration of pensions) had by and large failed to materialize because of government-imposed bureaucratic hurdles, such as having to submit birth certificates, property deeds, and records of employment. Much of this paperwork was lost or misplaced following the disruptions of the Civil War. The statement concluded with the demand that the government undertake reparations in a way that honored "justice and equality and that closes wounds without re-opening new ones." This could be accomplished "with a simple gesture like acknowledging the nation's gratitude and respect for all those who gave their lives and their liberty in defense of democracy."

Yet pleas for moral reparation fell on deaf ears as the PSOE administration firmly believed that delving into the past created nothing but trouble. Forgetting and moving on was the mantra adopted by the PSOE leadership, a point underscored by the party's most distinguished and influential voices. Writer Jorge Semprún, a member of the Republican exile who served as Minister of Culture from 1988 to 1991, asserted in a 1993 interview: "If you want to live a normal life, you must forget. Otherwise those wild snakes freed from their box will poison public life for years to come" (Michnik 1993: 13). To its credit, on entering office the González administration expanded the legal provisions to compensate Republican veterans for their service in the armed forces, something envisioned around the time of the enacting of the 1977 amnesty process but not fully delivered by the UCD government.[3] The government also returned the patrimony confiscated by Franco after the Civil War to the trade unions. Slower in coming was recognition of the sacrifices by foreign veterans on behalf of Spain. In 1995, just before leaving office, the González administration sponsored legislation that granted Spanish citizenship to members of the International Brigades, a promise made by the Republican government in 1938.[4]

But the PSOE did not spend any of its considerable political capital on making justice for the old regime a political priority. Under the González administration, the Ministry of Justice took no steps to modify the 1977 amnesty accord, somewhat surprising given that the ministry employed several notable jurists, including Baltazar Garzón, who in the late 1990s became celebrated around the world for his advocacy of transitional justice for the victims of South America's military regimes. As seen in Chapter 5, Garzón's innovative jurisprudence led to the successful indictment of Pinochet on charges of crimes against humanity, and allowed Chilean citizens to sue their former oppressor in Spanish courts to get around the limitations of Chilean amnesty laws. This bold jurisprudence was not displayed with respect to Franco's political crimes.

Nor did the González administration, as will be seen later, employ cultural and education policy to raise consciousness about the past, especially the repression of the Francoist period. If anything, the government deliberately sought to bury the past once and for all, a point tellingly suggested by the administration's handling of the commemoration of the fiftieth anniversary of the beginning of the Civil War, which fell on July 17, 1986. González's main dilemma was how to address the obvious need for an appropriate monument to honor the victims of the Civil War without disturbing the silence about the past imposed by the Pact of Forgetting. El Valle de los Caídos, Franco's memorial to the victims of the Civil War, is widely recognized as a one-sided monument to Franco's Nationalist crusade. Instead of erecting a new monument, the González administration altered one built for the heroes of May 2, 1808, marking Madrid's rebellion against the French occupation, with the addition of the inscription "Honor to all those who gave their lives for Spain," unveiled by King Juan Carlos, one of the few symbols of national unity in contemporary Spain. The intention of recycling the monument to those who resisted the French occupation was twofold: to tie the memory of a very controversial event within Spanish society to one that is universally cherished, and to mark the fiftieth anniversary of the Civil War with a monument that did not call attention to itself. Merely an addition to an existing monument, "it does not even alter the landscape of the city" (Aguilar and Humlebaek 2002: 126).

Oddly, the dedication of the "new" memorial took place not in 1986 but in 1985, the tenth anniversary of the restoration of the Spanish crown, a decidedly less confrontational event. In 1986, the nation observed the start of the Civil War with "a deluge of popular publications, television programs and films," and scholars organized "dozens of conference and collective publications whose primary purpose was to disseminate the results of scholarly research on the war" (Boyd 2008: 136). The government, however, abstained from observing the anniversary, contending in a message released to the media that the war's "fratricidal character" made it "unsuitable for commemoration."[5] The statement added that: "the Civil War is history and no longer a part of the reality of the country." Implicit in the statement was that there was no shame in forgetting the past; in fact quite the opposite was the case. According to Humlebaek (2011: 192): "The will to forget the negative or problematic parts of the past was clearly interpreted as something positive; an achievement parallel to and constituent part of the establishment of a democratic system."

The wholesale neglect of the past signaled by the government's handling of the fiftieth anniversary of the Civil War did not sit well with some left-wing public intellectuals, many of them supporters of the PSOE, who by the 1980s were complaining about the existence of a "pact to silence the past" that risked erasing Spanish history, and worse, threatened to whitewash the Franco era. José Antonio Gabriel y Galán, the noted cultural critic, in a stinging critique of the cultural policies of the socialist administration in *El País* on February 20, 1988, noted that

> My impression is that in the collective consciousness of the Spanish people—aided, among other things, by the pact of silence—has begun a process of revisionism of Franco and the dictatorship. A kind of *light* version is seizing history that slowly but surely is heading toward adulteration. At this pace, how many years will it take before we accept that Franco was a well-meaning leader who had to confront

> the horrible cruelty of the Civil War, that he faced the postwar period with bravery, steered the country toward economic development, provided jobs and security, who restricted civil and political leaders because he had no other choice and who died peacefully and in a Christian manner leaving everything in peace and order. So in fifteen years could we be saying that there was never a dictatorship and a dictator?[6]

Interestingly enough, the only widely recognized "breach" of the Pact of Forgetting in the González era came not to force the nation to confront the past but for gaining political advantage over the opposition once the PSOE's near-hegemonic grip on power began to wane. In 1993, after more than a decade in power, the PSOE won congressional elections by insinuating that a victory by the right-wing PP would mean a return to Francoism.[7] In mounting this campaign, the PSOE capitalized on the fact that many PP leaders had close associations with the Franco regime, which conveniently opened them to the charge of having a "Francoist attitude." The main target was new PP head José María Aznar, a former tax inspector and president of the regional government of Castilla-León, who during his youth had been a member of the fascist Falange and whose father, an ambassador to Cuba under the dictatorship, had been a close friend of Franco. The purpose of exposing the authoritarian past of PP leaders, as observed by Joaquín Estefanía, editorial manager of *El País*, was twofold: to cast doubt on the PP's democratic credentials—Aznar's in particular—and to help the PSOE battle the public's growing exhaustion from ten years of socialist rule.[8]

Governing While Ignoring the Past

During the parliamentary debate leading to the 2007 Law of Historical Memory, the PSOE was on the defensive for its support of the Pact of Forgetting. As might be expected, the most vigorous defense of the pact came from former members of the González administration, including González himself, who since leaving office in 1996 has made no apologies for his support of forgetting as a means for coping with the past. His defense of the pact pointedly stressed the main rationale employed by the political class after Franco's death for letting bygones be bygones: the fear of reopening old wounds. In a 2001 article in *El País* contrasting Spain's handling of the past with that of Argentina and Chile, González noted, rather defensively: "We the Spaniards did it well. Within the limits of what was possible, we attempted to overcome the past without rekindling old fires, under which sparks still flew."[9]

Echoed in González's statement are many of the reasons that compelled his administration to support the Pact of Forgetting after 1982, beginning with lingering concerns about the military's capacity to derail the new democracy. Only a year before the PSOE's historic victory in 1982, the military had staged a rebellion; thus, the specter of another military rebellion was never far from the minds of PSOE leaders. As contended by Francisco Espinosa Maestre of the University of Seville, "the effect of history's traumas on the behavior of the left during the transition to democracy ensued not from fears of another civil war but from the memory of terror imposed by the victors, a memory revived by the attempted coup of February 23, 1981."[10] The lesson of the failed coup, he added, was "to force the left into assuming once again the position of political passivity imposed by the transition." Accordingly, caution rather than confrontation was the operative word for the PSOE when dealing with the military after 1982, a point stressed by several studies. Vincent (2007: 227) observes that: "entrenched military hostility toward 'Reds' meant that the socialist administration had to tread carefully." Jaúregui and Menéndez (1995: 196) stress that the PSOE's aim after ascending to power with respect to the military was "to avoid any policy that even hinted at possible ideological prosecutions."

In choosing not to confront the military on the issue of the past, the PSOE was also banking on having an easier time at introducing reforms intended to professionalize the military. In defending the González administration decision not to purge the military after 1982, former defense minister Narcís Serra (2010: 153) noted that "This would have provoked a corporate reaction and prevented the assimilation, however limited, of the aims of the reforms." Serra's argument is, of course, debatable, but the evidence is on his side. Between 1982 and 1991, the government undertook a sweeping modernization of the armed forces. The reforms included growing the navy and the air force at the expense of the army, with the aim of producing "an efficient, highly trained, professional defense force, a move symbolized with the abolition of military governorships in the 1990s" (Vincent 2007: 227).

Yet another reason for the PSOE to adhere to the status quo with respect to the past was the need to continue and deepen the democratization agenda initiated by the previous UCD administration in a political environment that echoed the one into which democracy was born. Indeed, the many challenges facing the incoming socialist administration were the same that the Suárez administration encountered between 1977 and 1981, including the struggle against ETA terrorism, rising unemployment, and growing tension with newly created regional governments, especially in the Basque Country and Catalonia. Thus, it is not surprising that even though the PSOE (in contrast to the UCD) enjoyed a parliamentary majority, which made compromise with the opposition less compelling for the government, González was very keen on retaining the consensus-driven approach to policy making that the previous administration had employed rather successfully. Between 1982 and 1985, the new administration negotiated several social pacts involving the government, the trade unions, and the national employers' association that regulated labor and industrial relations and dictated wage and inflation policy. Although the economic legacy of these accords remains contested, they are credited with boosting the political stability of the new democratic regime (Bermeo with García-Durán 1994; Encarnación 1997).

The PSOE also came into office determined to enact a sweeping program of social modernization that was sure to rile up conservative actors in Spanish society, including the Catholic Church. Therefore, upsetting the right on the issue of the past did not seem like smart politics. The PSOE upset church officials by legalizing abortion, even though the law was highly restrictive, permitting termination of a pregnancy only in cases of rape, severe fetal deformity, and threat to the health of the mother. Nonetheless, the conservative opposition took the government to the Constitutional Court, which did not reject the legality of abortion but requested that the government take measures to ensure that a request for an abortion was in full compliance with the limitations of the law. The PSOE also sought to modify the church-state compromise embedded in the 1978 constitution by limiting church access to state funds to finance a wide range of ecclesiastic activities, including education. A PSOE-sponsored law secured greater regulatory powers for the government over providers of private sector education, whose primary target was the Catholic Church. This case also ended up in the courts, with another decision favoring the government.

Ironically, in implementing its modernization policies, the PSOE was hardest on its own constituencies. As it sought to modernize the economy in anticipation of admission into the EEC, the PSOE took on its closest ally, organized labor, by arguing, as González put it, that "We must undertake serious and profound reforms, which in principle are difficult from a socialist perspective. This government has the obligation of transcending party interests" (Gunther 1986a: 34). Rather than advancing El Cambio, the Marxist-inspired economic agenda that brought the PSOE to power in 1982—and called for wealth redistribution, expansion of the welfare state, and a robust state-controlled economy—once in office, the PSOE began to renege on its economic promises by embracing an expansive package of neoliberal economic reforms intended to correct many of the structural defects bequeathed by the Franco regime to the new democracy and largely ignored by the UCD administrations, most notably numerous inefficient public companies grouped around the National Institute of Industry (INI).

The PSOE's economic reform effort entailed shutting down factories, especially in the steel sector, privatizing state-owned companies, and relaxing the labor market, which under Franco had been one of Europe's most rigid and protected as a means to compensate the working class for the lack of political freedoms. Things got started in earnest with the 1984 Law of Reconversion and Re-industrialization, which in a single legislative stroke targeted eleven sectors for "re-conversion," entailing the elimination of 80,000 jobs or a quarter of the workforce in the steel, shipbuilding, and textile industries (Bermeo with García-Durán 1994: 11), with the bulk of the job losses concentrated in Asturias and the Basque Country. By 1986, the government had sold or dissolved more than 30 enterprises, many of them owned by INI, including banks, automobile manufacturers, utilities, energy companies and steel mills.

Another about-face took place in foreign policy. The PSOE had opposed the 1981 decision by the UCD government to incorporate Spain into the North Atlantic Treaty Organization on grounds that joining violated Spain's long history of neutrality in major international conflicts such as World War I and II, and ran contrary to the country's traditional image as a bridge between Europe and the Third World (Latin America and North Africa in particular). The party, aware that these positions were cherished by the left, promised during the 1982 campaign to put the issue of membership in NATO to a referendum in the hope that the public would choose to pull Spain from the organization. Once in office, however, González found it difficult not to make NATO membership a key component of his plan for Europeanization of Spain. In campaigning for Spain's continued presence in NATO, he argued that membership could advance foreign policy goals, such as membership into the EEC and enticing France to cooperate with the Spanish government in the fight against ETA. In the end, González succeeded in getting 52 percent of the vote on the NATO referendum, aided by a clause calling for the reduction of American military personnel in Spain. With the NATO controversy behind him, González successfully completed Spain's incorporation into the EEC in 1986, his greatest accomplishment on the international front.[11]

Europe and the Reimagining of Spain

The most powerful incentive for the endurance of the Pact of Forgetting past the 1982 elections, however, was the pact's utility to ease Spain's incorporation into Europe, a key goal of the architects of the new democracy. As noted by Farrell (2005: 215): "The newly constructed social democratic state was constructed in part around the myth of Europe, which epitomized everything that was modern. Among those who shared the myth was the belief that Spain must rejoin Europe, which was critical to the reinvention of a democratic consciousness." European integration promised untold economic riches through the Structural and Cohesion Funds intended to create socioeconomic parity across the EU, to say nothing of validating the democratic credentials of the new political regime. After all, it had been the long Franco dictatorship that for decades had kept Spain outside Europe. For the PSOE, European integration had the special advantage of facilitating a redefinition of Spanish national identity away from the historical and ideological markers of the Franco era. After 1982, the PSOE embarked on an ambitious project of national-identity building that aimed at debunking the Francoist view of Spain as a conservative, Catholic, culturally homogeneous nation with a history steeped in its imperial past, while boosting Spain's image as a European, modern, multicultural state.

The PSOE's deep discomfort with Spain's traditional image was rooted in a mix of complex factors, starting with the party's difficult relationship with the notion of *El Estado Español* (the Spanish state). For much of its history, the PSOE resisted this idea because of its strong affiliation with Francoist rhetoric. But the rejection preceded the Franco regime, as suggested by the party's support for regional rights during the Republican era. Republican leaders granted statutes of autonomy to Catalonia and the Basque Country prior to Franco's 1936 coup and were in the process of formulating one for Galicia when the Civil War broke out. During the common struggle against Franco, the PCE and PSOE developed strong ties with nationalists in Catalonia and the Basque Country; both were on record as endorsing the creation of a federation of the peoples of Spain and even self-determination for any region, a position recanted during the negotiations of the 1978 constitution, which affirmed the indissoluble unity of the nation even as it recognized a plurality of nationalities within it. After the inauguration of democracy in 1977, the PSOE was quick to rebuild a reputation as a champion of regional rights by frequently attacking the Suárez administration as a "rigid defender of Spanish centralism" (Gunther 1986a: 42).

More important to the rejection of traditional markers of Spanish national identity was the conviction that this image was intimately linked to the political and economic failures of the past. As argued by Balfour and Quiroga (2007: 82), "in the 1970s and 1980s, the vast majority of leftist leaders shared the idea that the history of Spain was the history of failure." In making this case, leaders such as González (1978) stressed Spain's social and economic backwardness, a legacy of having missed the first and second industrial revolutions, and the international isolation the country endured for much of the twentieth century. Even the Republican period, which was controlled largely by the left, was in for some rough treatment after the socialists came to power. For the PSOE, the Republic was the embodiment of historical failure. Javier Pradera, the anti-Franco activist and columnist for *El País*, captured this sentiment in 1990 when noting that for the socialists, "the Republican transition served as a negative model for the post-Francoist transition."[12] Accordingly, after 1982, the socialists began to promote the very dubious claim of the post-Franco regime being the first democratic period in Spanish history.

For PSOE leaders, especially González, only an aggressive project of political rejuvenation and economic modernization could change the course of Spanish history, a development that hinged on the country's incorporation into Europe. Europe was, as González himself put it in *El País*, "the frontier of our ambition," a statement that suggested that the Spaniards "could achieve little or nothing of their collective project beyond or without the EU" (Torreblanca 2008: 25).[13] The newspaper itself underscored González's point by contending that: "there can be no serious Spanish national project outside Europe" (Closa and Heywood 2004: 245). Such beliefs tied the PSOE to a long tradition of liberal thinking that saw Europe as the natural end point for Spain, the answer to the country's ills, from its economic backwardness to its provincialism to its fractured national identity. "Spain is the problem, Europe the solution," famously contended philosopher José Ortega y Gasset when making the case in the first half of the twentieth century that Spain's path to freedom and progress rested with Europe.[14]

For the PSOE, the strategy of remaking Spanish identity in Europe's image and the Pact of Forgetting proved mutually reinforcing. As seen previously, the left had long viewed Europe as a panacea, and after Franco's passing it saw tying Spain's fortunes to Europe as the best insurance against the return of right-wing authoritarianism. Moreover, Europe signaled a great national project that promised leaving the past behind and embarking on the future, an idea the entire political class could support. As observed by Magone (2011: 218), European integration became "a kind of escapism from the politics of the past, which had just been suppressed through the 'pacto del olvido.' . . . The unanimous support of the political elite for European integration reinforced and consolidated the 'pacto del olvido' and allowed for a new beginning in the EEC of democratic states."

For the right, however, embracing Europe was more problematic. Spanish conservatives have traditionally viewed Europe as a vortex of ideas at odds with Spanish values and institutions, and, therefore, as something best kept at a distance. Franco had quarantined Spain from the end of the Civil War through the 1960s, fearing that European influences would contaminate the country; he opened Spain to foreign tourism and investment after the failure of his plans for economic autarky proved near devastating for the economy and the political regime. The post-Franco right has also resisted the left's notion of Europe always being the answer to Spain's problems. In 1992, PP leader Aznar criticized the "infantile sickness leading people to believe that Europeanization is always good" (Torreblanca 2008: 38). But by the early 1970s, the right, led by the industrial and financial bourgeois class, whose members by then had come to see the Franco dictatorship as a hindrance to its ambitions, was fully on board with European integration. "An advanced West European economic status" was "the standard against which Spanish industrialists viewed themselves" (Martínez 1993: 115). And just like the left, political motivations were also at stake: for many conservatives, Europe provided the best warranty against the future radicalization of the left.

The PSOE's agenda for remaking Spanish identity in Europe's image also enjoyed strong support in the separatist-minded regions, whose leaders already saw themselves as more European than Spanish. Regional politicians such as Jordi Pujol, the long-serving president of the Catalan Generalitat

(1980–2003), championed the idea of "Europe of the Regions," a notion that sustained the view of Europe as a collection of regions rather than of nation states. Even the Spanish Crown embraced the idea of Spain as belonging to the European community of nations, believing that the country's history, culture and religion belonged squarely in the European tradition. "The idea of Europe would not be complete without reference to Spain. . . . We are Europeans," proclaimed Juan Carlos I in his first address to the Cortes after the restoration of the monarchy (Crespo 2000: 121).

More important, perhaps, the Pact of Forgetting aided Spain's adoption of a European identity by hiding or obscuring episodes of Spanish history, like the Civil War and the Franco dictatorship that had made the country decidedly un-European, in an attempt to meld Spanish history in a broader European historical narrative. The pact provided the government with something of a clean slate on which to project a new vision of Spain. As observed by Cazorla (1992: 85), "the attempt to 'forget' Franquismo and turn ourselves into 'Europeans' has involved to a certain degree the invention—by imitation—of a modern Spain and even a re-interpretation of our history." In this pursuit of historical reinvention, the PSOE employed an impressive array of policy initiatives, from boosting regional cultures in the nationalist regions, to revamping cultural institutions and creating new ones, to reframing the teaching of Spanish history.

Recasting Spanish Identity

In keeping with the desire to shatter the Francoist myth of cultural homogeneity, the PSOE provided an enormous boost to the consolidation of the *autonomías* (regional governments). With the blessing of the central government in Madrid, during the 1980s the autonomous regions moved aggressively to promote the use of local languages in education and the media. In Catalonia, where these efforts have been most pronounced and successful, the 1983 Law of Linguistic Normalization allowed instruction in Catalan in primary and secondary schools; provided subsidies for the publication of books, magazines, and newspapers in Catalan; and created a television station broadcasting exclusively in Catalan. In Galicia and the Basque Country, significant efforts were made to revive moribund indigenous languages, which unlike Catalan, had neither been standardized nor gained public acceptance.

The state's cultural institutions, most notably the Ministry of Culture, were reorganized to allow them to exercise greater autonomy and a higher public profile. New cultural institutions were created, such as the Museo Nacional Reina Sofía in Madrid, the Museo de Arte Contemporáneo in Barcelona, and the Guggenheim Museum in Bilbao, to showcase modern and cutting edge art and thus to counterbalance the conservatism of Madrid's Prado Museum, an encyclopedic compendium of Spanish art. New awards and national prizes in the fields of literature, history, painting, and music were established with an eye toward recognizing the latest artistic trends. In 1991, the Cervantes Institute was created to promote Spanish culture abroad, an expression of confidence in the desire of overseas audiences to learn the Spanish language and to consume the nation's new cultural productions, from fashion to food to film.

National symbols also received a makeover in a way that did not disturb the silence about the past but nonetheless injected something new into the country's image. After Franco's death, the PSOE and other left-wing parties led an unsuccessful campaign to make December 6 Spain's official holiday, commemorating the anniversary of the constitutional referendum, in place of October 12, El Día de la Hispanidad, which commemorates Columbus's "discovery" of the Americas. For obvious reasons, many on the left were eager to drop or downgrade October 12, formerly known as Día de la Raza. Hispanidad pays homage to the common historical destiny of all Hispanic peoples, an idea that became fashionable in the early 1930s among conservative thinkers.[15] In 1987, the socialist government reopened the debate over the national holiday, but did not press the idea of replacing October 12 with December 6, which surely would have angered the right. Instead, it passed a law that rechristened October 12 the National Holiday of Spain, with an eye toward erasing any reference to "conquest and colonization, to Christopher Columbus, and even to Latin America" (Aguilar and Humlebaek 2002: 137).

Nothing better suggests the PSOE effort to showcase Spain as a modern, European, forward-looking country than the cultural trifecta the government staged in 1992, widely promoted as "the year of Spain." That year the country hosted three major international events: the Barcelona Olympics, the World's Fair in Seville (Expo '92), and the European Capital of Culture designation for Madrid. The fact that these major international events were held in 1992 was not accidental, since the year holds special significance for the country and its reputation abroad, hardly any of it positive. That fateful year marked the 500th anniversary of the expulsion of the Jews and Moors from the Iberian Peninsula, and the beginning of Spanish colonization of the Americas. Thus, the government made a deliberate attempt to employ the 1992 commemorations as a new historical juncture in the evolution of Spain. As observed by Graham and Labanyi (1995: 406), the commemorations marking the anniversary of 1492 were "intended to celebrate Spain's coming of age as a modern, democratic European nation-state, marking the end of a period of political transition (and uncertainty) and the completion of an economic, political and social process initiated in the 1970s."

The 1992 commemoration events were very popular with the Spanish public; they accorded Spain and the various cities involved in the celebrations extraordinarily good publicity abroad. They were also very successful in projecting a new image for Spain. The Olympic Games, for example, were an observance of the marriage of Catalan and Spanish nationalisms. As noted by Vincent (2007: 233), at the Olympics "nation and region were on display simultaneously, sometimes with surprising results. The King of Spain's first words at the Olympic opening were in Catalan and the symbols of Cataluña—language, flag and anthem—were given equal prominence with those of Spain." Vincent (235) also described Expo '92 as "a showcase of nationalism, internationalism, and modernity." Spain's dazzling pavilion, which stood at the head of the Avenue of Europe, and those of the seventeen Spanish regions, celebrated the country's cultural diversity, and other countries' pavilions often featured the work of celebrated Spanish artists, such as architect Santiago Calatrava, in a deliberate effort to underscore and pay homage to the international appeal of all things Spanish.

Largely lost in the celebrations of 1992 was any direct connection to the complex events that made 1492 a benchmark in Spanish history. As explained by Graham and Labanyi (1995: 406), the anniversary celebrations represented Spain's new modern democratic identity "as if it were built on a *tabula rasa*, thus avoiding confrontation with the cultural, social, regional and political tensions that have plagued Spain since its emergence as a nation state." A deliberate attempt was made to downplay the imperial/colonial connotations of 1492 by shifting the emphasis of the commemorations from the conventional "discovery" of the Americas by intrepid Europeans to the more palatable "encounter" between Spaniards and Americans. The recasting of 1492 was on the whole successful in Spain, but did not play well across the former Latin American colonies, where many governments used the occasion to highlight the horrors of the conquest, especially the abuse and killing of indigenous peoples, a history many now consider as nothing short of genocide.

The PSOE also revamped the teaching of Spanish history to reflect Spain's new image as a modern, multicultural state. In 1991, nearly a decade into its fourteen-year rule, the González administration ventured into the delicate business of reconfiguring the history curriculum with the enactment of the 1991 General Law of the Educational System (LOGSE). This was the first comprehensive attempt since the end of the Franco dictatorship to reconsider what Spanish children were taught about such sensitive subjects as the Civil War. Not surprisingly, this attempt at education reform became the touchstone for the "history wars" of the 1990s. As shown in Chapter 1, the education system was a primary vehicle for political socialization after the Civil War ended; the Franco regime fully exploited education policy to convey its own version of the Civil War and promote many of its own myths, such as having saved the nation from the chaos and destruction of the Republican period. The textbooks of the democratic transition had their own myths to promote, such as collective culpability for the events that drove the nation into the Civil War, which meant, among other things, glossing over the repression of the Franco years. Promoting such myths was critical to the rise of the politics of forgetting. Thus at its core the LOGSE was intended to "prioritize historical knowledge over mythmaking and historical distance over passionate moralizing" (Boyd 2008: 139).

For the first time, textbooks discussed the origins of the Franco dictatorship as part of the military coup against the Republican government in 1936 and acknowledged the years of repression that followed the end of the war in 1939. But the LOGSE had more ambitious goals than introducing historical accuracy into Spanish history textbooks. The first was to teach students to *valorar críticamente* (critically evaluate) the realities of the contemporary world and the antecedents and factors that influence it" (Boyd 2005: 100). This pedagogical effort, as socialist education minister José María Maravall observed, "connected the reforms of the early 1990s with those adopted by the Second Republic during the 1930s, which emphasized rationality and citizenship."[16] A second point was to popularize the idea of Spain as a "nation of nations," by emphasizing the richness of the country's cultural makeup. The government paired this effort with a policy that granted considerable control (35 percent) over the content of the educational curriculum to the nationalist communities. This decentralization of educational policy led to the development of textbooks offering "identity-driven narratives" in which the history of the Spanish state was subordinated to the history of the region or community, and, in the most extreme cases, the Spanish state was "vilified for its continuous repression and victimization of the Catalan and Basque people" (Boyd 2008: 139).

Last, but not least, the PSOE gave Spanish history an Europeanist orientation in an attempt to incorporate Spain into the larger narrative of European political development. In new textbooks, the transition to democracy, the construction of the autonomías, and Spain's integration into the EEC were seen as part and parcel of a postwar European-wide movement of political and economic integration that converged around the unification of Europe—never mind the fact that, because of the long phase of authoritarian rule, Spain had remained completely marginal to the developments leading to European integration for much of the twentieth century, beginning with the creation of the EEC with the Treaty of Rome (1957). To assimilate Spain into the narrative of European amalgamation, the Civil War was treated as a domestic aberration created largely by European-wide tensions between democracy and fascism, and Francoism was seen as "a parenthesis in Spanish history, an anomaly proving Spanish backwardness, isolation temptation, and the incapacity of its elite to modernize the country" (Torreblanca 2008: 25).

The Waning of Disremembering

The González era came to an end with the 1996 elections, which brought the right back to power for the first time since the Franco dictatorship. By the mid-1990s, fatigue with the PSOE had set in with the majority of the electorate. But the real catalyst for the defeat was the wave of scandals that rocked the González administration during the mid-1990s, which crested with the revelation of the existence of the Grupos Anti-Terroristas de Liberación (GAL), a network of death squads operated by the security forces located in the Ministry of the Interior to eradicate ETA's leadership. The death squads battled ETA between 1983 and 1987 using ETA's own tactics—assassinations, kidnappings, and bombings—which targeted numerous civilians on both sides of the Spanish-French border, many of whom had no connection whatsoever to terrorism (Encarnación 2007).

Once exposed in the mid-1990s by the right-leaning newspaper *El Mundo*, the existence of the GAL became the biggest political scandal of the post-transition years and by far the "darkest page in the history of the PSOE governments led by Felipe González" (Muro 2008: 139). Although the opposition accused González of masterminding the whole operation, the investigations of the late 1990s exonerated him of direct involvement with the creation and operation of the GAL. They did, however, implicate many in the upper echelons of the González administration and the PSOE. In 1995, Enrique Rodríguez Galindo, an officer of the Guardia Civil, and Julen Elgorriaga, a top PSOE official, were sentenced on charges of kidnapping and murder. By the time the investigations were completed in 1998, Rafael Vera, secretary of state for security, and José Barrionuevo, interior minister, had been sent to jail for illegal detention and misappropriation of state funds.

Back in opposition for the first time in 15 years, the PSOE began to gradually withdraw its support for the pact to forget. Three main factors led the way, the first being the provocations of the new conservative government on cultural and educational policy. Although the PP's first term in office (1996–2000) is generally seen as signaling the rise of a moderate right in contemporary Spanish politics (Balfour 2005), the party's cultural and educational program was controversial in the eyes of many left-wing leaders. From its inception, Aznar's conservative administration moved decisively to reorient teaching of Spanish history in secondary schools with a new "humanities plan" drafted by academics selected by the Ministry of Education and intended to address the perceived calamitous state of Spanish history instruction. Education officials contended that PSOE educational policies had led to neglect of traditional historical subjects, arguing that students could complete "ten years of schooling without hearing the names Julius Caesar and Philip II."[17]

But the PP greatly miscalculated and its education reform plan was defeated in the Congress of Deputies, the result of an unexpected collaboration between the PSOE and the nationalist parties from Catalonia and the Basque Country (CiU and PNV respectively). The regional parties, although in formal coalition with the PP, were nonetheless very disturbed by what they perceived as an "an encroachment of Madrid into their nationalist principles" by attempting to establish a common curriculum on the historical events that shaped Spain.[18] Esperanza Aguirre, the national education minister, accused the PSOE, which had previously supported the humanities plan in the senate, of political opportunism in order to embarrass the government and curry favor with the nationalists."[19]

This early defeat did not deter the PP—quite the contrary. On gaining absolute control of the Congress of Deputies in 2000, the party embraced what it termed "Constitutional Patriotism," a cultural project intended to undermine the view of Spain as a multicultural and decentralized state, replacing it with the notion of Spain as a country whose identity is defined by a common history and its contributions to universal culture (Balfour 2005; Nuñez Seixas 2005; Muro and Quiroga 2005). Constitutional Patriotism also sought to eradicate the negative and pessimistic image of Spain as a backward, barbaric, and decadent nation popularized by the liberal intelligentsia. In its place, the PP promoted an image that emphasized Spain as a proud, civilizing state, as suggested by the great forces that shaped the nation: the genius behind the conquest of the Americas, when the country was ruled by Queen Isabella and King Ferdinand, and the golden age of Spanish history, the period dominated by the Hapsburg emperors Charles I and Philip II, when Spain's empire extended to Europe, the Americas, and Asia. The PP policy for "Constitutional Patriotism for the Twenty-First Century," approved at the party's fourteenth congress in January 2002 and penned by two prominent PP Catalan and Basque leaders, Josep Pique and Maria San Gil, notes that "Spain is a great country, a nation shaped through the centuries . . . .A plural nation with an identity that is not ethnically based, but politically, historically and culturally based, which developed through its contribution to universal History and Culture, its own constituting plurality, and its historical project rooted in two worlds: Europe and America."[20]

Oddly enough, the PP recasting of Spanish history had much in common with that promoted by the PSOE while in office, if only because both attempts employed the politics of forgetting to fashion new projects of national identity. Like the PSOE's mission of Europeanizing Spanish history, the PP's project of historical reinvention also hinged on whitewashing or underplaying the Civil War and the Franco dictatorship. In the case of the PP, the Civil War was interpreted as a conflict rooted in problems that the nation had fully overcome. More surprisingly, Constitutional Patriotism appropriated Spain's constitutional-liberal tradition in an effort to create a cohesive grand historical narrative—rather ironic considering the traditional demonizing of Republicanism by Spanish conservatives. Naturally, the constitution of 1876, conceived by conservative politician Antonio Cánovas del Castillo, was praised for its liberal and secular orientations and for having provided Spain with political stability under the Restoration regime

(1874–1931), aided by the system of *turno pacífico* (peaceful turn), the corrupt practice of alternating power between liberals and conservatives. Even the much-maligned Second Republic got a favorable interpretation, with many conservative intellectuals praising "the patriotic intellectual legacy of Republican president Manuel Azaña" (Nuñez Seixas 2005: 133). The most effusive praise, however, was reserved for the 1978 constitution, a document that many conservative legislators actually rejected during the parliamentary vote that preceded the constitutional referendum, praised as "the best in Spanish Constitutional, Liberal history." In particular, the 1978 constitution was credited with "bringing about the transition to democracy" by "integrating the nation while recognizing its plurality."

Constitutional Patriotism raised the ire of the left—the term itself had long been associated with leftwing, progressive politics both in Spain and in the larger European context. Indeed, many PSOE leaders saw themselves as followers of the German political philosopher Jürgen Habermas, who is generally credited with popularizing the term during the 1980s. For PSOE leaders, as for Habermas, Constitutional Patriotism referred to the means by which any government could unite a society around constitutional principles. Under this theoretical construction, the nation is defined not by its history, collective memory, or culture but rather by a common commitment to liberty, equality, and justice. The PSOE's failed attempt to make December 6, the anniversary of the 1978 constitution, the national holiday of Spain over October 12, with its overt association with the Spanish colonization of the Americas, can be seen as a prime example of the party's championing of the ideals of Constitutional Patriotism. PSOE party leaders also objected to the charge by the PP that the left did not care for the notion of Spain. As noted by José Bono, president of the regional government of Castilla-La Mancha, in 2003: "The PSOE is the only party that has Spain as part of its official name."[21]

Understandably, criticism of PP appropriation of Constitutional Patriotism was most intense among left-wing intellectuals from places like Catalonia. Toni Comín wrote in *El Mundo*:

> It is inconsistent to claim constitutional patriotism and have nationalist attitudes and oppose federalism, just like it is contradictory to promote those symbols and policies that reinforce a unique and homogeneous vision of Spanish identity. These are the very

> tasks that the PP devoted itself to when at its last congress it adopted constitutional patriotism as its official doctrine. Now we know with certainty that this was only for the purpose of better confronting peripheral nationalisms, and not because they have renounced the original Spanish nationalism inherited from times both old and recent.[22]

A second factor prompting the PSOE to rethink its support for the pact to forget was a surging "memory" movement in civil society that the party could not afford to ignore. As seen in the next chapter, for a variety of reasons civil society had been a "silent" accomplice with the political class in the pact to forget, but this began to change dramatically in the late 1990s. For the first time since the transition, popular organizations began to press the government on a wide range of issues regarding the past, especially assistance in exhuming Republican mass graves. This movement was given a big boost by the 1998 indictment of Chilean strongman Augusto Pinochet on charges of crimes against humanity. Pinochet's indictment and subsequent arrest in London flooded the public sphere with memories of the political abuses of the Franco era and revealed that the nation was strong enough to sustain a national conversation about the past and take steps to recover its historical memory. But the indictment, which the Aznar administration opposed as an egregious example of judicial overreaching, also put the government in the position of being seen as wanting to defend a dictator who like Franco had come to power by crushing a left-wing popularly elected government. This battle over Spain's right to prosecute another country's dictator fractured the consensus between left and right to let bygones be bygones in Spain's own dictatorial legacy.

The third factor pushing the PSOE into changing its stance on the pact to forget was the pressure exerted by the party's liberal flank. After the 1996, the liberal media, especially *El País*, began to push for a more aggressive stance on the issue of historical memory.[23] Common themes of many left-wing writers in *El País* were the complicity of the left in perpetuating Francoist myths and the need to restore historical memory to deepen the quality of democracy. Vicenç Navarro, one of Spain's best-known political scientists, in an essay titled "The Costs of Disremembering," wrote: "There can never be an authentic democratic culture in Spain until there is an anti-Francoist culture, for which we need a vivid historical memory."[24]

Reinserting the Past into Politics

As it sought to reinsert the past into politics, the PSOE adopted a strategy that, according to historian Charles Powell, forced the Aznar government "to disown Franco."[25] This strategy was amply displayed during the "season of anniversaries" linked to the Republic, the Civil War, and Franco himself that began in 1996 with the fortieth anniversary of Franco's coup against the Second Republic. These historic anniversaries provided the left the opportunity to undertake legislative initiatives that condemned Francoism and exalted the memory of the Republic. As Powell has noted, the rise of the PP was accompanied by a "new nostalgia for Republicanism" within the left that implied a moral superiority not just to Franco but also to the current political system.[26]

In 2000, to mark the twenty-fifth anniversary of Franco's death, the PSOE and Izquierda Unida (IU) a federation of left-wing parties led by the former communists, introduced a number of resolutions honoring Franco's victims. The first, approved unanimously by the Congress of Deputies on October 24, 2002, recognized "the tragedy of Franco's slaves," the individuals employed to build monuments to the old regime such as El Valle de los Caídos and public works projects such as dams, bridges, jails, and viaducts. This declaration was a prelude to a more ambitious resolution, also passed unanimously by the Congress of Deputies on November 20, 2002 (the twenty-seventh anniversary of Franco's death), denouncing the 1936 military uprising as an anti-democratic act and condemning the Francoist repression. It cited the "illegitimacy of violence in imposing political beliefs and establishment of totalitarian regimes."[27] The resolution also offered "moral support" from the state to all initiatives of the victims of the Civil War and the Francoist repression as long as these avoided "reopening old wounds or reviving the quarrels of civil confrontation." It also urged the government to undertake measures designed to aid and protect the victims of the Civil War and the dictatorship, including financial assistance to those forced into exile—the so-called "children of the war" (the children of the Republicans sent outside Spain after the war broke out). Furthermore, the resolution advocated restoration of Spanish citizenship and voting rights to these children and their descendants.

The second resolution came only after the Aznar administration secured a firm commitment from the PSOE and IU that its passage would mean the end of using the past as a political weapon, a promise that proved to be short-lived. Clearly, the very modest nature of the resolutions was as far as the ruling PP was willing to go. The resolutions, interestingly, do not assign responsibility for the Civil War. For the right, at least, the terms of the Pact of Forgetting, which clearly was unraveling, were still valid. A month after the passing of the second resolution, Aznar was asked if he thought the Spanish government should apologize to the victims of Francoism, to which he responded, "There is no reason why I should apologize for anything. The history of the Spanish transition is a history of profound reconciliation, and that is the basis on which we have to continue working" (Faber 2007: 152).

On November 30, 2003, to mark the twenty-fifth anniversary of the 1978 constitution, the left-wing parties organized an event "to prevent forgetfulness and poor memory" by convening a gathering of Republican Civil War veterans, surviving members of the International Brigades, including the 2,800 volunteers who formed the American Lincoln Brigade, exiles, ex-political prisoners, and former anti-Francoist guerrilla members. This was a clear provocation on the part of the left. Not surprisingly, members of the PP criticized the event as a "mothball revival" intended to incite old resentments, comments that outraged the victims and their families.[28] The PP skipped the event, the only party among the eleven present in the congress without representation at the event. The honorees, almost all octogenarians in various states of health, were treated to a lavish reception in the Spanish parliament, where they heard laudatory speeches about the sacrifices they had made for the Spanish nation. Remarking on the absence of PP leaders at the event, Tomás Caballero, grandson of a victim of a Civil War death squad, remarked, "mothballs are what they have in their own Francoist suits."

The anniversary resolutions foreshadowed the architecture of the 2007 Law of Historical Memory, widely regarded as the PSOE's full retreat from the Pact of Forgetting. The law reflects the new civil society activism embodied in the movement to recover the historical memory as well as the desire on the part of a new generation of left-wing leaders without any connection to the events of the democratic transition for a more honest treatment of Spain's dark past. Yet, as will be seen next, civil society activism on the issue of historical memory took decades to emerge. For years after the transition to democracy, civil society was a silent accomplice to the pact to forget.

CHAPTER 4

A Silent Accomplice: Civil Society and the Persistence of Forgetting

As they settled on a strategy of forgetting and moving on to deal with the dark legacy of the Civil War and the Franco regime, Spanish politicians appear to have enjoyed the complicity of "civil society."[1] Throughout the transition and its aftermath, none of the major players in Spanish civil society—organized labor, the Catholic Church, and professional organizations of lawyers and academics, to name but the most prominent, made transitional justice even a secondary priority in their endeavors. The only known effort by an organized group to dispense justice to the Franco regime took place in 1978, when a small group of intellectuals on the fringes of the Spanish Communist Party declared their intention to form an "international civic tribunal" to probe the political crimes of the regime (Aguilar 2008: 402). Largely a symbolic gesture, this aborted attempt at transitional justice was ignored as a publicity stunt by the political class, with politicians on the right and left fully invested in a pact to forget, and met a similar fate with the general public.[2]

More suggestive still, the Spanish transition did not engender grassroots movements devoted to addressing the human rights abuses of the old regime. To be sure, a variety of organizations concerned with the past did emerge during the transition. But, tellingly, retroactive justice toward the Franco regime was not among their demands. The mid-1970s saw the rise of Justicia y Paz (Justice and Peace), a movement that fought for amnesty for Franco's political prisoners triggered in part by the repression unleashed by ETA's assassination of Carrero Blanco in 1973, as well as a number of organizations demanding restoration of pensions for Civil War veterans and reparation for the victims of the Franco dictatorship. Notable among these organizations were the Association of Ex-Prisoners of Catalonia and the Society of History and Justice of Andalusia. It would be more than two decades after the democratic transition that the first organization devoted to bringing accountability to the Franco regime, the Asociación para la Recuperación de la Memoria Histórica (ARMH), emerged in 2000.

The absence of civil society activism in Spain on the issue of transitional justice stands out stands out for at least two reasons. On the one hand, during the transition Spain is thought to have experienced an explosion of civil society activism, a phenomenon captured in the expansive literature on the "return" of civil society after decades of Francoist repression (see Maravall 1978; Castells 1983; Pérez-Díaz 1993a,b; Encarnación 2001b; Threllfall 2008). The most influential of these studies (Pérez-Díaz 1993a: 32–35), made the argument that by the early 1970s there existed in Spain a political culture that was "hostile" to the Franco regime, alongside a "culture of protest" prevalent in universities, trade unions, and the legal establishment, among other sections of Spanish society, that made the Franco regime look politically anachronistic and out of step with the rest of society. This culture of protest has become an enduring and important feature of Spanish democracy given "the extraordinarily large role" that public protest plays in "channeling and defining" the participation of citizens in the political system (Fishman 2013: 1). On the other hand, the Spanish experience stands in striking contrast to other democratizing environments where civil society organizations played a starring role in putting transitional justice atop the agenda of the new democratic regime.

In Portugal, "powerful social movements" succeeded in pushing the government toward adopting an ambitious strategy of political purges designed to cleanse the state and society of authoritarian influences (Costa Pinto 2001: 71). Greek civil society "pressed for the administration of transitional justice" and the conservative government followed suit with military trials (Sotiropoulos 2010: 450). In Argentina, the case for justice against the military was led by Las Madres de la Plaza de Mayo, a group of mothers and grandmothers who demanded accountability for the disappearance of their children and grandchildren while in police custody (Navarro 1989; Brysk 1993). After a military court absolved the architects of the infamous *guerra sucia* (dirty war), the extrajudicial war waged by the military against political dissidents in 1976–1983, Las Madres were instrumental in forcing the government to pursue justice against the nation's top generals. In Uruguay, "the victims of repression, human rights organizations, opposition parties, and other social movements called for 'truth-telling' to counteract years of military denial of violations, and for trials of those responsible for abuse" (de Brito 2001: 120). Across the post-communist world, citizens' groups pushed for charging former oppressors with crimes against humanity and for lustration or disqualification of former communist leaders from holding office in the new democracy (Müller 2002; Garton Ash 2002; Friedman and Kenney 2005).

So what accounts for the seemingly puzzling complicity of Spanish civil society with the politics of forgetting? A suggestive explanation is that transitional justice was less an international phenomenon in the 1970s than in subsequent decades. Blakeley (2005: 45) notes that "The Spanish transition to democracy occurred in the 1970s at a time when the Cold War was still in existence, a framework of international human rights legislation was far from consolidated, and human rights themselves were certainly far from being the universal language that they had become by the late 1980s and 1990s." By contrast, Blakeley notes that when transitions to democracy began to take place in Latin America, Africa, and Eastern Europe, new features in the international and domestic political arena had evolved that facilitated transitional justice, such as a well-established network of nongovernmental organizations working in human rights both at a national and global level, the development of new communication tools like the Internet, and a growing array of mechanisms to aid transitional justice, such as the truth and reconciliation commissions pioneered in Latin America.

Blakeley's points are certainly valid, but they are weakened by the robust experience of transitional justice in Portugal and Greece, whose transitions virtually coincided with Spain's. To fully understand the absence of civil society activism in Spain during and after the democratic transition we have to consider, first, that, as with the political class, forgetting was the preferred way for the public to deal with the past. As shown in this chapter, the public entered democracy with no appetite for delving into the past. This was the outcome of a cocktail of social and political factors, including fears that revisiting old feuds could complicate and even undermine the nascent democracy, a collective memory of the Civil War that regarded this seminal conflict in Spanish history as a national tragedy for which everyone bore equal responsibility, and ambivalent sentiments among ordinary Spaniards about the legacy of the Franco regime, with a significant portion of the public unwilling to indict Franco for his political excesses, believing that he "had been good and bad for Spain." All the above made any civil society initiative designed to punish the old regime for its political sins an uphill struggle.

A less apparent factor was the impact of the transition itself. Largely invisible to the public, the transition in Spain afforded the political class remarkable autonomy from society in deciding how matters about the past would be settled. Moreover, unlike other transitions in Southern Europe and Latin America, the Spanish transition did not involve the active mobilization of the masses by either the left-wing parties or the Catholic Church; on the contrary, much of the success of a transition anchored on elite agreements depended on demobilizing groups, like the labor movement, that in other countries emerged as a foundation for demanding transitional justice. Finally, the overall success of the democratic transition not only underscored the wisdom of not having confronted the past in the eyes of many Spaniards, it also triggered an euphoric, forward-looking post-transition mass culture that made Spaniards quite uninterested in dwelling on the unpleasantness of the past, especially episodes like the Civil War and the Franco dictatorship that set Spain apart from other European states.

Fear and Forgetting

The most compelling sign of the general public's willingness to support the decision by the political class to let bygones be bygones was its approval of the amnesty policy proposed by the government. In 1975 an impressive 61 percent of the Spanish public supported the idea of a blanket amnesty, believing that this would be in the interest of democracy (López-Pintor 1980: 15).[3] The political behavior of the public also spoke volumes about the desire to deal with the past by not dealing with it at all. In 1976, through a national referendum, the public endorsed a law of political reform that had nothing to say about the political crimes of the outgoing authoritarian regime. The clear winner of the 1977 elections, Adolfo Suárez, was someone whose political background was intimately linked to the old regime and whose administration explicitly endorsed a policy of forgetting and moving on. By contrast, the public largely shunned the old Republican elite. Even "left-wingers" regarded the "fabled Republicans like creatures from another planet" (Hopper 1986: 273).

As happened with the political class, fear provided the glue that cemented the willingness of the Spanish public to want to leave the past behind. This point has been underscored by the leadership of the civil society organizations that since the early 2000s have made recovery of the historical memory a chief endeavor when asked to explain the general public's apparent acceptance of the politics of forgetting. According to Antonio Sánchez Marín, a spokesperson for the Memory Forum, "The democratic transition did not bring about an end to people's fear about the past. Everyone was painfully aware of the history of the two Spains."[4] "We have to take into consideration the context of the time," noted Ludivina García Arias, a spokesperson for the Association of Descendants of the Spanish Exile, adding that "the public was keenly conscious that the right-wing forces were the architects of the transition and that they remained in control."[5] These statements are supported by public opinion data of the era.

The most extensive study of public opinion conducted in Spain between 1966 and 1977, by the Instituto de la Opinión Pública, suggests that democracy was seen by the Spanish people as "a natural development" after Franco's death; only a small proportion of the public believed the authoritarian regime could survive (Wert Ortega 1985: 73). Acceptance of the democratic principle of government grew gradually, climbing from 35 percent in 1966 to 78 percent by 1976. As seen in Table 5, after Franco's death the majority of Spaniards (74 percent) thought their country should "evolve toward a democracy of the Western kind."

The theoretical acceptance of democracy by the Spanish public, however, did not imply that a smooth transition to democracy out of Francoism would be possible. By and large, the public anticipated the political transition as "a harsh and frightful experience, a sort of ordeal" (Wert Ortega

Table 5. Political Preferences After Franco's Death (percent)

More freedom of speech	72
Universal suffrage	70
Regional autonomy	61
Political amnesty	61
More political freedom	58
More democratic policies	58
Would like to see a Western democracy	74
Evolution to democracy is not possible without reforming the Fundamental Laws	60

Source: López-Pintor (1985).

1985: 74). Table 6, reveals that 58 percent of Spaniards awaited the future "with worry," 39 percent "with tranquility," and 3 percent "did not know." Yet the public greeted democracy with optimism: a reported 52 percent evaluated the country's situation as "very good" or "good" in December 1976, a reflection of the euphoria created by the Law of Political Reform, which put a peaceful end to the Franco regime (Wert Ortega 1985: 84). By 1978, as suggested by Table 7, however, the picture had become decidedly more negative with only 22 percent of the population viewing the nation's state of affairs as "very good" or "fairly good."

Fueling public worries about the future was fear that the chaos that led to the Civil War in 1936 would return. Despite the passage of time, this remained a top concern for most Spaniards. The memory of the horrors of the Civil War had been engrained in the minds of the general public since the end of the conflict in 1939 and was in fact an important explanation for the longevity of the Franco regime. As Tusell (1979: 558) has noted, the continuation of the Franco regime was not due primarily to the weakness of the opposition, or to the support of the Catholic Church, or the general public's

Table 6. Indicators of Concern About the Future, 1975–76 (percent)

Looking toward the future	*March 1975*	*June 1975*	*January 1976*
With worry	58	57	54
With tranquility	39	31	34
Don't know	3	12	12

Source: López-Pintor (1985).

Table 7. Evaluation of the Present and Future Political Situation (percent)

Evaluation	*1978*	*Future*
Very good	2	5
Fairly good	20	35
Unsatisfactory	39	18
Fairly bad	13	7
Very bad	4	2
Don't know	19	31
No answer	3	2

Source: López-Pintor (1985).

passive acceptance of the authoritarian state: "The decisive factor was that a large segment of the population lived haunted by the memory of the Civil War."

Memories of the Civil War were awakened four decades later by the violence that enveloped the democratic transition, which pointedly suggested the deterioration of public order. ETA's 1973 assassination of Prime Minister Carrero Blanco served as a preview of the violence that followed Franco's death in 1975. As seen in Chapter 3, ETA intended the killing of the man whom Franco had hoped would realize the strategy of "Francoism without Franco" (also often referred to as *continuismo*) to be the catalyst for the military's wholesale repression of society. Instead, this bold act of terrorism strengthened the resolve of the political class (especially the left) to avoid confrontational tactics of almost any kind. Nonetheless, Carrero Blanco's assassination was followed by a wave of right- and left-wing terrorist acts that killed some 400 people between 1975 and 1980, and left the public wondering if Spain was capable of organizing a peaceful change of political regimes (Reinares 1990: 390).

Media depictions of the political violence that marred the transition to democracy reinforced the image of a nation coming apart at the seams. New publications, like the magazine *Cambio 16* and its sister publication, an evening daily called *Diario 16*, featured provocative headlines and heavy photographic content devoted to workers' strikes, mass demonstrations, and gory depictions of those killed by political violence. A resurgent extremist right-wing press, which served as a mouthpiece for the dying Franco regime, did its best to stoke the public's anxiety about the future. It opposed democracy by cautioning against elections, resuscitating the same arguments Franco had used to impose his authoritarian rule following the end of the Civil War. "Doesn't Mr. Suárez realize that in Spain elections can still divide, as they are in fact doing, the Church, the military, and the families?" This was the question posed by an editorial in *El Imparcial*, a paper that reflected the political attitudes of many in the military and far right on the eve of the 1979 general elections (Roldán Ros 1985: 267). Another fear-fueling tactic of the extreme right-wing press was to demonize many of the left-wing leaders, especially Santiago Carrillo of the Spanish Communist Party. The daily *El Alcázar* habitually portrayed Carrillo as a war criminal whose intentions were to mobilize the Spanish working class in an effort to turn the country over to Moscow.

Not surprisingly, perhaps, the public opinion data of the transition period were quite clear in pointing to the public's preference for a transition to democracy that favored the gradual democratic evolution of the authoritarian regime. One of the most suggestive findings in Table 5 is the high percentage of the population (60 percent) that believed that the transition to democracy would not be possible without reforming the Fundamental Laws, the governing bylaws of the Franco regime.[6] This belief clearly entailed a preference for reforming the authoritarian regime from the inside out. Of those eligible to vote, 77.7 percent approved the law. The preference for gradual political change is also supported by a national survey that marked the tenth anniversary of Franco's death (CIS 1985). Of all options given to the respondents about "what you wish would happened after Franco," the response with the highest level of support (39 percent) was that "things would change gradually until we reach democracy little by little." Only 22 percent of respondents expressed a preference for "a rapid change to democracy," and a barely significant 2 percent of the public had a desire for "revolutionary" change.

The Shock of the Coup

Despite the peaceful general elections of 1977 and 1979, fear continued to percolate among the public. By 1979, concerns about the future emanated from the dreaded prospect of a military coup in reaction to some of the government's policies, such as the legalization of the PCE in 1977 and the extension of home rule to the Catalans and the Basques. These actions, combined with rising levels of violence on the part of the ETA, as well as extremist groups on the left and the right, and the ensuing perception that the civilian leadership had lost the capacity to protect the social peace, triggered the aborted military coup of February 23, 1981. The failed coup, televised live, followed by the spectacle of a military trial, "paralyzed Spanish society in fear, which had to wait silently and submissively for the conflict to resolve itself."[7] According to the polling data from the Centro de Investigaciones Sociológias (CIS), 61.5 percent of Spaniards feared the return of another civil war as a consequence of the events of February 23, 1981, considerably higher than the percentage of people who feared that polarization and disorder would trigger another civil war (CIS 2008).

Although *El Tejerazo* failed to derail democracy, it did play a major role in deepening the process of repressing the past initiated by the transition. In particular, fears of a military coup succeeded in casting a pall over nascent efforts by civil society to recover Spain's historical memory that began shortly after the democratic transition, specifically after the 1979 elections. The first municipal elections of 1979 were read by the public as a sign that the country was on the right track toward long-term democratic stability. The elections came on the heels of the enactment of the democratic constitution in 1978, along with some gains by the PSOE over the center-right UCD. As documented by Humlebaek (2007: 8), many people saw the left's gains across a number of cities and towns as "the signal they had been waiting for to begin a public recuperation of the memory that had been hidden for over four decades." Most disturbing in people's minds was the state of the mass graves of Republicans killed by the Nationalist army, which had gone unmarked for the entire Franco dictatorship. In many instances, the relatives of the victims knew the precise locations of many of the graves, but the repression of the Francoist era had prevented them from exhuming the bodies and giving them a proper burial. After the 1979 elections, a number of local governments now in the control of the left began to dig up the unmarked graves. This was an egregious breach of the Pact of Forgetting, with some people, according to Humlebaek (2007: 8), "even starting to demand justice, gathering at the front door of the executioners."

The most notable incident reported by Humlebaek took place in the village of Torremejía, in Extremadura, a region on the Spanish-Portuguese border, where in 1979 the bodies of 33 Republicans killed by Franco's nationalist army were exhumed and reburied. These actions landed the village's mayor in court, not merely because he had authorized the exhumations but because he had used public funds to conduct them. The case was eventually dismissed, but lingering fear about the future put an end to the illegal exhumation of unmarked Republican graves. After the failed military rebellion, the digging up of unmarked Civil War graves came to a screeching halt. The fear instigated by the aborted military coup triggered the return of the repression of memory to which people had been conditioned under the Franco dictatorship. No exhumation of Republican graves would take place between 1981 and 2000.

The military coup also shaped the public's reception of the fiftieth anniversary of the start of the Civil War in 1986. Like the government's own reaction to the anniversary, silence characterized the public's response. This was most tellingly suggested by the absence of obituaries placed in national newspapers by the relatives of those who died in the war. As seen in chapter 6, such notices (*esquelas*) became quite popular decades later, especially around the seventieth anniversary of the start of the Civil War in 2006. Reflecting on the contrast in the popularity of anniversary obituaries published by the relatives of the victims of the Civil War between 1986 and 2006, a reporter from the newspaper *El Mundo* wrote: "Not even in 1986, with the half-century anniversary of the Civil War, did obituaries of this type appear in the leading papers of the time, *El País*, *ABC*, and *Diario 16* because of the prevailing fear that gripped Spanish society, embarked still on a delicate transition to democracy with the wounds of the coup of February 23 not yet healed."[8]

Fear of the Past

Other social fears, independent of the violence that accompanied the change in political regimes and the threat the military posed to the stability of democracy, further encouraged Spaniards to accept the idea of forgetting and moving on. First of all, they feared the past itself and were unsure about what its full exposure could reveal. An important factor helping Franco succeed in institutionalizing his repression was the willing participation of many Spaniards who fervently believed in his cause. Many of them were affiliated with the bureaucratic apparatus of the state through the Falange, which controlled many social service agencies, or the Catholic fundamentalist organization Opus Dei, which controlled the education and economics ministries. Still others assumed the role of passive collaborationists by becoming state secret informants, and benefited directly from the cover the Pact of Forgetting provided. Graham (2004b: 324) has explained how these fears about the past interacted with the rise of the politics of forgetting:

> The "pact of silence" was needed not only because of the Francoist elites, but also because of the wide complicity of "ordinary Spaniards" in the repression—not only the civilian militia, or local priests across Spain, but hundreds of thousands of people who for political reasons and many other sorts of reasons, had responded to the regime's enthusiastic encouragement to denounce their neighbors, acquaintances and often even family members—denunciations for

> which no corroboration was either sought or required. So it was widespread social fear that underlay the "pact of silence": the fears of those who were complicit, the fear and guilt of the families and heirs of those who denounced and murdered, as well as of those who were denounced and murdered. Fear, in short, of the consequences of reopening old wounds that the social and cultural policies of Francoism had, decade on decade, expressly and explicitly prevented from healing.

Fear also manifested itself in the internalized shame of those victimized by Franco. The bodies of those who had died in support of Franco's Nationalist crusade were exhumed after the end of the Civil War and their graves inscribed with the phrase *Caídos por Dios y por España* (Those who fell for God and for Spain). By contrast, those who died from the Republican side were demonized and humiliated by Francoist discourse and had to make do with unmarked graves. This shame imposed a silence upon the survivors of Franco's victims. As reported by Elkin (2006: 43), "The children and siblings of victims learned how to not talk about it, as if it were a stain on their families. They learned to live with the burden."

The Myth of Equal Culpability

The memory of any nation's history, especially of controversial events, is almost always contested. This is the case of the Spanish Civil War, whose causes remain hotly debated by scholars and by the descendants of those who fought the war (see Juliá 2006). But some interpretations of history, regardless of whether or not they correspond to historical reality, are more successful than others at lodging themselves into the national consciousness and in creating a shared knowledge about the past—in other words, a collective memory. As some have argued (Halbwachs 1992), collective memory represents a curated or edited social representation of the past, a highly subjective interpretation of events that privileges some memories over others in creating a dominant narrative. As such, collective memory is capable of determining what is remembered (as well as what is forgotten) and of influencing the public's behavior by becoming part of the larger political culture.

Around the time of the transition, the collective memory of the Civil War emphasized a set of core assumptions that represented an imagined social representation of what actually transpired during the war and its aftermath. Widely shared by society, these assumptions predisposed the public during the transition to want to set the past aside. The most interesting of these assumptions was that both sides in the Civil War bore equal responsibility for the bloodshed and its long-term consequences. This sanitized narrative of the Civil War, which masks the facts that Franco's coup was a vicious attack by a reactionary minority upon a popularly elected government, and that the human cost of the war and the dictatorship fell disproportionably on specific sectors of society like the working class and the left, engendered the argument that *todos somos culpables* (we are all guilty). This sense of shared responsibility led to the logical conclusion that the Civil War was best forgotten, since no one side was to be blamed for it. As argued by Benedicto (2004: 295),

> This re-interpretation of historical memory started in the later years of the Franco regime, relying on the idea that the war had been a collective tragedy, a fight in which both sides had made mistakes and which both had ultimately lost. Stripped of its character as a symbol of disunity, the war turned into a historical experience from which important lessons could be learned; "never again" were the mistakes of the past to be repeated. Yet at the same time, it was better to forget this experience. In other words, it was a source of political learning for the new stage, but of amnesia when it came to its origins and causes.

The problematic notion of equal culpability remains very much alive in the consciousness of the Spanish public even decades after the democratic transition and in the face of significant research that shows, among other things, that the number of killings perpetrated by the Nationalist side far exceeded the number attributed to the Republican side (see Casanova 1992; Juliá 1999b). According to the CIS national polling data (2008), when asked which side generated more killings, the majority of respondents (35.0 percent) answered "both sides were the same." More suggestively, perhaps, when asked who was responsible for triggering the Civil War, the majority (39.9 percent) answered that the "the left and the right are equally to blame."

Interestingly enough, the roots of the myth of equal culpability rest deep within civil society, especially the so-called "mid-century generation," the influential anti-Franco intelligentsia that emerged during the 1950s and

1960s, composed of dissident artists, writers, filmmakers, and thinkers (see Besas 1985; Jordan 1995; Juliá 2004). This attests to the importance of elite agents in originating, advancing, and disseminating what eventually comprises the collective memory of any event. The origins of the mid-century generation have been debated intensively among Spanish scholars. Theories about its emergence include the relative openness of the late Franco years facilitated by the liberalization of the economy; the entry of Spain into international organizations like the United Nations; disillusionment with the rigidity of the intellectual environment created by Francoist institutions, such as the student syndicate, the radicalization of some sections of Spanish society traditionally supportive of the Franco regime (especially Catholic organizations); and, most intriguingly, the rise of a generation gap created by the trauma of the Civil War within families from the winning side of the war.

While those who won the Civil War and controlled the dictatorship viewed the events leading to the Civil War in stark black and white terms (e.g., the policies of the Second Republic bore ultimate responsibility for the Civil War, and Franco valiantly stood up to the Republic to save the nation from chaos and destruction), this was not always the case for their children. As noted by Jordan (1995: 246), the next generation of those who won the Civil War often saw themselves as "innocent spectators and hapless victims of a monstrous, bloody, and damaging conflict"; moreover, their formative years in the 1940s were influenced "by the tragic and repressive aftermath of the war, as well as international isolation, economic dislocation, shortages, rationing and censorship." Thus, according to Jordan, the mid-century generation was generally not interested in taking sides; instead, it sought to "overcome the divisions created by the war, to heal the divide between the winners and losers." In keeping with this intention, the Civil War was regarded "as an abstract moral outrage, a wild orgy of blood-letting, whose appalling effects are visited upon a whole generation of innocent children, irrespective of social and class differences." This nonpartisan reading of the causes and consequences of the Civil War did not imply a desire to whitewash history—on the contrary. In Jordan's view, the economic, social, and political disparities of postwar Spain became so acute that some of the more privileged offspring of the winning side felt compelled to assume responsibilities ignored by their parents and "correct the errors of the older generation."

The student protests of 1956 at the Complutense University of Madrid (which led to the closing of the university) marked the arrival of the mid-century generation. Juliá (2004) has argued that the protests began a process of distancing the children of the victors of the Civil War from the Franco regime, alongside the beginning of new debates about Spanish history. Dissatisfied with the founding myth of the dictatorship (that it had saved the country from chaos and destruction), and frustrated with the inability of the regime to pull Spain from the postwar doldrums, the children of Falangists and Nationalists began to offer alternative frameworks for understanding the causes of the Civil War and ways to alleviate its dire consequences. The members of the intelligentsia realized that "their social, intellectual, and artistic concerns could not find an answer within the current institutional structures and that the founding myth of the regime, the Civil War, had been a 'collective madness' which everyone had been responsible for and which required reconciliation between the victors and the defeated" (Chuliá 2007: 169).

Several political and social currents made the problematic arguments about the Civil War set forth by the new intelligentsia embodied by the mid-century generation quite influential. It certainly mattered that these arguments represented an internal challenge to the authoritarian regime. For the first time there were Spaniards belonging to the winning side of the Civil War producing "an alternative discourse to the official one on the history of Spain" (Chuliá 2007: 109). This willingness to dissent from the official story gave credibility to the members of the mid-century generation in the eyes of the Francoist opposition. More important, the arguments advanced by the mid-century generation reminded the public of the very high price that the nation had paid for its political excesses as democracy was approaching, a point underscored by the cultural output of the late Franco period.

The early novels of Juan Goytisolo (*Juegos de mano*, 1958; *Duelo en el paraíso*, 1955) and Ana María Matute (*Historias de la Artamila*, 1961) portrayed lives irreparably damaged by the horrors of the Civil War and the economic dislocation of the postwar years. Similar themes are explored in the late dictatorship films of the early 1970s. Inspired by the masters of postwar Italian cinema (De Sica and Rosselini in particular), these films contrasted sharply with the nationalistic epics favored by the state film company (CIFESA) or the frivolous comedies that dominated Spanish commercial film making after 1959. The so-called "new Spanish cinema" dealt with such themes as the suppression of memory and the consequences of political repression (Kinder 1993; Besas 1985), albeit often obliquely because of the prevailing Francoist repression; until 1976, the state required that all scripts be scrutinized by state-approved inspectors. The indisputable master of such films was Carlos Saura, whose work dramatized the twilight of the Francoist era. In some of his best-known films, such as *Ana y los lobos* (1972), *La prima Angélica* (1973), and *Cría Cuervos* (1975)—prototypes of the so-called "Children of Franco" films—Saura skillfully used children to convey the costs of the Francoist dictatorship and to show a glimpse of hope for a democratic future (Evans 1995: 307).

Equal culpability for the Civil War was also emphasized by a new generation of Spanish academics that came to professional maturity during the 1960s and 1970s. Boyd (2008: 136) credits these scholars with taking ownership of the study of the Spanish Civil War from foreigners, and has argued that for them "scholarly research was a form of political activism whose target was the official Francoist memory of the war as a crusade against the godlessness, anarchy, and anti-patriotism of the Second Republic." The work of this generation aided in debunking the myth of Francoist salvation of Spain while assisting in the rise of a new myth concerning who bore responsibility for the Civil War. Boyd adds (136) that after the 1960s the new historical paradigm, greatly influenced by Marxist and structuralist analyses, argued that social backwardness (especially a weak bourgeois class) was at the root of the country's failures since the early 1800s. The Civil War was accordingly seen "as the result of a prolonged structural crisis, an interpretation that sustained the myth of the war as an inevitable collective tragedy."

Framing the Civil War as an event lacking a clear culprit was not abandoned until the 1990s, when scholars began to rescue the Second Republic from "the infamy" to which it had been subjected under the Franco years and from the image of "dysfunctionality" inherited from liberal and Marxist scholarship. They instead assigned responsibility for the Civil War to "its most approximate cause: the military uprising against the Republic of July 1936" (Boyd 2008: 136). The case for Francoist culpability was strengthened by new research showing conclusively that the numbers of victims of the Nationalist repression vastly exceeded those killed by the Republican side; a blow to the myth of equal responsibility.[9]

The Complicated Remembrance of Francoism

Memories of the political crimes of the Franco regime around the time of the transition were complicated by a variety of factors. For one thing, there was the passage of time and the demographic changes that this had brought about. Most Spaniards who lived through the transition to democracy were born after the Civil War and did not experience its horrors first-hand, and those who masterminded the political transition were the children of those who fought the war. It is hardly surprising, then, that the scholarship on the Spanish historical memory makes note of a "generational memory gap" between those who actually lived the war and those who experienced its consequences (Gálvez Biesca 2006: 27). Memories were most vivid among those old enough to have experienced the Civil War and fuzziest among those who learned about it second-hand. Also, many who had survived the worst of the violence of the Civil War and the ensuing Francoist repression had already moved on with their lives—quite literally in the case of the exiled Republicans, who by the time of the transition had remade their lives outside Spain, in Europe, Latin America, and elsewhere.

Also relevant was the complexity of the Francoist legacy of repression. On the one hand, the bulk of the Francoist repression took place during the early phase of authoritarian rule (1939–1959). This made for far less contentious demands from society about retroactive justice during the democratic transition than those witnessed in other countries, because, by the time of Franco's death in 1975, the memory of the post-Civil War repression was fast receding into history and many of those who had the most legitimate claims of abuse against the state had already passed away. On the other hand, with the exception of the Basque Country—which serves as a reminder that Franco's rule remained oppressive until its very end—during the late Francoist period (1959–1975), repression ceased to define the character of the old regime.[10] It is reported that "by the mid-1970s, it was practically impossible to find any person still in prison for matters related to the Civil War. Many had been executed and the rest had benefitted from the successive pardons that had been issued during the Franco period" (Aguilar 2002: 191).

Finally, people's assessment of the Franco period was colored by the dramatic social and economic changes experienced by Spain during the period of the late dictatorship (1959–1977). Per capita income in Spain rose from $400 in 1960 to $1,300 by 1974; GDP grew during the decade of the 1960s at an average of 7.5 percent, a rate bested only by Japan (Borja de Riquer i Permanyer 1995: 262). This economic expansion has been credited with triggering a radical transformation of the country, from a "mainly rural and agrarian society" to "a new society—urban, industrialized, and service-oriented" (Bernecker 2007: 67). Perhaps the most obvious change was the relentless drive toward urbanization. The number of Spanish cities with a population of over 100,000 went from twenty in 1960 to forty in 1975, occasioning the internal migration of some 6 million Spaniards. This period also saw the rise of the mega-metropolis in Spain. Between 1955 and 1975, two million people migrated to Madrid and 1.8 million to Barcelona seeking better economic opportunities. By 1981, the percentage of Spaniards living in cities larger than 100,000 reached 42 percent, making Spain as urbanized as the average European country.

The dramatic economic take-off of the 1960s also brought about the rise of a society obsessed with upward mobility. Having escaped poverty for the first time, millions of Spaniards on their way to middle class status were only too content to enjoy the fruits of their changing economic fortunes. In 1960, one year after the state created a government-run television service, only 1 percent of Spaniards could afford this new technology, but by 1974 85 percent of Spanish households had a television; in 1960, only 4 percent of Spanish households had a refrigerator, but by 1974 82 percent had one; automobile ownership rose from 500,000 (one car per fifty-five inhabitants) in 1960 to over 3,300,000 (one of every nine) by 1974 (López-Pintor 1980: 6). Recognition of the public's awareness of its improving fortunes was quite evident during the democratic transition. By 1976, a clear majority of Spaniards (42 percent) admitted they were better off than five years earlier, with only a small minority (14 percent) saying they were worse off.

A by-product of the economic boom of the 1960s was to encourage a culture of distancing oneself from the past. The twilight of Francoism witnessed the advent of an expansive consumerist culture dominated by television and football, among other forms of mass entertainment, which directly helped Spaniards evade difficult questions about the past. Richards (2006: 88) argues that "there was a great contrast between the enormous hardship of the early post-Civil War years and the consumerism of the 1960s, which preceded the transition. This contributed to the relegation of the past as a subject of concern to most people and, at a personal level, there were good psychological reasons for trying to forget the sheer awfulness of the war and its aftermath." Thus, according to Richards (2006: 88), the 1960s were a period of "looking forward rather than back," with "normalization" reduced to "forgetting" through the alignment of Spain with Western European consumer societies and Americanism.

On the other hand, the association of the dictatorship with unprecedented order and economic prosperity created very ambivalent attitudes about the past within the general public. In a way, affluence gave the dictatorship a kind of retroactive legitimacy, as people were willing to overlook decidedly negative aspects of the Franco era, such as the denial of basic political and civil freedoms for the economic and social progress associated with the late Francoist period. At the very least, affluence diminished the desire within some sectors of society for reprisals against Francoist authorities during the democratic transition. As argued by Aguilar and Humlebaek (2002: 132), "the relatively low negative evaluation of the Franco period" helps explain "the absence during the transition of social movements demanding policies of retroactive justice." As will be seen next, the public's collective memory of the Francoist era is certainly complex, and it is especially revealing for the extent to which the general public has been unwilling to offer wholesale condemnation of the Franco regime.

Table 8 illustrates the conflicted sentiments among Spaniards about Franco in 1979, only a few years after the dictator's death; a high percentage of the public (a collective 30 percent) gave him high marks as a political leader. This ambivalence also explains the apparent anguish expressed by the public on Franco's death. According to a Gallup poll of November 22, 1975, two days after the dictator's death, 53 percent of Spaniards confessed to feeling "pain and sorrow," and an additional 29 percent felt "an irretrievable sense of loss" (López-Pintor 1980: 11).

Broader and longer views of people's recollection of Franco and his regime are provided in Tables 9 and 10. Commenting on these data, Montero (1993: 150) notes that "for various historical reasons, evaluations of Franco were more ambiguous than was typical of other contemporary dictators. The image was basically negative, but it was not a clear black-and-white image." The public's ambivalence about Franco appears to be rooted in the popular perception that Franco was both good and bad for Spain, a point

Table 8. Public Opinion on Franco's Legacy (1979) (percent)

I totally approve of his performance	9
All in all he performed very well	21
He was mediocre but did not commit many errors	13
He made many errors that could have been avoided	21
I disapprove completely of his performance	25
Don't know	6
No answer	5

Source: CIS (1979).

Table 9. Changing Public Attitudes Toward Franco (percent)

	1977	*1979*	*1982*	*1998*
(1) Which of the following corresponds most closely with your ideas?				
Francoism	29	16	15	–
Anti-Francoism	36	49	52	–
(2) What are your sentiments toward Franco?				
Sympathetic	–	27	29	–
Neutral	–	18	18	–
Hostile	–	54	53	
(3) Agree or disagree: *Franquismo* is a political tendency that best defends your interests	12	6	6	6

Source: Montero (1992: 150).

Table 10. Evaluations of Authoritarianism in Spain, Portugal, Greece, and Italy (percent)

	Spain	*Portugal*	*Greece*	*Italy*
Overall, it was good	18	13	6	6
Partly good, partly bad	46	44	31	43
It was only bad	27	29	59	37
Don't know/No answer	9	14	4	13

Source: Montero (1992: 150).

not unrelated to the relative peace and prosperity that the Spanish people enjoyed during the late Franco period. In the years since Franco's death, this mixed perception of the dictator appears to have enjoyed surprising endurance. According to various surveys from the CIS, from the mid-1980s through 2000, almost half the Spanish public acknowledged "both positive and negative" aspects to the dictatorship. The percentage expressing such sentiments went from 46.2 percent in 1985 to 44.6 percent in 1987, 48.9 percent in 1995, and 44.4 percent in 2000.

The Paradoxical Legacies of the Transition

Notwithstanding the strong predisposition of the Spanish public toward forgetting and moving on, it was the transition itself that proved most effective in ensuring that civil society fell in line with the politics of forgetting by undermining the rise of social movements willing and able to help the public overcome its fears about the past and to challenge the elite's proposal for political amnesia. It is a paradox of Spanish democratization that while a transition anchored in political negotiation and moderation was beneficial for ensuring a peaceful and orderly introduction of democracy, it was also detrimental for building a strong civil society. This has led to some to argue that "the viability of Spanish democracy has been achieved at some cost to its quality" (McDonough, Barnes, and López Pina 1998: 1).

In multiple ways, the reformation of Francoism from the inside out all but precluded the rise of civil society activism on the issue of transitional justice. The pivotal events of the transition took place not in the streets but behind closed doors, in places unknown to the general public where the political class convened to work out myriad political compromises, including the Pact of Forgetting, without any direct involvement from civil society. This "invisibility" of the transition allowed political leaders "to pursue their own strategy for dealing with the legacy of the past without due concern about grassroots opposition" (Rigby 2000: 78). This criticism about the secrecy of the transition is echoed in widespread complaints around the time of the transition of the existence of "a shadow government" that made all the decisions concerning Spain's future away from public scrutiny, a point that resonates with the present-day movement to recover the historical memory.[11] "At no point during the transition was the public aware of what was being bargained away and the impact of that bargaining on those of us most directly affected by the actions of the old regime," observes Luís Berlinches Raso of the Association of Ex-Prisoners and Anti-Franco Political Dissidents.[12]

Elite unity on the desire to set the past aside further dissuaded those who might have been inclined to press for transitional justice. Any attention to the past contradicted not only the national consensus to forget, as defined by the political elite, but also the collective memory of the Civil War, which, as seen already, stressed equal responsibility for the war and a determination to prevent another war. On the other hand, acceptance of the pact to forget by the communist and socialist parties meant that the left would play no role in channeling societal demands for justice through the political system: quite in contrast to other countries, especially those with non-negotiated transitions, such as Argentina, Greece, and Portugal. Whatever leadership the left exerted on the issue of the past, it stressed forgetting rather than confronting the past. As seen in the previous chapter, from the onset of the transition the Spanish public was treated to a steady diet of exuberant exaltations about the virtues of forgetting.

The elite's consensus on forgetting was echoed in the media, which pointedly encouraged the public to let go of the past and move on. Led by *El País*, the nation's emerging liberal press wholeheartedly endorsed letting bygones be bygones. On the first anniversary of Franco's death, in 1976, *El País* praised the nation's willingness to forget by declaring Franco "the most forgotten man of the post-Francoist era."[13] This statement was strikingly similar to several made in the conservative press, such as *Ya*, a Catholic newspaper with links to the right, whose editorial marking one year since Franco's passing noted that "Francoism ended with Franco."[14] The media also endorsed the comprehensive amnesty enacted in 1977, which *El País* hailed as "a real indication of having overcome the Civil War" (Aguilar 2002: 194). More telling yet, the media pointedly ignored inconvenient stories that could resuscitate memories of the past, such as the digging up of mass graves that erupted in the late 1970s. "The issue did not receive much attention," a reflection of the media's agreement with the "tacit agreement" between the major political parties to forget (Humlebaek 2011: 191).[15]

Forgetting and moving on was also encouraged by the Catholic Church, an advocate for transitional justice in parts of Latin America and post-communist Europe. From the earliest days of the democratic transition through the bitter debate that resulted in the enacting of the 2007 Law of Historical Memory, the Catholic Church remained steadfast in its opposition to any digging into the past. There was a lot of self-interest in this stance, given the symbiotic relationship of the Church with the Franco regime. It was not until the late 1960s that Church officials began to distance themselves from the authoritarian regime, a decision that acknowledged the growing modernization of Spain and reflected concern about an increasingly unpopular government (see Brasslof 1998). Of course, as an extended branch of Francoism, the Church had no moral standing on which to criticize the old regime for its human rights abuses.

Any potential attempt by civil society to make the past a political issue during the transition was also undermined by the dynamics of a transition that was devoid of a prolonged struggle against the authoritarian state, the result of the left's consent to the self-reformation of the Franco regime. Once

Adolfo Suárez convinced the left that "democratization could be achieved through the reform process that he proposed rather than through a complete break [*ruptura*] with all of the Franco regime's institutions, as originally demanded by the left," the principal opposition groups engaged in "tactical demobilization" (Gunther 2011: 30). This demobilization affected the public at large and targeted the strongest and most visible civil society groups during the transition, those that in other countries' transitions endeavored to mobilize the public around the issue of transitional justice.

By some accounts, the tactical demobilization of the public by the PCE and other groups on the left that accompanied the transition was an expedient and efficient affair. Gunther (2011: 13) reports that "in most parts of the country, where massive street demonstrations in support of democracy were common during the first six months of 1976, mass mobilization virtually ceased, as private negotiations among party representatives became the main vehicle for far-reaching political change." Hipsher (1996: 228) notes that the vibrant neighborhood association movement that began appearing in Madrid and other urban centers by the late 1960s "abandoned its former tactic of confronting the authorities through street protests and demands" after the PCE shifted political tactics in favor of negotiation. Other groups controlled or influenced by the PCE (most notably the trade unions and student associations), were prevented from engaging in "excessive mobilization" and were encouraged to moderate the political and economic demands for the sake of an orderly transition (Encarnación 2001b: 76).

A cynical reading of the demobilization of civil society during the Spanish transition would be that it was undertaken to prevent the masses from spoiling the work of the political class. In reality, however, it was a by-product "of the ethos of tolerance and bargaining that pervaded the transition from Francoism," which although "not hostile to civic engagement was often indifferent to it" (McDonough, Barnes, and López Pina 1998: 1). In either case, the outcome was the same: to weaken civil society by occasioning a durable case of "civic anemia" (1–2). One of the hallmarks of this phenomenon is the "pervasive cynicism" that distinguishes the post-transition political culture in Spain (Gunther, Puhle, and Diamandouros 1995: 22). This is best suggested in the data on "interest in politics," generally defined as "how frequently people discuss political matters with their friends." According to data from the Eurobarometer survey, between 1985 and 2004, the percentage of Spaniards professing to have an interest in politics has rarely exceeded 25 percent versus the EU average of above 40 percent (Martín Cortés

2007). During the early 1990s, the percentage of the population professing an interest in politics actually fell to the mid-teens, an all-time low for the post-transition period.

Another sign of civic anemia in Spain is low levels of mass involvement in politics. It has been reported that "two decades after the passing of Franco the fraction of the population identifying with a political party was about the same as in Eastern Europe following the collapse of Communism" (McDonough, Barnes and López Pina 1998:1). The picture for all kinds of social organizations is no more encouraging. According to the data from the Comparative National Elections Project, which examines electoral politics in nineteen newly democratic countries, the percentage of Spaniards claiming no organizational affiliation of any kind climbed from 64 percent in 1978 to 80 percent by 2004 (Gunther 2007: 30).

The Residual Authoritarian Power

After the transition was securely in place, the government could rely on the residual authoritarian power left in place by the transition to promote forgetting. Former Francoist bureaucrats continued to run the state's cultural and educational ministries—neither was significantly affected by the transition—and thus were able to shape how Spanish history was taught and remembered for years to come, a point underscored by the textbooks in use during the transition. Valls's (2007: 158–59) analysis of the textbooks of the transition years (1975–1985) notes that "The predominant interpretation in textbooks continues to have a markedly moralistic character that is also only slightly fact-based in nature." He adds that the textbooks "barely address the more severe persecution of the Franco dictatorship," and concludes that "History pedagogy only began to undergo significant change in the mid-1980s, and the more progressive pedagogy became the rule rather than the exception with the entry of the socialist educational administration in the early 1990s." By then the reforms of the socialist era were giving the autonomous governments control of approximately 35 percent of the content of the school curriculum, 45 percent in communities with their own languages, such as Catalonia and the Basque Country.

Valls's findings and contentions are echoed in public opinion data on people's recollections of the education system under Franco. As revealed in the survey data collected by the CIS (2008) national survey on the memory of the Civil War and the Franco regime, a clear majority of Spaniards did not think their primary education included sufficient information about the Civil War and the Franco dictatorship. Only 4.3 percent of respondents claim to have received a lot of information about the war and the dictatorship, versus 44 percent who claim little attention and 25.3 percent who claim no attention at all. In light of these findings, it is not surprising that a principal rationale for the recent surge in civil society advocacy for policies of historical memory stresses Franco's manipulation of history. According to Miguel Muñoz Molina, president of the Memory Forum, "The people were deceived about the past under Franco; there was no means for them to know the facts."[16] Of special concern to Molina and other "memory" activists is the legacy of Francoist propaganda that depicts the Civil War as a "rescue" by a well-meaning section of the population from godless, foreign-influenced radicals and haters of Spain.

Also due to the transition, control of major cultural and educational institutions, including museums, universities, national archives, and libraries remained for years firmly in the hands of former Francoist civil servants. Such control of these institutions made it considerably easier for governments in the post-transition era to shape debates about the past without resorting to censorship, which was never a component of the Pact of Forgetting. A case in point is the fortieth anniversary in April 1977 of the bombing of the Basque town of Guernica, one of the most emblematic episodes of the Civil War and a "mythical reference-point for the defeated" (Aguilar 2002: 200). As might be expected, the anniversary reignited the longstanding argument of who bears ultimate responsibility for Guernica's destruction—the Germans whose planes bombed the village; Franco, who secured Nazi assistance for the bombing; or the Republicans, who the Nationalists claimed torched the town as they were fleeing. This controversy was the subject of much chatter in the media and the public, including a gathering of experts in Guernica in April 1977. But the Suárez administration, with the backing of all the public institutions, refused to give access to the official records, contending that it saw no point in helping revive a historical controversy, leaving the issue of culpability for Guernica unresolved, at least officially.[17]

The Suárez administration also decided against locating Picasso's masterwork *Guernica*—the iconic painting commissioned by the Republican government for the 1937 Paris World Fair to publicize the violence of the Civil War, and today widely regarded as a universal symbol of the horrors of war—in the Basque Country, once the painting was returned to Spain in 1978 from New York's Museum of Modern Art, where it had hung since the 1950s in keeping with Picasso's wishes that the painting be given to Spain once the country had restored political liberties and democratic institutions. Although public opinion sided with the Basques' claim that the painting belonged in Guernica, the Suárez administration chose to keep it in Madrid to prevent the Basques from "monopolizing a symbol as powerful as the bombardment of Guernica" (Aguilar 2002: 3). Subsequent requests for relocating the painting to the Basque Country have been denied by the government, most recently in 2007 to coincide with the seventieth anniversary of the bombing. At the time the Basque government argued that a temporary showing of the painting at Bilbao's Guggenheim Museum would help bring peace to the Basque Country, an argument that provoked culture minister Carmen Calvo to say that she did not wish to link *Guernica* to terrorism.[18]

The governments of the post-transition era have also availed themselves of the control of the media inherited from the old regime in order to forget and/or obscure the past. A free press emerged in Spain with a new press law that went into effect on April 13, 1977.[19] But even after this law was enacted, the possibility for frank discussion of the past in the media remained seriously circumscribed. Until at least the mid-1980s, the state retained a national monopoly over virtually all television and radio reporting, "so that news generally reflected the views of the government" (Roldán Ros 1985: 261). Spain's first privately owned television station, *Antena 3*, would not begin broadcasting until 1990. The press law also included the provision that the government "could seize any audio or visual materials that contain news, commentaries or information considered contrary to the unity of Spain, that constitute an attack on the monarchy or royal family, and that in any manner attempt to decrease the institutional prestige or the public regard of the armed forces" (261).

Such limitations led the editors of the daily *Diario 16* to complain: "Why this obsession with maintaining taboos and silent zones where only the official dogma can tread?" (Roldán Ros 1985: 262). This same publication was one of the first to test the new law by publishing, ten days before the 1977 elections, a series of articles highly critical of Manuel Fraga Iribarne, the former minister of information and tourism under Franco, and the head of the neo-Francoist Popular Alliance (AP). The government responded by seizing the 201st edition of *Diario 16* for its article on Fraga. Around the same time, another publication called *Posible* published an exposé of former prime minister Arias Navarro, who in 1977 was an AP senate candidate. The article recalled his activities as a war prosecutor under Franco and linked him to the execution of 1,880 persons in the province of Malaga in 1936. Under the new press law, Arias Navarro sued the paper for slandering his reputation.

Racing for Modernity and Europe

It was the almost instant success of the transition, however, that guaranteed that any civil society initiative to dispense justice against the Franco regime or to reconcile the historical record of the Civil War would be met with indifference (if not hostility) by the general public. Successive elections in 1977 and 1979, to say nothing of the successful enacting of a new democratic constitution in 1978, all but erased the Francoist myth of the ungovernable Spain, and wiped out people's worries about the country's democratic future. Thus, it is hardly surprising that the democratic transition rapidly became a cultural touchstone for projecting the arrival of a thoroughly democratic and modern Spain. As observed by a study of Spain's cultural landscape of the 1990s, "The political and historical phenomenon known as "the Transition" carried Spain away from its old image as a backward, slightly bumbling country toward a new image as a modern, democratic, chic, and vigorous and cultural center" (Gies 1999: 1).

For the Spaniards, modernity under democracy had a very distinct European orientation. Indeed, democratization and Europeanization were virtually indistinguishable. After Franco, democracy came to mean "achieving a political ideal of individual and collective freedom through a political system based on popular sovereignty, rather than dictatorship and authoritarianism. Yet, at the same time, democracy also represented a distinctive vision of modernity, a form of society represented by Western European countries" (Benedicto 2004: 293). Spaniards embraced membership in European institutions in 1986 with considerable gusto. According to the survey data from Eurobarometer, Spaniards have for years been more enthusiastic about the European Union (EU) than have other member states. Data from 2006 reveal that 72 percent of Spaniards agreed that "belonging to the EU is a positive thing" compared to the 55 percent average in the rest of the member countries.[20]

As with the case of the political class, especially the left, the public's eagerness for belonging in Europe was rooted in the desire to overcome feelings of inferiority toward Europe, feelings exacerbated by the Francoist dictatorship, itself the culprit for the exclusion of Spain from the EEC since its creation with the Treaty of Rome in 1957. Balfour and Quiroga (2007: 83) have observed that closing the door on the past allowed the Spaniards to "cast off their inferiority complex towards other Europeans and embrace a positive view of their past and present as a peaceful, European and modern nation." Intensifying the desire to be part of Europe was the fact that by the mid-1980s Europe was no longer an abstraction but rather a concrete reality with the emergence of the EEC. Vincent (2007: 228) has observed that while "Europeanization" in Spain had traditionally meant "everything and nothing," by the late twentieth century "the existence of supranational European institutions meant that such aspirations acquired context."

One of the most evident consequences of the "dual" transition to modernity and Europe was to engender a forward-looking mentality fueled by the sentiment that too much time had already been wasted. "It is hard to avoid the impression that post-Franco Spain is marked by a sense of catching up with the future," wrote cultural critic Jo Labanyi (1995: 396) when observing the eagerness of the Spaniards to leave behind their Francoist past. The desire to catch up with modernity and Europe was echoed throughout the leading cultural movements of the post-dictatorship era. Partly in rejection of the rigid conservatism of Francoism and partly in reaction to the advent of new civil liberties, during the years of democratic transition Spain experienced a delayed sexual revolution. In what was baptized as *el desmadre sexual* (debauchery or uninhibited revelry), the Spaniards went on a sex binge. As noted by journalist John Hopper in his portrait of 1980s Spain (1986: 186), "Objecting to sex in almost any form short of child molestation has become as much of a taboo as sex itself."

A related movement of the era was *el destape* (the opening), which began with the lifting of the censorship that, during the Franco regime, prohibited movies from showing any kind of sexual content (even kissing) and forced newspaper and magazine editors to hire *retocadores* (retouchers) to reduce the size of women's breasts and conceal naked male torsos. The movement produced policies and behavior rare even for mature democracies: sex advertisements in the most reputable newspapers; sex shops anywhere in town, irrespective of zoning; sale of pornographic material in public markets; and, perhaps most memorable, a rush by the rich and famous to pose nude on the cover of popular magazines such as *Interviu*. The point of many of these posed pictorials (for both the person posing and for the publisher) was not just to make money, but also to shock the public with what was now permissible.

Also notable, at least because of its impact on Spain's image abroad as a cultural innovator, was La Movida (literally the movement; conceptually the vibe or the stirring), a group of Madrid-based artistic innovators that reinterpreted punk-rock culture led by filmmaker Pedro Almodóvar. La Movida brought together actors, singers, and fashion designers (many of whom appeared in Almodóvar's films), leading to the creation of a "mutual admiration society that has its own magazines, its own clubs, and its own galleries and shops" (Coad 1995: 377). The movement's cultural output, especially Almodóvar's earliest films like *Pepi, Luci, Bom y otras chicas del montón* (1980), *Laberinto de pasiones* (1982), *Entre Tinieblas* (1983) and *Qué he hecho yo para merecerme esto* (1984) drew on Hollywood and Spanish comedies of the 1950s, the so-called "Spanish National Cinema," which is often criticized for being "intellectually worthless, aesthetically valueless, and industrially paralytic (Hopewell 1986: 57), much in contrast to the politically committed films associated with the mid-century generation. This association of La Movida with the most vapid and commercial aspects of Francoist popular culture underscores the often noted frivolous and escapist nature of post-transition Spanish popular culture, as suggested most notably by Spanish television, generally dismissed by literate Spaniards and foreign observers as "teletonta and telebasura" (numbing TV and trash TV) (Smith 2003: 14; Maxwell 1995).

By doing what it did as much as by what it did not do, the national media served as a cheerleader of the post-transition euphoria. Almodóvar's films—the face of post-Franco Spanish cinema at home and abroad, according to the cultural critic Marshal Kinder (1997: 3)—"pretend that the patriarchal Franco never existed." At the same time, contends Kinder, Almodóvar's films established the new cultural stereotype for a hyper liberated socialist Spain. "They displaced the stereotypical macho matadors and gypsies of the Andalusian *españoladas* with an outrageous libertarian array of transgressive sexualities, including gay couples, transsexuals, bisexuals, lesbians, and liberated women" (Kinder 1997: 3). For decades after the transition, Spanish television exercised a virtual blackout on the Civil War and the dictatorship. *Cuéntame como pasó* (Tell Me How it Was), the first television show to provide a reasonably accurate portrait of life under Franco, did not commence broadcasting on the national television network RTVE until 2001. It tells the story of the middle-class Alcántara family in the twilight of the dictatorship, and its struggle with the Francoist repression.

The printed media was also complicit in celebrating forgetting and in encouraging the public to continue to look forward, as suggested most tellingly by the coverage by Spain's leading papers of the twenty-fifth anniversary of Franco's death (observed in 2000). *El País* led the way with a distinctly celebratory, forward-looking angle, described by the Spanish social critic Fernando León Solís (2003: 61) as "the myth of re-foundation of the Spanish state" designed to sever "the spatial and temporal links of modern Spanish society with its Francoist and 'transitional' past." The title of a special supplement to the November 19, 2000 issue devoted to the anniversary was especially revealing: *Aquella remota dictadura* (That Remote Dictatorship).[21] In it, some of Spain's leading intellectuals ponder the nation's trajectory since 1975 and the state of the memory of Franco and his regime. According to Javier Pradera, Spain has undergone "a profound transformation," adding that: "Nothing of substance remains of the Francoist repressive apparatus, having been replaced by a democratic state comparable to the other members of the European Union." Jesús Rodríguez made note of "the twenty five years that feel like a century." Franco is "a ghost," "a distant, ugly, stranger to the lives of the young." Luis Carandell referred to the norms and values of Francoist Spain as "things that make us laugh." "Franco no longer hurts," wrote Arcadi Espada.

Understandably, in the post-Franco years the public has shown a remarkable lack of interest and even curiosity about the past. To be sure, the Civil War has always been a source of interest to academics and cultural critics. But for years, intellectuals have complained about the apathy of ordinary Spaniards toward their work. Aguilar (2008: 21) has written that, when she started her doctoral investigations in the early 1990s, many seemed surprised and even upset by her choice of subject. She was repeatedly asked: Have we not spoken enough about that subject already? Should not we leave the subject alone? The disdain for the past is tellingly captured in public opinion polls. The CIS (1985) survey on the tenth anniversary of Franco's death has a plurality of Spaniards (52 percent) claiming to have "distant and faint" recollection of the former dictator. The memory of the Civil War appears to have fared even worse. A CIRES survey from June 1991 reported that "a nearly total disinterest concerning everything related to the Civil War was displayed by respondents, including a lack of identification with either of the two sides in the struggle, and even a frequent lack of basic knowledge of this matter especially among the young" (Cazorla 1992: 85).

A lengthy profile of the so-called "Eurogeneration" by *El País* describes this group of Spaniards born after 1986, the year Spain joined the EEC, as "having very little interest in the past.[22] "I have never stopped to think about what Spain was like 20 years ago; my biggest concern has been finding a way to make a living doing what I love," are the telling words of someone identified as a radio announcer and singer. Interestingly, one of the reasons given by the sample of youth interviewed by the newspaper is that "they already have heard too much hype about the democratic transition" and "they would rather think about the future that awaits them."

CHAPTER 5

Pinochet's Revenge: Awakening the Memory of Civil War and Dictatorship

Having remained frozen for decades, memories of the violence of the Civil War and the repression of the Franco dictatorship began to thaw in the late 1990s with the emergence of a vigorous movement devoted to the recovery of the forgotten historical memory. This movement powerfully signaled the end of civil society's complicity with the Pact of Forgetting. It is tempting to see the surge in civil society activism on the issue of the past as a reflection of the passing of fears among the public of another civil war or dictatorship, or of the international tentacles of the transitional justice movement finally catching up with Spain. These are compelling explanations, but the issue of timing seriously weakens both. By the time memory organizations began to emerge in 2000, Spain had enjoyed two decades of stable democracy, its future as a democratic society was all but ensured by incorporation into the EEC in 1986, and long before 2000 the transitional justice movement had already made its mark on international politics in Latin America, South Africa, and the post-communist world.

Instead, the end of civil society's complicity with the Pact of Forgetting is best understood as a by-product of the collapse of the elite consensus on the past that materialized with the democratic transition. It was only then that civil society demands for some kind of recognition of the past began to get some traction in the public sphere. The obvious catalyst that shattered the elite consensus on the past was Spain's indictment in 1998 of Chilean general Augusto Pinochet for his role in the bloody military coup that crushed the democratically elected government of Salvador Allende in 1973. Pinochet was arrested in London on October 16, 1998, while on a private visit to England to consult with physicians about a back problem. The charge was "crimes against humanity," key among them genocide, that most heinous of contemporary political crimes, with its powerful association with the Jewish Holocaust. With poetic revenge, the Spaniards' indictment of Pinochet just before his arrest unleashed a chain of unintended repercussions that contributed significantly to the undoing of the political agreement that since 1977 had made discussions of Spain's painful and difficult past an enduring political taboo. In sum, in seeking to punish Pinochet, Spaniards ended up forcing themselves to confront a past many thought had been effectively put to rest.

As shown in this chapter, the Pinochet affair dealt a one-two punch to the Pact of Forgetting. First, the Pinochet indictment triggered what Wilde (1999) has called "an irruption of memory," a sporadic event that, for whatever reason, upsets the collective consciousness of a society by reminding the political class and the public of the unforgotten past. Pinochet's arrest unleashed a worldwide charge of moral hypocrisy, seeing Spain demanding justice for another country's dictator while allowing the political crimes of its own dictator to go unpunished only two decades earlier. This in turn generated considerable societal introspection about the limitations of the Pact of Forgetting in fully reconciling the political excesses of the past. Pinochet's arrest also triggered considerable curiosity about Spain's dark past with dictatorship, especially for Spaniards who did not experience the change in regime in 1975–1977 and the political compromises it entailed.

Second, the Pinochet affair created what Tarrow (1994) has referred to as "political opportunity structure," a change in the political landscape that allows for the rise of collective action. The controversy over whether Pinochet should stand trial in Spain divided the political class along ideological lines, with the left advocating for the general's extradition to Spain and the right dead set against it. Inevitably, perhaps, this discord fractured the political consensus to keep discussion about justice for past wrongs away from the usual deliberation of politics, with the left accusing the right of defending impunity for Pinochet just as they had done for Franco regime. All this signaled to the public that it was safe to engage in debates about Spain's own past. Many citizens became mobilized by what they perceived to be a double standard in the Spanish justice system: its willingness to go after the political crimes of another country's dictatorship while refusing to investigate those of its own former dictatorship. Eventually, the activism that grew out of the effort to ensure that Pinochet would pay for his crimes gradually began to turn its energy toward Franco's crimes. This set the stage for a public demand to revisit the transition-era decision to forget the past.

The General's Arrest

It is very fitting that General Pinochet would feature so prominently in the demise of the Pact of Forgetting in Spain. Those familiar with Chilean and Spanish history would find it hard to miss the striking historical parallels in the rise to power of Pinochet in Chile in 1973 and Franco in Spain in 1936. Franco and Pinochet both came to power through bloody military coups that put an end to popularly elected left-wing regimes (the Second Republic in Spain and the Allende government in Chile). Both followed their military victories with widespread repression of the left aided by conservative groups such as the military, the Catholic Church, and the business community. Moreover, Pinochet fashioned his political regime, which came to power during the twilight of the Francoist era, on the Franco template, right down to the influence of Catholic fundamentalist organizations like Opus Dei. Less known, at least outside Spain, is that Pinochet was one of only two foreign heads of state to attend Franco's funeral (the other was the king of Morocco). These historical parallels and associations provide a context for understanding the strong case of "political projection" the Spaniards expressed following Pinochet's arrest. It was as if they wanted to punish Pinochet for Franco's political crimes.

Pinochet's arrest in 1998 was set into motion two years earlier by the legal maneuverings of Baltasar Garzón and Manuel García-Castellón, two Spanish judges known for their liberal jurisprudence and penchant for the media spotlight. From their perch at the Audiencia Nacional, a court traditionally concerned with "serious" matters such as political violence and terrorism, Garzón and García-Castellón agreed to hear claims of human rights abuses by Latin America's Southern Cone dictatorships. These claims came to the judges' attention as a consequence of a unique aspect of Spanish law, the principle of *acción popular* (popular action), which permits any Spanish citizen (who may or may not be the injured party) to pursue a case in the public interest provided he or she can convince a judge of the merits of the case. The earliest cases brought to the Audiencia Nacional concerned the disappearances of Spanish citizens or those holding dual citizenship in Argentina and Chile during dictatorships in these countries.[1] This was, as

Golob (2002: 27) noted, "a nod to the reality that national courts are more open to prosecuting crimes perpetuated abroad by foreigners upon nationals (the principle of passive personality)."

Eventually, the scope of the case against Pinochet was broadened dramatically and came to include the systemic torture, murder, illegal detention, and forced disappearance of more than four thousand Chilean and Argentine citizens. All these claims were consolidated into a single case of genocide and terrorism heard in Judge Garzón's court and handled by Carlos Castresana, a public prosecutor and head of the Unión Progresista de Fiscales. Castresana launched a thorough investigation into the crimes of the Pinochet regime, relying largely on the so-called Archivos del Terror, a treasure trove of documents detailing Operation Condor, the trail of murders throughout South America that entailed hunting and killing enemies of the Pinochet regime with the help of other military regimes in Argentina, Paraguay, Bolivia, Brazil, and Uruguay. Pinochet, assisted by the infamous Dirección de Inteligencia Nacional (DINA), Chile's state secret police, was charged as Condor's main architect.

Propelling the Spanish judges into action (and before them the relatives and friends of the victims of repression as well as the human rights organizations that assisted them) were the legal limitations on transitional justice set by the series of laws passed by Pinochet before relinquishing power in 1990, following a national referendum in which 55 percent of Chileans voted "no" on continuation of Pinochet's rule, opening the way for a transition to democracy. A 1978 law bestowed amnesty to all persons engaged in politically motivated acts during the state of emergency between 1973 and 1978. For years, this law "ensured impunity for Pinochet and his subordinates" and guaranteed that "the vast majority of the thousands of suits filed with the courts (including a number naming Pinochet himself) were thrown out or halted by application of the amnesty law" (Davis 2004: 266). This amnesty was part and parcel of the *leyes de amarre* (binding laws), a package of legislation designed to allow Pinochet and his allies a significant role in shaping Chilean politics in the post-Pinochet era.[2]

An International Maelstrom

On learning of Pinochet's visit to London, Judge Garzón asked British authorities about the possibility of questioning the former dictator on the disappearance of Spanish citizens residing in Chile during his regime. The British government responded that this request would have to be preceded by an order of arrest, which Garzón promptly issued through Interpol. To legitimize the claim, Garzón claimed competency over Operation Condor, which allowed him to charge Pinochet as an individual rather than his regime as a whole for crimes against humanity, a point highlighted in the order of arrest. "Reaching out across borders to bring Pinochet to justice seemed appropriate," wrote Golob (2002: 28), "given that the dictator had reached out across borders to advance his own form of transnationalized law enforcement." Pinochet's arrest by Scotland Yard on October 16, 1998, while he was recuperating from spinal surgery at a private clinic in London, created an international legal maelstrom. His lawyers immediately claimed immunity, based on the fact that Pinochet carried a diplomatic passport. British authorities dismissed this claim, since the general's visit to Great Britain was of a private nature, and ordered Pinochet to remain under house arrest until Spain's case for extradition could be fully examined by the British courts.[3]

For good reason, human rights activists around the world cheered Pinochet's arrest, as it was the first time a foreign leader was arrested abroad on the charge of crimes against humanity. Human Rights Watch responded to Britain's two successive rulings that denied Pinochet his immunity, noting: "These historic decisions were evidence of a growing consensus in the international community that human rights transcend national boundaries, limiting the immunity of former heads of state and even the prerogatives of national sovereignty" (Brett 1999). Following Pinochet's detention, a number of countries including Switzerland, Belgium, France, and Argentina joined Spain in seeking Pinochet's extradition, making the Pinochet affair a landmark case in international jurisprudence.

There were two notable exceptions to the international euphoria surrounding the news of Pinochet's arrest in London. One was the United States, which did not support Spain's actions. Although the Clinton administration claimed neutrality, it clearly favored the return of Pinochet to his homeland, a point Secretary of State Madeleine Albright stressed to the British government.[4] Garzón himself has publicly complained about the lack of cooperation on the part of American authorities, especially State Department and Central Intelligence Agency officials.[5] Surely, the United States was leery of supporting any legal action that might cast light on American government actions that aided the rise of the Pinochet regime in 1973, to say nothing of not wanting to help create a precedent in which one country could detain the former leader of another country on charges of crimes against humanity. The other country that opposed Pinochet's arrest was Chile. Although 63 percent of Chileans considered Pinochet guilty as charged, they were deeply divided as to what this meant for Chilean democracy, with 44 percent viewing the deposed dictator's arrest as "good" and 45 percent as "bad" (Angell 2003: 81). This mixed response reflected the ambivalence many Chileans still felt about their former dictator—not dissimilar from the mixed sentiments of Spaniards toward Franco after the end of his regime, as shown in the previous chapter.

Pinochet's prestige remained "high among a significant proportion of the Chilean public, particularly business sectors that continued to benefit from his economic legacy" (Davis 2004: 266). Indeed, many at home and abroad, especially in conservative circles, treated him as a respected senior statesman. He was openly admired by Jesse Helms, influential chairman of the U.S. Senate Foreign Relations Committee, and by former British prime minister Margaret Thatcher, for his anti-communist credentials and vigorous advocacy of neoliberal economics. On the other hand, following Pinochet's fall from power, Chilean politics, much like Spanish politics after Franco, had reconnected with remarkable speed to its democratic past. In fact, as fate would have it, at the time of Pinochet's arrest Chile was in the midst of a presidential campaign. Thus, for many Chileans, as for Spaniards before them, the arrest brought up unpleasant memories of an authoritarian past that many thought had already been put to rest.

Furthermore, many Chileans also shared the view that Pinochet's arrest was a gross and reckless violation of national sovereignty and a sign that the international community regarded Chile's democracy as inadequate to handle its own affairs. "Chile is being treated like a colony," declared the conservative newspaper *El Mercurio* in Santiago in a fit of transcontinental rage.[6] Such comments had a strong psychological impact in Spain, as shown below, by couching the debate about Pinochet in terms that related directly to how the Spaniards treated their own past, and by extension, their dictator. This introspection was undoubtedly aided by the apparent hypocrisy of Spain's decision to search for justice for Spanish victims of Pinochet while refusing to pursue justice for its citizens victimized by Franco.

An Irruption of Memory

As noted previously, the Pinochet affair undermined the Pact of Forgetting in two distinct ways. First was the advent of "an irruption of memory," an instance of public consciousness reminding the nation that questions about the past had not yet been fully resolved. The opening argument in the discursive link between Spain and Chile over Pinochet's arrest came quickly from Chilean president Eduardo Frei, who did not hold back from questioning Spain's moral authority in asking for Pinochet's extradition. On the day of the general's arrest, while attending an international gathering of Christian Democratic leaders in Bayonne, France, Frei noted that Chile "did not question the legitimacy of the democratic system born in Spain forty years ago and we wish that Spain would accord us the same respect." He added that

> Spain is showing signs of poor memory; here is a country with an authoritarian government that persisted for 40 years from which the current democracy spawned. This democracy did not recognize the processes of human rights that it presently demands from the Latin American countries. What would be the reaction in Spain if another country questioned how Spain dealt with the one million dead from the Spanish Civil War, or the war against terrorism or the infamous process of the GAL?[7]

Frei's charges of hypocrisy, which were followed by cancellation of a planned trip from Bayonne to Madrid and the recall of the Chilean ambassador to Spain, had a deep impact among the Spaniards but hardly the one the Chilean president intended. Rather than rallying around the notion of national sovereignty and the related argument that Pinochet deserved to be judged by his own people, Spaniards seemed convinced that this was their chance to take revenge on their own former dictator. A clear majority of the Spanish public supported Pinochet's extradition to Spain (64 percent according to a poll by the Center of Sociological Investigations), and public discourses on the Pinochet indictment, as some have pointed out, had "some kind of psychological transference factor at work—the impulse to do to Pinochet what was not done to Franco" (Davis 2005: 869). And in a veritable case of "transnational civil society" activism, many private citizens and groups became directly involved in helping the exiled Chilean community in Spain and human rights groups in Chile gather the testimony used to prosecute Pinochet. The human rights branch of the IU and the Union of Progressive Jurists, working in concert with the Chile-based Salvador Allende Foundation, coordinated the collection of documents needed for Pinochet's prosecution.

Across major Spanish cities, mass rallies—which in contemporary Spain have become an important venue for the citizenry to partake in politics—demanded Pinochet's extradition from Britain to Spain (rather than to Chile) to ensure his conviction. These demonstrations were notable for at least two things. The first was the obvious thirst for justice prevalent in Spanish civil society, a point stressed at a Madrid rally on October 28, 1998. Some statements from civil society leaders in attendance were striking in light of the passivity with which these same groups had welcomed Spain's pact to forget during the democratic transition.[8] Antonio Gutiérrez of the Workers' Commissions noted that "an assassin cannot get away with impunity." José Ricardo Martínez, of the rival General Workers Union, argued that "crimes have to be paid for. It is important in a democratic society that Pinochet be judged for the crimes he committed." Esteban Ibarra, leader of the Youth Against Intolerance, declared himself "proud that Spain would take the initiative for global justice." Numerous editorials and op-ed pages, such as one by the political commentator Francisco Umbral, stressed the point of psychological projection. He keenly observed that "for the Spanish people, the Pinochet arrest is the vicarious dream of a historical impossibility, that of Franco being arrested in bed" (Malamud 2003: 157).

The second interesting aspect of the general's arrest was how it effectively served not only to bring back memories of the Franco dictatorship and repression, but also to highlight the limitations of Spain's approach to dealing with the past. Some of the demonstrators (especially the relatives of the victims of the Civil War and the Franco regime) made a point of reminding the nation that while Spanish society at large had moved on, many were still struggling with the their own memories of the past. Their suffering was exacerbated by the apparent paradox of seeing Spain devote so many legal resources to prosecuting the political crimes of another country's dictator while choosing to ignore those of its own. At the heart of this complaint was the desire to bring about justice for crimes that had gone unpunished as well as the need for recognition of what had happened in Spain. The need for public recognition of Spain's past political excesses was undoubtedly prompted by the discomfort some felt at not being free to discuss the fate of their loved ones, while, paradoxically, stories about the findings of truth commissions in Central and South America, and the prospect of a trial for Pinochet on Spanish soil, flooded the Spanish media. "They go on about other countries but nothing about us: we have suffered much more and longer," one of Franco's victims remarked to the BBC.[9]

The Spanish media focused obsessively on Pinochet's case, with one study estimating that *El País* alone published "several hundred articles on the issue between 1996 and 1998" (Davis 2005: 868). On the whole, the Spanish media supported the right of the Spanish judiciary to bring Pinochet to justice. This was especially the case for the nation's leading newspapers (*El País*, *El Mundo*, and *Cambio 16*), which, perhaps reflecting public opinion, exerted considerable pressure on the government to secure Pinochet's extradition to Spain. Surprisingly, one of the strongest stances for prosecution came from the conservative paper *El Mundo*, which, in a somewhat tortured analysis, took President Frei to task for failing to see the differences between the Chilean situation and that of Spain after Franco. In an editorial, the paper noted that, first, Spanish judges "do not make politics; they apply the law." Second, nobody during the Spanish transition pretended that the Pact of Forgetting was supposed to be a new dogma of international jurisprudence." Third, the paper contended that between 1977 and 1998 the world had changed a great deal, and now there was an international legal framework that allowed prosecutions for human rights violations regardless of national sovereignty.[10] *ABC* and *La Vanguardia* assumed a less strident position, contending that Pinochet was not the only cruel dictator alive deserving of justice, that it would have been preferable for an international criminal court to have acted instead of the Spanish justice system, and that it was advisable to work in support of Latin American stability, which could be affected by the extradition (Malamud 2003: 164).

Pinochet's arrest also put the members of the political class in an uncomfortable position, especially the left-wing leaders, who were forced to recall their participation in the suppression of memory prevalent during the Spanish transition. The most vocal in expressing his thoughts on the Pinochet case was former prime minister Felipe González, whose government between 1982 and 1996 went to great lengths to prevent the past from encumbering his policies of political and economic modernization. Writing in *El País*, González acknowledged his embarrassment at seeing Spanish leaders "giving lessons in democracy to others, willing to dictate how to do things in other people's houses."[11] This kind of thinking led González to oppose Pinochet's extradition to Spain, a position that put him directly at odds with his own party, which went on record as favoring extradition. González characterized Pinochet's arrest in London as a potential "abuse of power by one country over another," adding that the courts' decision to seek Pinochet's extradition was one that he hoped that Spain "would not regret in the future."[12]

More nuanced perspectives came from other left-wing leaders, who attempted to justify their support for retroactive justice in Chile—but not in Spain—by highlighting the very different conditions in which Spain found itself during its transition to democracy. Catalan socialist leader Jordi Solé Tura, in an expansive essay aptly titled "Franco y Pinochet," argued that in Spain the transition had begun with Franco's death, whereas the Chileans had to initiate and manage their transition "with their own Franco alive."[13] Additionally, forty years had passed since the end of the Civil War in Spain, whereas in Chile the memory of the military coup that ended democracy was still fresh. In Spain, a new generation had come onto the scene and memories of the horrendous Civil War, while vivid, were no longer a part of people's daily lives. The military was a residue of Francoism not in a position to impose a military dictatorship, and the country was part of a new Europe, ready to embark on a path of peace and prosperity. In Chile, Solé Tura argued, the wounds of human rights abuses had not healed, the military was still a fundamental factor in the political life of the country, and the United States was "feeding a cold war that did not cede any grounds and that grouped anything that it did not like under the box of international communism" across Latin America.

Fracturing the Political Consensus

The real political debate about the Pinochet affair was not within the left but rather between the left and the right. With the left strongly in favor of Spain's role in adjudicating Pinochet's fate and the right wishing the case would simply go away, the general's arrest deeply divided the political class along partisan lines. During the sixteen months between Pinochet's arrest in October 1998 and the decision by the British government in March 2000 to let him return to Chile, after he was declared unfit to stand trial on the basis of his age and physical frailty, Spanish politicians engaged in a battle of scurrilous accusations that effectively served to fracture the consensus not to use the past for partisan political purposes.[14] Playing a vigorous offense was the left, led by the PSOE, which saw in Pinochet's arrest the opportunity to make up for the missed chance to pursue transitional justice against the Franco regime. Malamud (2003: 157) has noted that the PSOE message about Pinochet's arrest to the general public was clear: "It was not possible to punish those who repressed us, given the exigencies of the democratic transition process in Spain, but now that it is possible, let's do it to others, in this case Pinochet and the Chilean people, irrespective of their own process of transition." Underscoring Malumud's point was the reaction of PSOE spokesman Alfredo Pérez Rubalcaba to the news of Pinochet's arrest: "If only we could have done the same with Franco" (157).

PSOE chairman Joaquín Almunia struck a more artful tone in his formal remarks on Pinochet's arrest. He stressed that Pinochet's extradition to Spain was "an expression of Spanish leadership in the globalization of justice and a meaningful step toward maintaining that crimes against humanity have no frontiers," and added that "the government should not put any difficulty to Pinochet's extradition and should ensure that the dictator has the opportunity to respond to his crimes in a court of justice."[15] Party officials also noted that Felipe González's words in favor of "territoriality in the application of the law," which asserted that Spain had no right to intervene in the affairs of another country and insisted that each country is responsible for dealing with the consequences of its own actions, represented "a personal opinion" of the former prime minister and not that of the party.

Prime Minister José María Aznar, who headed Spain's first conservative government in the post-Franco era, sought to distance himself and his administration from the case, even though the Spanish justice system had initiated the chain of events leading to Pinochet's arrest. The case pitted Aznar against Frei, a fellow center-right president, and threatened Spain's lucrative relations with Chile. Since the early 1990s Spanish multinational companies, including Telefónica, Endesa, and Banco Santander, have been heavily invested in the Chilean economy, as has the Spanish government through a variety of profitable military contracts. Moreover, the Pinochet case threatened to undo much of the political work Aznar had done to advance the modernization of the Spanish right.[16] For the Aznar administration, the prospect of putting Pinochet on trial in Spain was terrifying. Surely, any trial held in Spain that dealt with Pinochet's atrocities also would spark an interest for retroactive justice with respect to Franco's atrocities, since Pinochet's abuses of power were eerily similar to those by the Franco regime (especially the killing and disappearance of political enemies).[17] So it must have come as a great relief to Aznar when the British allowed Pinochet to return to his homeland.

In his first comments to the media on October 18, 1998, Aznar urged "prudence in relation to the arrest of the general and possible extradition to Spain" and expressed his respect for the judicial decisions of Garzón's court, but noted that his government "would not be rushed into action by anyone or anything."[18] In remarks understood to convey his ambivalence about the case, Aznar added: "We will receive the petition for extradition which may or may not be studied; but do not ask me to do anything without knowing the fundamental, solid facts about the Ministry of Justice's request for extradition." Eventually, Aznar declared himself neutral on the prosecution of Pinochet and agreed to pursue the course of action dictated by the Spanish courts. His position, however, apparently did not deter his government from actively endeavoring to undermine in a variety of legal and political ways the work of the Spanish courts to dictate universal jurisprudence.

Almost immediately following Pinochet's arrest, Eduardo Fungairiño, Spain's director of public prosecutions, ruled against the general's extradition, a decision widely seen as reflecting the wishes of the Aznar government. Fungairiño declared the international arrest issued by Spain to be "null and void in the full legal sense" (Malamud 2003: 157). In his deliberation of the case, Fungairiño (often portrayed in the Spanish media as Garzón's nemesis) contended that Chile's crimes were politically motivated, a condition that put the case outside the parameters of Spanish law's definition of genocide, which he understood to apply to "a national, ethnic or religious group." Garzón successfully appealed to the full court of the Audiencia Nacional, which flatly rejected Fungairiño's arguments. The eleven judges unanimously agreed with Garzón's interpretation of genocide, which was more in line with international legal standards than with Spanish law, and understood "national group" to apply to any group in society that did not conform to the ideology of the ruling regime. This cleared the way for justice officials to forward to Britain a formal request to extradite Chile's former dictator to Spain.

The Aznar administration also endeavored behind the scenes to undermine the work of the Spanish courts. One government argument employed early on was that Garzón might have broken with protocol in bypassing the Spanish Ministry of Foreign Affairs by directly approaching Interpol when transmitting his request for Pinochet's extradition from Britain. Later, government officials contended that Garzón had failed to notify the attorney general's office of his intention to request an extradition from Britain, and that in any case the extradition violated Pinochet's diplomatic immunity. More revealing yet, Britain's decision to allow Pinochet to return to Chile was readily (perhaps eagerly) accepted by the Spanish government, even though Garzón had publicly announced his intention to appeal any negative response to his extradition request.[19] When word came from Britain that Pinochet would be allowed to return to Chile, Aznar communicated to the British authorities that his government would support the decision, a reaction widely seen as a rebuke of Garzón. Within hours of Britain's pronouncement, Pinochet was on his way to Chile, far from the reach of the Spanish justice system.

As might be expected, Aznar's reluctance to side with the Spanish courts on Pinochet's extradition left him vulnerable to attacks from the opposition. PSOE spokesman Pérez Rubalcaba, attempting to explain why the Aznar administration appeared reluctant to follow Garzón's orders, recalled that in articles written twenty years previously, "Aznar had professed support for Pinochet" (Malamud 2003: 160). PSOE congressional deputies complained that the Aznar administration's legal maneuvering to impede the general's extradition to Spain revealed that the government was staffed by people "not fit to work in a country with a consolidated democracy."[20] IU deputies went a step farther in their criticism, accusing Aznar of "protecting the ex-Chilean dictator" and wasting an "opportunity to demonstrate that he (Aznar) was a democrat."[21] The message conveyed by such comments was that the Aznar administration was protecting Pinochet, just as Franco would have done, a rather sensitive accusation given that Aznar's Popular Party was founded by former Francoist ministers. The new boldness of the left's attacks on the Aznar administration, which clearly included questioning government officials' democratic credentials by suggesting an authoritarian mentality in handling the Pinochet affair, represented the most egregious breach of the Pact of Forgetting to date.

The left did not stop at verbal attacks against the Aznar administration. Hoping to pressure the government into requesting Pinochet's extradition to Spain and to rally the citizenry to exert the same demand, left-wing leaders employed a variety of political institutions and forums. The PSOE leadership promised to hold hearings in the Congress of Deputies to investigate any likely obstruction of justice on the part of the administration, a threat that never materialized. At the request of the PSOE and other liberal parties, the European parliament adopted a resolution urging the Spanish government to request Pinochet's extradition, should this be the wish of the courts. In town halls across Spain and in the governments of the autonomous regions, the IU introduced declarations in support of extradition and played a pivotal role in organizing civil protests.

The Aznar administration counterattacked by charging the left with using Pinochet's arrest as a cynical ploy to gain political advantage and to incite political passions about Spain's own past. "This is a chance for the Spanish left to live vicariously the process of revenge they feel they missed out on after General Franco's death, when Spaniards decided to move ahead from dictatorship to democracy and forgive the sins of the past," remarked an unnamed PP official to the *Guardian*.[22] The Aznar administration also asserted that it needed no lessons in human rights from the PSOE, citing the damage to Spanish democracy from the socialist sponsorship of the GAL in the fight against Basque terrorists during the mid-1980s. This was another below-the-belt hit in the fight between the PP and PSOE, intended to suggest that the left was not morally fit to criticize the government. "The scant sensitivity of the PSOE for the transgression of human rights (with respect to the GAL), undermines the opposition party's demands from the government in relation to the request for the extradition of Augusto Pinochet," contended Luis de Grandes, the PP parliamentary spokesman (Malamud 2003: 160).

Tellingly, few sectors in Spanish political society sided with the Aznar administration's position on Pinochet. Iñaki Anasagasti, spokesman for the Basque Nationalist Party, urged the government "not to place economic interests above human and democratic rights," while Jordi Pujol, president of the Catalan Generalitat, praised Pinochet's detention as "morally positive," adding that "the years of dictatorship have not been forgotten."[23] Spanish jurists criticized the government for interfering with the deliberation of justice. For instance, Aznar's initial argument that the government had to first examine the merits of the extradition case before acting on it was widely seen as an obstruction of justice by the Spanish judicial community, even by conservative jurists, who argued that the role of the Aznar administration in the matter was simply to act as "the messenger" of the extradition request.[24] Political commentators also noted the fact that in failing to support the Pinochet extradition, Aznar was wasting an opportunity to move his party toward the center and away from its Francoist origins. An essay in the op-ed pages of *El Mundo* noted that Aznar was obviously failing to realize that "the march toward the political center is not possible by supporting dictators."[25] Predictably, the only source of solid support for the government position came from the far right. Manuel Fraga, minister of information and tourism under Franco and founding father of the PP, declared the detention of the ex-Chilean dictator "an offense to civilization," adding that during "an extraordinary period like that of Spain during the Civil War, societies should forget the past."[26]

A Window of Opportunity

The second blow to the Pact of Forgetting brought on by the Pinochet affair—the creation of conditions that allowed voices in civil society to demand attention to the past—benefited from important changes in both the domestic and international environment. On the domestic front, as already shown, the intensity of the political debate triggered by Pinochet's arrest and the many legal twists and turns the case took had shattered the political elite's consensus to refrain from using the past as a political weapon while awakening the political ghosts of Spain's past in the Spanish population at large. In a striking departure from past political behavior, civil society groups once cowed by fears of reopening "old wounds" were now willing to make their demands public, regardless of the consequences. On the international front, the work of nascent human rights associations in Spain was greatly facilitated by the growing popularity of the transitional justice movement, whose own rise had benefited tremendously from the notoriety of the Pinochet affair and the legal innovations Garzón introduced in his prosecution of the Chilean dictator. Indeed, in the wake of "the Garzón effect," Spain would have had a difficult time ignoring pleas from its citizens for action with respect to Spain's own political excesses.

By 1999, the Aznar administration began receiving requests by human rights organizations, local and regional governments, and universities for public assistance to exhume and rebury the remains of those killed by Franco's army still resting in unmarked graves. These demands were met with outright disdain from government officials, even though these groups did not seek vengeance or retribution, only financial assistance in identifying the remains buried in the graves. "Of course the government recognizes the right of families to privately re-bury their dead, but we see no point in reopening old wounds that afflicted Spanish society; these matters are for historians, not politicians" observed a PP member of parliament.[27] At the party's 2003 national convention the PP reaffirmed this position with Fraga proclaiming: "We have had enough of unburying the dead" (Gálvez Biesca 2006: 31).

Leading the way in making the issue of the past a salient one in Spanish politics was the Association for the Recuperation of the Historical Memory (ARMH), an organization formed in 2000 by journalist Emilio Silva. Like many other Spanish "memory" advocates, Silva's interest in Spain's "forgotten" recent past was motivated by being "perplexed by the public's enthusiastic response to Pinochet's prosecution for his political crimes while being seemingly disinterested in investigating similar acts committed by Franco."[28] Silva had a personal connection to the issue of Franco's political crimes, especially the so-called *desaparecidos*, those who vanished while in the custody of the state and were eventually killed, including Silva's own grandfather, shot by Franco's army in October 1936. Yet for much of the post-Civil War period, Silva's grandmother had deliberately kept the details of her husband's death from her son and other relatives. Silva eventually located the remains of his grandfather in an unmarked grave in the province of León.[29]

Other organizations devoted to the recovery of the historical memory soon followed, such as the Memory Forum (linked to the IU) and victims' groups such as the Association of War Children, Association of Ex-Political Prisoners, and Association of the Descendants of the Spanish Exile. Currently, according to one study, more than 160 associations working at the national, regional, and provincial levels constitute the movement to recover the historical memory (Gálvez Biesca 2006: 34). Most of these groups are located in three regions: Madrid, Catalonia, and Andalusia. Memory associations have little if any presence in Cantabria, Navarra, Castilla-La Mancha, and the archipelagos of Baleares and Canarias. This distribution clearly suggests that the memory associations are most prominent in Republican strongholds and in the places where the Civil War was fought most intensively and less visible in regions where Francoism was strong or the population was relatively unaffected by the war.

Since its creation, the activism of the ARMH (and that of related organizations) has been devoted to advancing the following: (1) the promotion of initiatives seeking moral, judicial and financial reparation for the victims of the Civil War and the Franco dictatorship; (2) complete annulment of all judicial proceedings, both military and civilian, that took place under

Franco; (3) exhumation of Civil War graves; (4) removal from public view of monuments to the old regime; (5) creation of a national archive of the Civil War and the dictatorship with access to all documentation related to the Francoist oppression, including military and church archives and private collections.

In working to raise awareness about the issue of historical memory and to force the government to respond to its demands, the ARMH shrewdly began to look beyond Spanish borders. In August 2002, leaders of the organization appeared before the UN Office of the High Commissioner for Human Rights in Geneva to inform this body of their work; that same month Montserrant Sans, a lawyer for the ARMH made the association's case to the United Nations Working Group on Enforced or Involuntary Disappearances.[30] The ARMH called for the Spanish government to pay for the exhumations, to give remains of the bodies exhumed a proper burial, and to establish a commission to investigate the facts surrounding the fate of those who disappeared during the Civil War. The result of this international advocacy was the inclusion of Spain in the UN list of countries that had yet to resolve the issue of state crimes and repression. In November 2002, the UN urged the Spanish government to investigate the fate of Republicans killed following the Civil War and undertake the exhumation of known graves of the disappeared. A few years later, the ARMH collaborated with Amnesty International on a 77-page report titled *La deuda pendiente con las víctimas de la guerra civil española y del regimen franquista* (The Pending Debt with the Victims of the Spanish Civil War and the Francoist Regime) asking Spain to adhere to the international principles contained in the international treaties to which Spain was a party.[31]

The ARMH did not wait for the government to respond to the pressures exerted by international bodies to start digging up the 30,000 unmarked graves of people the group claims Franco summarily executed.[32] With the aid of private financing and volunteer work, the organization made headlines in October 2000 with the exhumation of thirteen bodies from a mass Civil War grave in the province of León. By 2006, the ARMH had exhumed some forty gravesites containing the remains of 520 bodies. These exhumations spoke volumes about the savagery carried out by Franco's army: the decomposed bodies showed that the victims were tortured before being shot in the head and were buried in freshly dug graves by the roadside or in remote fields. Even the burials were an act of revenge. Some bodies were buried face down—an insult in Catholic culture—in keeping with Franco's view of Republicans as "unbelievers" and "godless communists." Interestingly, many of the recovered remains were not of Republican soldiers but of ordinary people killed after the Civil War because they were suspected of aiding the Huídos, the Republicans who took to the hills rather than surrender to Franco, and subsequently the Maquis, the exiles who began to reenter Spain after the end of World War II with the hope of toppling the Franco regime.

Perhaps more shocking to the public than the exhumation of mass graves were the oral histories the ARMH collected from the survivors of the Civil War and its aftermath. The collective testimony gathered by the ARMH staff tells of the fear many relatives of Franco's victims still feel about revealing what they know about the Civil War graves. Many confessed to discovering unmarked mass graves shortly after the killings but keeping details of their location secret for more than sixty years. Others tell of paying anonymous visits to the graves to clean them or simply lay flowers on them. An article in *El País* with the macabre title "The Earth Returns Its Dead" chronicles the poignant tale of an eighty-seven-year-old woman giving her son a map of where her two brothers were shot by Franco's army in 1937 for fear she would die before their graves were exhumed and the remains re-buried.[33]

Re-Politicizing the Past

A final consequence of the Pinochet affair in Spain was to politicize or, more accurately, to "re-politicize" the past. A case in point is the observation of important historical anniversaries. Prior to 1996, political actors and society at large approached historical anniversaries with utmost sensitivity, careful to avoid anything that could offend either faction that fought the Civil War, as was the case with the fiftieth anniversary of the start of the Civil War in 1986. But since the late 1990s, as seen in the previous chapter, anniversaries have become a golden opportunity for the left to score points over the right. More telling, perhaps, is the re-politicization of the past evident in Spanish popular culture in the aftermath of the Pinochet affair. Since 2000, there has been an outburst of books, films, and exhibits devoted to the Civil War and the Franco dictatorship. Indeed, in the eyes of some observers, such as the novelist Isaac Rosa, the vastness of the artistic and cultural works about predemocratic Spain coming in the wake of Pinochet's indictment has led to an *empacho de memoria* (a memory binge), "which like candy is quite fattening but not especially nutritious."[34]

Broadly speaking, the artistic and cultural work attached to the movement for the recovery of the historical memory has sought to move the debate about the Civil War and the Franco dictatorship beyond the old question of who bore ultimate responsibility for this conflict (the radical policies of the left or the reactionary behavior of the right) and toward new concerns such as who suffered the most during the war, which side endured the most devastating consequences of the dictatorship, and what could be done to recover the loss of memory occasioned by the years of forgetting. The aim of a new generation of writers, scholars, journalists, and filmmakers is to show that Franco's 1936 coup was not an act of national salvation as depicted in state policy under Franco, but rather a vicious attack by a reactionary minority on a popularly elected government. The latter claim undermines the sanitized, neutral reading of the Civil War constructed by the mid-century anti-Francoist intelligentsia (and which prevailed throughout the democratic transition and the post-transition years), which emphasizes collective culpability for the war.

Those who have examined in detail the cultural work devoted to exposing the horrors of the Civil War and Franco dictatorship, such as Faber (2007: 152), note that its rhetorical power rests in presenting "truths that have been hidden or ignored. . . . They claim to tell the reading and viewing public of something important it did not know: newly discovered proofs, facts that might have been common knowledge among specialists but not among others; puzzle pieces that had not been put together; and testimonies that no one ever heard before." Moreover, many of these works place Spain in a broad comparative perspective in an effort to underscore the horrors of the past. As Faber (152) notes, "whether deliberate or not, much of the new cultural work on the past links Francoist Spain to the worst political excesses of post-war Latin America while highlighting striking parallels with Hitler's Germany."

Several works are worth noting, if only because of their influence in shaping popular discourse about the past. Santos Juliá's edited volume *Víctimas de la Guerra Civil* (Victims of the Civil War, 1999) "established the paradigm for discussing the civil war and the dictatorship in terms of victimhood" (Labanyi 2008: 124). Carlos Elordi's *Los años difíciles* (The Difficult Years, 2002) describes the hardship of the Civil War years as seen through wartime memorabilia such as the diaries and letters to relatives of those individuals executed under the Franco regime. *Las trece rosas* (The Thirteen Roses, 2003), by journalist Carlos Fonseca, details one of the most infamous episodes of repression of the postwar period: the torture and gruesome murder of thirteen girls on August 5, 1939, on charges of aiding the Republican rebels. This episode spawned a 2003 novel by Jesús Ferrero and a 2007 film by Emilio Martínez-Lázaro. Isaías Lafuente's *Esclavos por la patria* (Slaves for the Fatherland, 2002) chronicles the misery of Franco's labor camps while Javier Rodrigo's *Los campos de concentración franquistas* (Francoist Concentration Camps, 2003), depicts the existence of Francoist camps in 1936–1942.

The television documentary *Los niños perdidos del franquismo* or *Els nens perduts del franquisme* in its original Catalan (The Lost Children of Francoism, 2002), directed by Montse Armengou and Ricard Belis, traces the tragic fate of the children of Republican families snatched by Franco's social workers from Auxilio Social, Franco's largest charity, and given to Nationalist supporters to raise, or sent to orphanages where they died of abuse, neglect, and hunger. *Les fosses del silenci* (The Graves of Silence, 2003), marketed in the United States and Britain as *The Spanish Holocaust*, by the same directors, is a harsh indictment of Spain's delayed attention to the thousands of unmarked graves that have remained forgotten by the nation since the return of democracy. Javier Corcuera's documentary *La guerrilla de la memoria* (The Guerilla of Memory, 2002) describes the brutal repression and eventual eradication of the Huídos, those who refused to surrender to Franco's rule and instead took to the hills in the hopes of overturning the dictatorship by means of a popular uprising.[35] Pau Vergara's *Más allá de la alambrada: La memoria del horror* (Beyond the Barbed Wire, 2004), describes the story of the 8,000 Republican prisoners at the Nazi concentration camp at Mauthasen, in upper Austria, between 1939 and 1945, including interviews with twenty-three survivors.

Another notable intellectual endeavor is the attempt to reconstruct the Civil War as "a class war" by reiterating the origins of the Civil War in class struggle, and more specifically the oppression of the majority by a politically and economically powerful oligarchy; but, more important, perhaps, by pointing to the social and economic consequences of the Civil War. The latter point has the goal of emphasizing the disproportionate oppression that the working class and workers' organizations bore under Francoism as a means to suggest that not everyone suffered equally under the old regime, another myth underpinning the politics of forgetting. As summarized by

Piqueras and Sanz Rozalén (2007: 3), the new "social history of Spanish labor" is mindful of the fact that "the country lived under a long, very strict dictatorship (1936–1977) which during its first twenty-five years continuously and systematically repressed working-class organizations and left-wing organizations in general." They added, "The dictatorship physically eliminated numerous members of parties and trade unions, sent others to jail and dissolved their organizations, confiscated and destroyed their files and books and persecuted their traditions and intellectuals." This singular repression, it is pointed out, was not recognized until at least the 1990s, a development due not only to the traditional neglect of the working class by historians, but also to the limitations on research imposed by the dictatorship and the appeal of new historical narratives that arrived with the democratic transition.

A Rightwing Countermovement

The historical revisionism prevalent in the wake of Pinochet's indictment and subsequent arrest met its match with the rise of an intellectual countermovement intended to revisit the Francoist era and recast it as the foundation of Spain's democratic present, giving rise to intense debates over how to interpret Spain's past, especially the Civil War. A network of media outlets and cultural institutions, including the newspaper *El Mundo*, the magazine *Razón Española*, and the publisher La Esfera de los Libros, is today invested in a "neo-Francoist" historiography. Prominent among its leaders is Pío Moa, a former left-wing radical turned right-wing intellectual agitator, and author of a string of best-selling books that reject the generally accepted view that Franco overthrew democracy in Spain in 1936.[36] "The coup of 1936 terminated a democracy that had already been destroyed by the left," Moa has famously argued.[37] In his view, Franco did not rebel against a democratic government but rather ended an extreme revolution. Moa has also argued that the left has exaggerated the number of victims of the Civil War and the dictatorship, in order to turn Franco into a vengeful and bloodthirsty dictator, and has characterized the International Brigades, who joined the left in defending the Republic, as anti-Spanish communists. He has also praised Franco, who he claimed "liberated Spain from World War II and left a prosperous and reconciled nation, free of the hatreds of the Second Republic."[38] These views form the core of his best-known book, *Los mitos de la guerra civil Española* (The Myths of the Spanish Civil War, 2003).[39]

Moa also allied himself with the PP in criticizing the PSOE and IU for their decision to break away from the Pact of Forgetting by insisting that the left's interest in reviving the past was a political ploy to discredit the rise of a legitimate conservative party in Spain.[40] In his words, the Civil War was resurrected by the left "as a weapon to disqualify its conservative opponents by accusing the party of Aznar of being the direct heir of Franco."[41] Indeed, the work of Moa and others served to legitimize the very aggressive reorientation of the teaching of Spanish history after the party gained an absolute majority of parliamentary seats in the 2000 elections. As shown in the previous chapter, in 2003 the Aznar administration unveiled a comprehensive philosophy destined to "shape the values of new generations of Spaniards along traditionalist lines" (Balfour 2005: 158). Baptized "constitutional patriotism," and approved by the PP at its fourteenth congress in 2002, this new policy attempted to recast Spanish historicism in a fashion that echoed the thinking of Spanish conservatives of the late nineteenth century.[42]

Accompanying the PP policy of constitutional patriotism was a series of high-profile political provocations of the left and of the nationalist-regionalist parties of Catalonia and the Basque Country. These provocations signaled not only an open disregard for the commitment to avoid politicizing the past, but also a challenge to Spain's new image as a multi-cultural state. In 2003, Aznar spent millions for the exhumation of Russian graves belonging to several corpses of the members of La División Azul (the Blue Division), the Spanish battalion sent by Franco to support Nazi troops during World War II, and the repatriation of the remains from Russia to Spain. Before leaving office in 2004, the Aznar administration authorized several grants from the Ministry of Culture to the Francisco Franco Foundation, whose mission is to promote the memory and accomplishments of the ex-dictator.

Most upsetting to socialist and regional nationalists, however, was the Aznar administration's campaign to revive the importance of national symbols in the everyday life of Spaniards, believing that they served the purpose of promoting national unity and democratic coexistence. In 2002, Aznar raised eyebrows everywhere when his government planted an enormous Spanish flag at Plaza Colón in Madrid's Salamanca district, home to embassies, government offices, and the city's best-known department stores. The government also began to require that the Spanish anthem be played during the king's travels throughout Spain. National holidays, especially October 12, became the occasion for extravagant displays of Spanish nationalism.

These patriotic gestures were intended to remind the public that "Spain was still one nation."[43]

Popular Discourses and Memory Wars

Taking their cues from the politicians, ordinary Spaniards followed suit with their own debate about the past. A bizarre setting for this debate was the obituary pages of the nation's major newspapers, which by the mid-2000s had become a popular venue for the public to relive the painful events that led to the Civil War. In what the Spanish media dubbed *la guerra de las esquelas* (obituary wars), the relatives of those killed during the Civil War appeared to be fighting the war all over again.[44] In keeping with the politics of interwar Spain, the obituaries are written from the perspective of the two sides that fought the Civil War (defeated "Republicans" from the left and victorious "Nationalists" from the right) and tell emotionally charged tales of political violence and revenge that echo the intensity of the ideological polarization prevalent around the time of the war. Underscoring the politically charged rhetoric of the obituaries, those honoring the Nationalist dead would usually appear in conservative papers like *El Mundo* while those honoring the Republican dead were most commonly found in the liberal *El País*.

The first Civil War obituary to appear was published by Carlota Leret in *El País* on July 17, 2006, to honor the memory of her father Virgilio Leret, a pilot with the Republican army who is remembered today as Franco's first victim. The obituary was timed to mark the seventieth anniversary of the beginning of the Civil War. It read: "Commander Virgilio Loret was a victim of Francoist terrorism. He was shot at dawn on July 18, 1936 after surrendering. As a result of a pact of silence unacceptable in any democratic society, Spain is still in debt with its justice, the truth, and the memory of the victims." Published at the cost of approximately $12,000 and covering half a page, Mr. Leret's obituary triggered a flurry of similar notices from both sides of the Civil War in newspapers across Spain. Asked what prompted her to memorialize her father seventy years after his death, Ms. Leret observed:[45]

> During seventy years the newspapers had profusely published Francoist obituaries honoring those "fallen for God and Spain," and I feel

> that we, the victims of their intolerance and repression, also have the right to remember our dear ones, those who gave their lives in defense of democratic legality. I wanted to let democratic Spain know that to this day there are a lot of people who do not want to recognize the black legend of this country, and that the losers of that war, to this day, have not had the opportunity to remember in a public fashion our dead ones. And I wanted to remember that the first episode of the Civil War took place on 17 July 1936, in Melilla, when the fascists attacked the air base of Al Atalayón. This is the event that began the Civil War.

Much has been said in the Spanish media about the shockingly incendiary language employed in the Civil War obituaries, with epitaphs such as "red hordes" and "Francoist terrorists," bandied about with remarkable frequency and ease, adding up to a very uncivil discourse about the remembrance of the violence of the Civil War. The characterizations of the killings are usually accompanied by explanations for them. Left-wing sympathizers usually include a political explanation such as "killed defending the legitimate government of the Republic and the Constitution," while right-wing sympathizers generally offer a religious explanation such as "vilely murdered because of his faith and devotion to God."[46] Some provide rich details about the pain of being unable to locate the remains of loved ones and for "the three horrible years lived in Madrid." Others regard publication of a death notice as closure for a long and painful ordeal. ARMH founder Emilio Silva noted that his family decided to write a death notice for the exhumation and reburial of his grandfather's remains "because it is a form of normalizing a person's death."[47]

As would be expected, the media took an interest in the phenomenon of the Civil War obituaries, which allowed them to pass judgment on the timing and purpose of the public's discourses on the remembrance of the past. For the conservative daily *ABC*, memorializing Civil War victims in the national papers defied political reason. In a strongly worded editorial, the paper argued: [48]

> Why these remembrances, these necrologies, we ask ourselves, given that it has been seventy years since that collective curse. Had we not negotiated intelligently a transition that we set forth as an example to the world—named Concordia—in which we agreed to turn the

> page of history leaving the dead to rest in peace? Someone has to explain the sociopolitical reasons why ten years ago when we marked sixty years since the beginning of the Civil War with José María Aznar as President of the Government of Spain this controversial phenomenon did not take place. Just like it did not happen in 1986, with half a century since the beginning of the Civil War with Felipe González re-elected President after winning a parliamentary majority in the Congress of Deputies. In 1976, in the midst of the transition to democracy with Adolfo Suárez busy reforming the Fundamental Laws, nobody thought of looking backward with vengeance through the rear-view mirror.

El Mundo, and especially *El Pais,* took a more positive view of the appearance of the Civil War death notices, often resorting to academic proxies from the nation's leading universities to make their points. In a lengthy profile, *El Mundo* sought a balanced view, noting that the phenomenon was a direct result of the "instrumentalization of the historical memory of the present government," and its attempt to make "angels of one side of the war and criminals of the other," as historian and journalist César Vidal pointed out.[49] On the other side, the relatives of the "reds" never had the chance to place obituaries during the Francoist era. "Those who criticize the Republican obituaries thought that everything was neatly tied up and that nobody would have any questions about why and where their relatives were killed," said journalist José Torres, the author of several books on the Civil War. *El País* uniformly praised the death notices as a positive contribution to Spanish society. "It is good that the taboo about the Civil War should end, that we finish off the fears about the War. There should be freedom of expression, and people should feel free to remember their dead," observed Antonio Alorzo of Madrid's Complutense University.[50]

El País also took note of the imbalanced way the Civil War had been remembered during the Franco era and the immediate post-Franco years, and saw the death notices as an effective way to remedy this.[51] "The victors also suffered, but they had forty years to pay homage to their dead. The defeated had no such choice," wrote José Antonio Martín Pallín, a jurist with the Supreme Court. Writers for *El País* also drew distinctions between the death notices of the Republicans and those of the Nationalists. "There is a great difference between the death notices and that is what we are studying," remarked anthropologist Francisco Ferrándiz. "In the Nationalist ones, there is a determined rhetoric that was already established by the Francoist regime. Vilely murdered by Marxists hordes and the red hordes, this is language that comes from the rhetorical repertoire of the dictatorship." Ferrándiz added: "The Republican death notices have a more intimate, personal tone."

The lively debate about the past encapsulated in the war of obituaries overlapped with the national debate about the past triggered by the 2007 Law of Historical Memory, which, as seen in the next chapter, was the government's attempt to address the obvious yearning for official policies with respect to the past. It is unclear, however, the extent to which the war notices were meant to influence the debate over the law. According to Emilio Silva, "this movement does not respond to a political strategy . . . they are a byproduct of the past being elevated in the public's consciousness, which in turn has created two currents that want to remember and honor their relatives."[52] He analogized the phenomenon to Germany in 1968, when young people began to confront their parents over their involvement in the Holocaust. Others are less sanguine in their interpretation. Florencio Dimas, president of Amigos de los Caídos por la Libertad (Friends of Those Fallen for Liberty), an organization composed of children and grandchildren of those killed by the Nationalist army, blamed the right for creating "an artificial war," pointing to the "vengeful" tenor of the death notices in the right-wing media, in contrast to those by the members of his organization. The key difference, he argued, between the right-wing and left-wing obituaries was that Nationalist side had "forty years to publish as many *esquelas* and hold as many funerals as they wished without impediments from the state, while those from our side could not even hold a mass."

CHAPTER 6

Post-Transitional Justice in Zapatero's Second Transition

On October 31, 2007, the thirtieth anniversary of the transition to democracy, the socialist administration of José Luis Rodríguez Zapatero enacted the Law of Historical Memory. Heading into the March 14, 2004, elections, which brought the PSOE back to power after two resounding defeats by the right-wing PP (1996 and 2000), few could have anticipated that this law was in store for Spain. For one thing, Zapatero is often referred to as an accidental leader, because his rise to power is intimately linked to the political fallout over the March 11, 2004, bombing of Madrid's Atocha train station. This was the worst act of terrorism in Spanish history and the bloodiest single attack on civilians on European soil since the end of World War II; the attack killed 190 people and left more than 1,500 wounded. PP Prime Minister Aznar mangled his response to the attack by putting the blame on ETA, even as evidence was pointing to Moroccan terrorists affiliated with the Al Qaeda organization (the mastermind behind the terrorist attacks of September 11, 2001). This misstep made what had been predicted as a narrow victory for the PP into a resounding triumph for the PSOE.[1] With allegations of a government cover up mounting, Zapatero emerged as the undisputed victor of the 2004 electoral contest, with almost 1.3 million votes more than the incumbent party.[2] The PP vote plunged from 44.52 percent in 2000 to 37.64 percent in 2004; the PSOE vote soared from 34.16 to 42.64 percent.

Furthermore, despite rising public interest in the Civil War and the Francoist era, the past was not an issue during the 2004 campaign. In any case, Zapatero did not come into office with any clear intention of overturning the Pact of Forgetting. References to historical memory in the PSOE 2004 platform are oblique. This document only commits the party to establishing a National Center for Documentation and Investigation about the Civil War and the Franco dictatorship with the purpose of "reinvigoration of the cultural patrimony from the standpoint of making it an object for the recuperation of the historical memory."[3]

All that said, Zapatero's decision to undo the Pact of Forgetting with the introduction of the Law of Historical Memory could hardly be deemed a surprise. By 2000, several regional governments had already established commissions to investigate the living conditions of Civil War veterans, and for the first time in the post-Franco era, a thriving civil society movement existed to lobby the government on behalf of "restoring" the political memory lost during the democratic transition and its aftermath. As noted previously, some 160 "memory" groups led by the ARMH were already active by the mid-2000s, many of them with left-wing sympathies. Another factor pointing toward a potential memory law was the international spread of transitional justice by the early 2000s, and the way its absence in Spain made the country seem at odds with international human rights norms or, worse yet, in defiance of them. An important strategy that groups like the ARMH used to get attention from government officials was partnering with international organizations like the UN and transnational NGOs like Amnesty International to criticize the way Spain had failed to address the legacy of political violence of the Civil War and the repression of the Franco years. Zapatero, whose administration set for itself very lofty standards of ethics and social progressivism, simply could not afford to ignore the demands of human rights advocates both at home and abroad.

The socialist electoral triumph in 2004 also signaled a notable generational shift in political leadership in Spain, one of great consequence for how questions about the past would be dealt with by the new government. Zapatero was part of a new generation of professional left-wing leaders whose political socialization was not shaped by the struggle against Francoism or the political exigencies of the democratic transition. Indeed, he was the part of "the first generation to approach the past without fear or trauma."[4] This background explains some of the arguments Zapatero employed to justify his memory policies. During the 2004 campaign, he contended there was a flaw in the democratic transition: *mucha concordia y poca memoria* (much agreement and little memory).[5] Only a few years earlier, such a criticism of the transition would have been considered unacceptable for a member of the political establishment.

Less apparent, as suggested in this chapter, is that Zapatero's bold venture into memory politics embodied a clearly delineated political project, the so-called "second transition," a set of social and cultural policies which made the Zapatero administration the most controversial since the restoration of democracy in 1977 (see Kennedy 2007; Encarnación 2010; Field 2010). The goal of the second transition was twofold: to complete the unfinished business of the transition out of Francoism of the late 1970s and to reinvigorate the Spanish socialist brand after the beating it took during the Felipe González era. The second transition, however, did not entail a full embrace of transitional justice. In fact, notwithstanding characterizations of the Law of Historical Memory as an instance of "post-transitional justice" (Aguilar 2009), it is questionable that the label fully applies, given the notable shortcomings in the law with respect to accountability toward the old regime. Although the intent to end the Pact of Forgetting is apparent, neither retribution nor reconciliation, as conventionally defined, is reflected in the legislation.

Indeed, the ambiguity of the Law of Historical Memory suggests a marked timidity on the part of the Zapatero administration to completely overturn the Pact of Forgetting. To some extent, the law demonstrates significant continuity with the pact. This aspect belies attacks from the right depicting the law as radical and potentially damaging to political stability, while it contradicts assessments of Zapatero's policies as signaling a break with the politics of consensus of the transition. Oddly enough, the memory law itself is a notable example of political compromise. Because the government lacked a majority of seats in parliament, and because the main opposition party, the PP, was resolute in its opposition to the law from the start, the government was forced to compromise on a wide range of issues with a cluster of left-wing parties and important regional-nationalist parties. The negotiations were difficult and at times contentious, which explains why the Council of Ministers took two years to approve a draft bill on July 28, 2006, and more than another year for the bill to get parliamentary approval on October 31, 2007.

Contextualizing Zapatero's Memory Politics

During Zapatero's first term in office (2004–2008), the government introduced nothing short of a social and cultural revolution that went well beyond overturning the Pact of Forgetting, a remarkable achievement considering that the PSOE failed to get a parliamentary majority in 2004. Within its first 24 months in office, the Zapatero administration moved to strengthen separation of church and state by abolishing the practice inherited from the Franco era of showing religious symbols in public places, such as crucifixes in prisons, courthouses, and military buildings, and by shelving a law by the previous administration that called for compulsory religious instruction in public schools. New laws were passed that liberalized divorce, authorized stem cell research from embryos created for fertility treatment but no longer wanted by their owners, created a path to Spanish citizenship for millions of illegal immigrants, and made Spain only the third country in Europe, after the Netherlands and Belgium, to legalize same-sex marriage.

The Zapatero administration also passed a flurry of laws designed to bring gender equality in government and the workplace, including the Law of Equality Between Women and Men, which requires political parties to field lists of candidates for national and local office that are at least 40 percent of each sex and grants preferential treatment to companies with the highest percentages of female executives. Last, but not least, the administration endorsed Catalonia's controversial new compact of regional governance (the so-called Nou Estatut), which contends that Catalonia's powers of self-government emanate from the Catalan people rather than from the Spanish Constitution, and grants the region more control over such issues as tax collection, immigration policy, and judicial affairs.

Politics, as much as anything else, was a driving motivation behind Zapatero's second transition policies. On gaining the PSOE presidency, Zapatero eagerly embraced the notion of rebuilding the PSOE, believing that "Felipe González lost the 1996 elections not only because of scandals but because the PSOE's political project was exhausted."[6] In announcing his new team at the PSOE's thirty-fifth congress in July 2000, Zapatero stressed the idea of a new beginning for the party in eloquent but decisive terms: "I have always thought of socialism as a transit between nostalgia and hope. Our nostalgia, Felipe, is 1982. I am welcoming you to a new great hope: the hope of 2004."[7] The party's new political project hinged on what Zapatero termed "Citizen's Socialism," which advocated "near pacifism in foreign policy, expanding civil rights, and a preference for following rather than guiding the will of the people."[8] This new vision of socialism benefited from the fact that the odds for a socialist victory in the 2004 national elections were slim at best. It is a popular theory in Spain that Zapatero knew in his heart that he had no hope of winning the 2004 election, and therefore decided to go out on a limb and construct a kind of utopian socialist project that probably would never be implemented but could give a boost of energy to the PSOE and genuinely embodied his own political views (Encarnación 2010).

After Zapatero's unexpected win in 2004, the PSOE's ability to stay in that power depended on solidifying the electoral coalition that had brought the party back, a good share comprised young voters, many of them (about 530,000) first-time voters, and non-PSOE left-wing voters from the IU (which incorporates the former communists) who had voted for Zapatero in 2004 to ensure defeat of the PP over its mismanagement of the Atocha terrorist attack. (This shift in party preference by the "far left" explains the drop in support for the IU from 5.96 percent of the vote in 2000 to 4.96 percent in 2004, and the decline in parliamentary representation from eight seats to four.) A result of these shifts in electoral patterns was a new profile for the typical PSOE voter. During the 1990s, support for the party came mainly from "rural areas, the working class and the economic inactive groups (pensioners, the unemployed and housewives)," but after the 2004 general election the party began to draw clear majorities from the young, the middle classes, and those with university degrees (Méndez-Lago 2006: 433–34). There was little Zapatero could offer these new constituencies on the economic front to distinguish his administration from the previous one, since the PSOE and the PP had a consensus on the economy going back to the 1990s, but he could certainly veer left on social and cultural policy to appeal to new voters. After all, social progressivism was in his political DNA.

The left-wing background of Zapatero's family is often credited with inspiring his progressivism, especially with respect to the issue of the past. His grandfather, Captain Juan Rodríguez Lozano, was executed by a Francoist firing squad for refusing to join the rebellion against the Republican government. This family connection to the Civil War gave Zapatero's "memory" policies the aura of a personal crusade. In speeches and rallies during the 2004 elections, Zapatero revealed that his interest in politics was piqued at age eighteen, when he read the handwritten testament his grandfather wrote just 24 hours before his execution. In this document, Captain Rodríguez Lozano asked his family to forgive those who were about to execute him and to clear his name when the appropriate time arrived. Zapatero's inaugural speech powerfully invoked his grandfather's memory. The speech incorporated the closing passage of Rodríguez Lozano's final letter to his family. It read: "An infinite yearning for peace, love of good and the betterment of those less fortunate."[9]

Zapatero himself has credited his progressive policies to a variety of schools of thought that emphasize an active role for government and the law in society with the goal of strengthening "the idea of citizenship" to make "a more creative, more tolerant society."[10] The best known of these schools of thought is that espoused by Irish political theorist Philip Pettit, widely known as Zapatero's guru.[11] In his book *Republicanism: A Theory of Freedom and Government* (1997) Pettit embraced the idea of "non-domination," which suggests that no one should impose his or her will on the choices made by others, and that the law can be effectively employed to disperse power within society and prevent the repression of women and minorities. Pettit has also called for what he has termed "civic republicanism," a deep and constant engagement by the citizenry in public affairs (Marti and Pettit 2010). Explaining Pettit's influence over Zapatero's political program, PSOE spokesman José Andrés Torres Mora, said: "We had simple political and theoretical instincts and Pettit offered us the analytical framework which helped place them within a systematic framework" (Kennedy 2007: 191).

Fittingly, during the debate over of the draft bill of the Law of Historical Memory, the government characterized the law not as a long-deferred moral obligation but as a component of the philosophical program of the government to create a more inclusive and open democracy. As Torres Mora noted in the Congress of Deputies, the draft bill was "a reflection of the policies of recognition and extension of rights followed by this government during this legislature."[12] In any case, almost immediately on taking office, Zapatero began incremental steps to undermine the Pact of Forgetting—steps that, in retrospect, can be seen as having set the political-legal framework for the 2007 memory law. Perhaps naively, Zapatero's expectation was that a gradual approach to legislating the recovery of the historical memory "would heal wounds without reopening them."[13]

Legislating the Recovery of the Historical Memory

Zapatero's first meaningful step toward revisiting the past was the creation of an inter-ministerial commission in September 2004 to study the circumstances of the victims of the Civil War and Francoism and consider measures that would compensate them for their suffering. In a powerful sign of the importance Zapatero assigned to the commission's work, the commission itself was approved by royal decree. Zapatero also put Deputy Prime Minister María Teresa Fernández de la Vega at the helm of the commission. The commission's final report, which called for the "moral and legal rehabilitation of the victims," issued on July 28, 2006, served as the blueprint for the 2007 Law of Historical Memory.[14] In December 2004, the Zapatero government, as part of its planning for the 2005 general state budget, upgraded Civil War pensions, and in March 2005 it increased economic and health care benefits for "war children" based on the recommendation by the inter-ministerial commission. In October 2005, an old law was amended to accelerate the return of trade union assets confiscated by Franco. The following month, a new law authorized the return to Catalonia of documents pertaining to the prosecution of Catalans under the Franco regime, which the Catalan government had been demanding for years.

In December 2005, by executive order, the Zapatero government established regulatory bases for awarding financial reparations to victims of the Civil War and Francoism, another recommendation by the inter-ministerial commission. Also in December 2005, as part of the law that approved the 2006 general budget, the government authorized expenses related to removal of Francoist symbols from public buildings and allowed a personal income tax exemption for reparation payments to victims of political repression by the old regime. In June 2006, a law declared that year "The Year of Historical Memory," and in June 2007, by royal decree, the government established the Center for Historical Memory in the city of Salamanca, which already hosted the Spanish Civil War archives. Also in June, the Zapatero administration introduced the project law for the recognition of the victims of the Civil War and the repression of the Franco regime that resulted in the Law of Historical Memory.

The legislative initiatives outlined above were paired with symbolic gestures intended to heighten the importance of recovering the historical memory. In December 2004, while traveling to Russia to discuss terrorism policy with Russian President Vladimir Putin, Zapatero met the "children of the war," the group of Spaniards residing in Russia after being evacuated from Spain by their Republican parents at the onset of the Civil War. He pledged to augment their pensions (to a minimum of 6,000 euros annually) and promised to meet with them again in May 2005, on the occasion of the sixtieth anniversary of the end of World War II. In May 2005, Zapatero also paid a visit to the Mauthausen extermination camp in Austria, the first time a Spanish prime minister had done so, to pay tribute to the 8,000 Spanish Republicans who had been detained there and mark the sixtieth anniversary of the liberation of the camp.[15] In an emotional ceremony at Mauthausen, Zapatero lamented that the Spanish Republicans held there had "suffered twice," having endured exile from their homeland brought on them by Francoism, followed by the harshness and inhumanity of Nazism.[16] In October 2007, the Zapatero government awarded the Gold Cross of Social Solidarity to former Mexican First Lady Amalia Solórzano de Cárdenas (wife of President Lázaro Cardenas, 1934–1940) in recognition of her contribution to helping exiled Spanish children in Mexico.

The Law of Historical Memory

The preamble to the Law of Historical Memory enacted by the Congress of Deputies on October 31, 2007, praises the spirit of "reconciliation and consensus" that guided the democratic transition and facilitated the democratic constitution that gave birth to the current regime. It then condemns Francoism by quoting from the November 20, 2002, parliamentary report that unanimously declared its rejection of "totalitarian regimes" and the March 17, 2006, report of the parliamentary assembly of the Council of Europe that noted "the serious violations of human rights committed between 1939 and 1975."[17] This wholesale condemnation of the Franco regime, a priority for the parties of the left, was nonetheless carefully crafted to avoid offending the right, perhaps in the hope of obtaining support for the law from PP parliamentarians. No direct blame for the violence of the Civil War is attributed to any particular section of society.

Article 1 states that the general purpose of the law is to "recognize and expand the rights of those who suffered persecution and violence for political, ideological or religious reasons during the Civil War and the Dictatorship; to promote the recuperation of personal and family memory; and to adopt measures destined to suppress elements of division among the citizenry with the goal of promoting cohesion and solidarity across the different generations of Spaniards around constitutional principles, values, and liberties."[18] To those ends, articles 1–10 establish a series of rights for those seeking to obtain a declaration of personal reparation and recognition, including those sentenced under Franco's "illegitimate" courts, and creates a new category of victims: those who gave their lives during the establishment of democracy in the years leading to Franco's death. This section of the law also improves the pensions for Civil War veterans (in both amounts allowed and eligibility), including indemnification for years in prison of 6,000–10,000 euros. It also provides for a lump sum compensation of 135,000 euros for the beneficiaries of those who died "between the period of January 1, 1968 and October 6, 1977 in defense of the rights and liberties of democracy."

Articles 11–14 compel the government, at all levels, to undertake responsibility for the exhumation and reburial of unmarked Civil War graves, a provision that applies almost exclusively to Republican graves since Franco had already exhumed the bulk of Nationalist graves. Articles 15–17 deal with the legacy of the Franco regime: article 15 calls for the removal of Francoist symbols from public spaces, article 16 bans public demonstrations at El Valle de los Caídos, and article 17 orders a census of buildings and public works built with forced Republican labor. Article 18 concerns the extension of Spanish citizenship to the members of the International Brigades. No longer will the brigadiers be required to renounce their current nationality in order to gain Spanish nationality. Articles 19–22, the last four, establish a national archive of the Civil War and the Franco dictatorship and regulate access to public records related to them. Additional amendments that end the document expand on the benefits of Civil War victims, such as granting Spanish citizenship to the descendants of the Republican exile.

Almost every aspect of the law proved controversial, and at several junctures in the negotiating process it seemed that the whole thing might fall apart. Government negotiators stressed this point after concluding a meeting with some forty civil society organizations, noting that dealing with the complexity of the issues was "like picking cherries, you pull one and many others fall out."[19] An early point of contention between the government and memory advocates was the exhumation of Civil War graves. The provision in the law that makes state agencies responsible for this gruesome business went through several iterations, from an initial resolution acknowledging government responsibility for financing the exhumation of the graves, to a commitment to draw up plans to locate the graves and establish protocol for regulating the entire exhumation process, from the opening of the graves, to the removal of the remains, to the preservation of the site. This was a hard-won victory for memory advocates since prior to the law's passage, the exhumation of Civil War graves was in the hands of private groups such as the ARMH, which relied largely on voluntary labor and grants from the autonomous governments of several regions, including Asturias, Catalonia, Extremadura, the Basque Country, Navarra, and Andalusia, to carry out this difficult and expensive endeavor.

As would be expected, another controversial matter was the provision in the law dealing with the removal of Francoist monuments from public spaces. To give teeth to this provision, the final version of the law empowered the government to deny public funds for organizations that refuse to comply with the law. The primary target of this "threat" was the Catholic Church, one reason why the Spanish Conference of Bishops opposed the law. Numerous churches and monasteries continue to display Francoist symbols, including the ubiquitous phrase *Caídos por Dios y por España* and the coat of arms of the Franco dictatorship. Given the clout of the church, the law's provision that Francoist monuments and memorials be removed from public spaces was a hard-won victory for the federation of left-wing parties comprising IU, which threatened to withdraw its support for the law (without which passage was uncertain if not impossible) unless this was a core component. Just before the laws' presentation in the Congress of Deputies, the government dropped the requirement on Francoist memorials and monuments, hoping this would happen voluntarily, by arguing that it did not have the constitutional authority to make it compulsory. This prompted IU leader Gaspar Llamazares to complain that "we have recently passed laws in this country that ban sexist and racist advertising but we cannot prohibit glorification of Spanish fascism."[20]

Nonetheless, the law makes exceptions for buildings of "historical or cultural significance," a last-minute loophole inserted by the Catalan party CiU. It is likely that this provision will leave such major Francoist memorials as El Valle de Los Caídos untouched, although not altogether unaffected. The law criminalizes pro-Franco demonstrations at the monument, stating that "acts of a political nature or that exalt the Civil War, its protagonists, or Francoism will not be allowed to be carried out in any part of the grounds." This settlement on El Valle de Los Caídos deeply disappointed many who had hoped for something bold and dramatic, such as the monument's transformation into a research center to highlight the horrors of the Civil War and the Franco regime. Jaume Bosch of the Catalan Green Party, which promoted this proposal, argued: "Auschwitz has been converted into a learning center; Argentina has turned its torture prisons into places for explanation. Too many years have passed for us to simply leave El Valle as the Franco regime left it."[21] At the very least, some hoped the law would mandate removal of Franco's remains from the site. According to Luís Berlinches Raso of the Association of Ex-Prisoners and Anti-Franco Political Dissidents, "Franco was oppressor number one and as such he does not deserve such a magnificent monument. His body should be exhumed and reburied in an ordinary cemetery."[22]

Undoubtedly, the Zapatero administration was well aware that any attempt to "reconsider" El Valle would raise the ire of the sectors of Spanish society that still venerate Franco and probably cause an upheaval from the right. The proposed ban on tributes to Franco at the monument that eventually became law triggered attacks on PSOE legislators from radical right-wing groups, including one notable act of vandalism. *El Valle no se toca* (The Valley is not to be touched) was the warning painted on one legislator's front door. But many on the left are unsure about how El Valle can be successfully reinvented. Those who bemoan the absence in Spain of proper venues to mourn and remember the Civil War dead or those who died victims of some of the acts of the violence that marred the transition to democracy, and who understand that, in other countries, places traditionally associated with repression have been converted into national places of remembrance, are unsure about how El Valle would fit that role. Aguilar (2008: 432) has noted that "many are of the view that it is not worth it to try to convert El Valle de los Caídos, believing that the monument is unrecyclable." Among the many vexing problems noted by Aguilar is the religious character of the monument, which means that any effort to "reconsider" it would require negotiations and accommodations with the Catholic Church, which is not fond of the memory law, to say nothing of the fact that Franco's remains would have to be transferred to another location. In any case, as noted already, El Valle is now protected from alteration, as stipulated in the section of the law that protects buildings with cultural or historical significance.

A related issue that arose alongside the stipulation calling for removal of Francoist symbols was the use of the phrase "the two factions," a phrase in the draft version of the bill that called for removal of Francoist symbols "that exalt only one of the two factions that fought the war." This reference troubled many on the left for at least two reasons. The first was that it posed the possibility that symbols linked to the Second Republic, such as monuments to Republican leaders, could be potential targets for removal by the right. But the real objection rested in the moral equivalence the phrase "two factions" drew between the Nationalist rebels who staged the 1936 uprising, which triggered the Civil War and went on to impose the dictatorial regime, and those fighting to preserve the popularly elected government of the Republic, a point stressed in a letter to the inter-ministerial commission by a number of human rights associations.[23] This proved a winning argument with the commission since, as seen already, the final version of the bill calls for the removal of symbols associated with the "military uprising" and the ensuing "dictatorship."

The most controversial matter handled by the legislators, however, was the thorny issue of the sentences delivered by Francoist courts, including verdicts handed down by kangaroo courts established during the Civil War that resulted in hundreds of thousands of Spaniards being convicted of political crimes (see Chapter 1). This issue was of great importance not only to memory advocates but also to many on the left and the regional-nationalists, who in meetings with government representatives demanded an outright nullification of Francoist sentences, "just like what happened with the Nazi regime and Italian fascism."[24] Nothing short of that, a spokesperson for the memory advocates demanded, would push them to seek support from international courts in the hope of forcing the hand of the government. These demands for a blanket nullification of Francoist sentences were not new. In 2002, while in the opposition, the PSOE failed in an effort to declare null the verdicts issued by the Francoist courts; in 2004, the Catalan parliament unanimously approved a resolution petitioning that the verdicts of those sentenced for their political affiliations (including Masons and Communists) be revoked.[25] It included, most notably, the court-martial against Lluís Companys, president of the Republican Generalitat of Catalonia, who was executed in 1940.

But the government stood firm in its opposition to an automatic nullification of Francoist sentences, fearing that a flood of claims against the state would create "unmanageable judicial insecurity," to say nothing of stressing an already overburdened judicial system.[26] As explained by Ramón Jáuregui Atondo Álava, the PSOE spokesman for the Constitutional Commission of the Congress of Deputies, "Here we cannot, and should not—I add—in one fell swoop do away with all the judicial certainty developed over 40 years, annulling thousands of judgments, even if we do all acknowledge the lack of justice and judicial guarantees thereof."[27] The government was also mindful of charges from the right that the left was undermining the rule of law by overturning four decades of Francoist jurisprudence, since a blanket nullification of Francoist sentences would not have distinguished between sentences given for political-ideological reasons and for common crimes.

To appease its critics within the left, civil society, and the regional-nationalist communities, the government proposed creation of a "committee of five notables" appointed by parliament to review the cases of those seeking nullification, a proposal that was met with almost universal derision because, ironically enough, it reminded many of Francoist practices for resolving issues of bad conduct. In the end, an agreement was reached to declare Francoist sentences "unjust" while absolving the state from any legal and economic liability. The final bill also included procedures for overturning individual verdicts (a tall order that requires an appeal to the Supreme Court) in search of what the law termed "moral reparation."[28] The law, however, clearly states that moral reparation does not constitute admission of responsibility or guilt on the part of the state, and does not entitle individuals to "any indemnities of a financial or professional kind."

Debating the Past

Despite Zapatero's best intentions to secure a broad political consensus for reconciling Spain's past, the debate over the final draft of the Law of Historical Memory was divisive and rancorous. The debate pitted the government not only against its right-wing opposition (the PP), which opposed the law from the outset, but also against allies on the left like the IU, which kept pushing the Zapatero administration for as robust a law as possible. In the end, the law was approved without any significant PP support. Since the law was voted on not as a single piece of legislation but by individual articles, PP parliamentarians were able to cherry-pick the articles they felt they could support, such as the provisions concerning improvements to compensatory schemes (save that which included those who died defending democracy) and the depoliticization of the Valle de los Caídos, while rejecting the bulk of the law. The left, led by the PSOE and the IU (save for Esquerra Republicana de Catalunya, ERC), supported the law, joined by two major nationalist-regionalist parties from Catalonia and the Basque Country (CiU and PNV), and an assortment of small parties.

Oddly enough, while the Zapatero administration bemoaned the lack of support from the PP, this resulted in a stronger law, since the administration was forced to accommodate the demands from the parties on the far left and the nationalist regions to secure enough votes to see the bill enacted. Indeed, the months spent fine-tuning the law were consumed by intense bargaining between the PSOE, on one side, and the IU, ERC, and nationalist parties, on the other. From September 8, 2006, when the bill was introduced in parliament, through October 31, 2007, when it was approved, the IU, ERC, and CiU presented more than 300 amendments. Out of this flurry of amendments emerged some of the most important (but controversial) provisions in the law, such as the condemnation of the Franco regime, removal of Francoist symbols from public view, and straightforward language acknowledging the old regime's human rights abuses. It is probably the case that, had the PP been willing to support the original, very timid version of the law introduced by the government in 2006, much of what gives the law its strength would not have made it into the final legislation, a great irony to be sure.

PP opposition came fast and furious. A central theme PP leaders employed to attack the law was that it was redundant and potentially unconstitutional. During the first plenary debate PP spokesman Manuel Atencia argued that the time for retroactive justice had passed, especially the time for extending the category of new victims, and that in any event the past had been effectively settled "with the transition and the Constitution."[29] Atencia also accused the PSOE of breaking the agreement not to use the past for political purposes (a commitment Zapatero had renewed in 2000, after the parliament endorsed a resolution condemning the Franco regime), and more generally of shattering the culture of political consensus born with the democratic transition. "The law exists because Zapatero has chosen to forget the pact that we reached in 2002, when the congress in unanimity, under a PP government, approved the resolution to condemn Francoism. . . . What we are doing is using history as a political weapon. This law is a strike against the democratic transition. There was no pact of silence, there was a conscious forgetting, intended to avoid repeating the elements that brought failure to Spain in the past."[30] Atencia concluded that "the badly-named historical memory is an attempt by the government to use history in a partisan way. For the PP the key word is reconciliation not memory."[31]

Atencia's charges were echoed by former Francoist minister of information Manuel Fraga, a PP founding member and the public figure of the post-transition era most closely associated with the old regime, who accused Zapatero of "not respecting the Pact of Forgetting signed by the left and the right during the transition."[32] He added that "ex-president Felipe González and the president of the Communist Party Santiago Carrillo abided by the Pact of Forgetting with the intention of forgetting the dictatorship and the

Civil War. I do not understand why Zapatero will not do the same, he is making a mistake." The mistake that Fraga was alluding to was another civil war, a specter raised most directly by other PP leaders when accusing Zapatero of bringing back *las dos Españas* (the two Spains). "Zapatero is looking to open the wounds of a fratricidal war," was the charge of María Dolores de Cospedal, the PP's secretary general, recycling the metaphor popularized during the transition to democracy to justify the Pact of Forgetting.[33]

Allies of the PP in the media and civil society also opposed the proposed law. The conservative media led by the daily *ABC* accused the Zapatero government of "distracting the nation" and "opening old wounds that can only destabilize the country."[34] The Catholic Church, a staunch supporter of the Franco regime, charged the government with wanting to "change the course of history," as Francisco Pérez, archbishop of Pamplona, put it.[35] This stance was backed by the Vatican, which fully exploited the debate of the memory law in Spain to highlight the anti-clericalism of the Republican period and the violence the Republicans directed toward the Church during the Civil War. The 1931 Republican constitution, it is worth recalling, established strict separation between church and state and stripped the Church of most of its property, and the Republican side was responsible for many unspeakable acts against the Church, including raiding and burning numerous monasteries, convents, and churches and killing an estimated 7,000 priests, nuns, and monks.[36] In remembrance of these events, in October 2007, three days before the Congress of Deputies passed the law, the Vatican beatified 498 Catholic martyrs. The honorees, now all on the path to sainthood, were members of various Catholic orders, all killed by the Republicans in the Civil War. During the ceremony at St. Peter's Square, Catholics clashed with protestors holding reproductions of Picasso's *Guernica*, the Basque village bombed by the German Luftwaffe in support of Franco's army, and many demanded to know why the Church was not extending beatification to the clergy who died fighting the Nationalists for the Republic in Catalonia and the Basque Country.

The Zapatero administration also fielded attacks from parties to the left of the PSOE. Although the IU backed the proposed law from the start, the ERC did not, denouncing it as "regrettable, humiliating, an offense to anti-Francoist heroes" because it failed to end "the system of impunity installed with the transition."[37] For ERC leaders, the spirit of the Pact of Forgetting is effectively carried over into the new law given the continuing validity of the 1977 amnesty accord enacted during the democratic transition. In their view, only a policy of "denazification" can erase the last vestiges of Francoism. Human rights organizations, while elated by Zapatero's efforts, found much to criticize in the proposed legislation. Although the ARMH criticized opponents of Zapatero's memory project of possessing a "Francoist" mindset and wanting to keep a veil over "the Spanish Holocaust," it nonetheless made it clear that the government's efforts were not enough.[38] "The law is a first, limited step in Spain to forge a collective memory about the horrors of the past," notes Emilio Silva, president of the ARMH.[39] "The law treats Franco's political crimes as if they were not illegal since it does not regard the Franco regime as illegal," according to Pedro A. García Bilbao, a professor of political science at the Juan Carlos University in Madrid and an affiliate of the Memory Forum. He added: "The Spanish model of forgetting and impunity remains in place."[40] "A positive but insufficient step" was the verdict of Ludivina García Arias of the Association of Descendants of the Spanish Exile, adding that "the law upholds impunity; it does not condemn the Franco regime."[41] "We are not in agreement with the law," remarked Gregorio Ortíz Ricoll of the Association of Ex-Prisoners, noting that while his organization agrees with the reparations, no mechanism, such as a truth commission, exists to investigate the killings committed during the Civil War and the dictatorship.[42] Equipo Nizkor, a group that claims to represent more that 70 organizations of Francoist victims, argued that the proposed law was out of step with UN legislation by protecting the anonymity of anyone involved in a claim of a human rights violation, a provision eventually dropped in the final version of the law.[43]

As might be expected, the final vote on the Law of Historical Memory in the Congress of Deputies was an emotional one, attended by the surviving victims of the Civil War, victims of the Franco regime, and notable players in the democratic transition such as former communist leader Santiago Carrillo. Curiously, Zapatero was absent for the vote. Deputy Prime Minister Fernández de la Vega, widely credited as the main architect of the law, represented the government. Right before final the vote she defended the law by noting: "There is not a single line in the text of the law that cannot be supported in its entirety by any democrat. This law takes care of the victims and its families, and it leaves history to the historians and to the judges what belongs to the judges."[44] Eduardo Zaplana, the PP spokesman, retorted: "For the first time under the new democracy, the government and its allies have decided to use Civil War graves as a propaganda argument."[45] Other PP parliamentarians were even less kind, deeming the law "unnecessary, hypocritical, legally irrelevant, and a mistake" and promising to challenge its provisions in the courts.[46] These words were echoed by Mariano Rajoy, the PP presidential candidate for the 2008 general elections, who pledged that "When I get elected this historical memory will be finished. . . . The people want to look to the future, and not to the prehistory since we are in 2007 and the world has changed at a great speed and we have to talk about what's happening now and not about the past."[47]

Intellectual Discourses from the Left, the Right, and Beyond

Predictably, the Law of Historical Memory split the Spanish intelligentsia along partisan lines. Right-wing intellectuals, like Pío Moa, have complained about the historical revisionism of the Civil War suggested by the law. For Moa, the Zapatero administration's memory law and its pretense of seeking "moral reparation" for the Civil War victims conceals other political motives, coming just as the nation was overcoming the trauma of "the great tragedy."[48] In Moa's view, the law has created a new "sectarianism" that refuses to leave the Civil War in its historical context believing that the history of Spain is one of perpetual civil war. "Why was it needed for Zapatero to open old wounds just as they appeared to have healed?"

For left-wing intellectuals, the right's opposition to the law amounts to nothing short of a defense of Francoism. "Why is the democratic right so reluctant to repudiate Franco?" asks the Spanish historian Alberto Reig.[49] The brutal repression after the war, Reig notes, sought to eradicate the left and planted a deep-seated fear in the country that did not end until the emergence of new generations who had not experienced the war. "In Germany nobody presumes that the Nazis were as respectable as the rest of society," adds Reig. The left's response to the memory law and the broader debate about the past also included a great deal of introspection and indeed self-criticism. For Vicenç Navarro, the left, since the democratic transition, has been complicit in the policies of forgetting—at a great cost to the nation. This has allowed the Nationalist side to "monopolize the historical memory, and as a consequence of this young people do not identify the left with the struggle for freedom, democracy and pluralism, which would have been the case if the left had kept alive the memory of the Second Republic."[50]

But even as it fiercely defended the Law of Historical Memory against the right, the left was less than unified in its embrace of the law. The most common complaint among left-wing activists was that the law did not go far enough in encouraging Spain to develop a deeper awareness about the past. In particular, many lamented that the absence of a truth commission would deprive the nation of an official narrative about the political abuses of the past. Silva has observed that in the absence of an official narrative it is unlikely that those most directly responsible for the abuses of the past will own up to them.[51] For example, he doubts that the state will ever admit to any wrongdoing or remorse for the Francoist repression; that Spanish businesses that benefited from the dictatorship (through preferential treatment or by partaking in the system of labor camps created by the regime) will ever openly acknowledge this, much less offer to make amends (as German businesses have done to compensate for cooperating with the Nazis); and that the Spanish Catholic Church will ever apologize for its complicity with the Franco dictatorship, as the Argentine Catholic Church did for supporting military rule.

Silva also lamented that while the law's heavy emphasis on "individual reparations" might mollify some, it will deny "collective justice" to those victimized by the Francoist state. This, Silva contended, "limits the law's capacity to construct a national narrative about the horrors of Francoism and hinders the country's democratic culture." Silva's comments are echoed by Spanish educators, who have argued that an official narrative about the past would be a useful tool for battling the public's apathy and ignorance about the past through the incorporation of this narrative into school curricula and textbooks. An official narrative, some feel, is needed because an entirely new generation of Spaniards has been raised generally unaware of the sacrifices and suffering of an earlier generation, mainly due to the silence over the past imposed by the transition. Valls (2007: 170) has decried the absence among the Spanish youth of "a more vivid and human sense of empathy for the suffering of so many Spaniards during the civil war and the long dictatorship due to violence and political persecution." This problem, Valls argues, is compounded by the way history is taught in Spain. "Many academic historians and secondary school teachers without regard to generation still do not integrate material on daily life into their history teaching, which remains based on classical historiography focused on political and institutional history."

A very different critique of the law came from the left-wing intelligentsia, including the danger of replacing history with memory in an attempt to forge an official historical narrative. "History," according to Juliá (2006b:

16–18), "is about finding the truth," whereas "memory," by contrast, is "story-telling" at its best, and at its worst a "selective and subjective" treatment of the past. This reasoning led Juliá to publicly attack the memory law in *El País*.[52] He described the law as "absurd and contradictory" because it reveals a "totalitarian" intention; there can never be only one account of the past because no past, especially a difficult one, can have the same meaning for everyone in society. He further argued that Spain would be better served by "taking the issue of the historical memory away from the hands of the politicians," by "forgetting about creating centers for remembering and instead strengthening archives and libraries," and by "renouncing an interpretation about the past intended to make people feel good with the promotion of knowledge and debate about history." Juliá has also criticized the movement for the recovery of the historical memory because of the movement's advocacy that the testimony of the victims of the Francoist repression, their own personal memory, should be treated as a legitimate representation of the past. He writes (2006: 7): "nowadays we are not as interested in the past as we are in its memory—not in the facts but rather in its representations."

The writer Antonio Muñoz Molina, who from his platform as a columnist for *El País* has criticized both the government's memory politics and the excessive attention to the Civil War on the part of the general public, echoed Juliá's arguments. In a 2010 interview with an Italian newspaper that received much attention in the Spanish media, Muñoz Molina bemoaned the Spaniards' inability to talk about anything except "the Civil War and bullfighting, even in the climate of an economic depression." In this same interview, Muñoz Molina criticized the Law of Historical Memory for "pretending that we can talk about the Civil War as if the Spaniards are as divided as we once were," adding that "too much time has passed," and that in any case delving into the past should be "left to the historians and not the judges and the politicians."[53]

Such criticisms highlight a marked divide (mostly but not exclusively generational in nature) within the Spanish left between those who, like Juliá and Muñoz Molina, believe that the left was right in its support for a policy of forgetting and moving on, and those who support Zapatero's stance that the moderation of the transition did not entail erasing Spanish history; and that, in any case, some reckoning with the past is both long overdue and of potential benefit to society. Typical of the latter view is that of the historian Pablo Sánchez-León (2006: 131), who sees a lot of value in the work of the memory movement, in part, he argues, because historians since the transition have largely failed to find much subjective meaning in their scholarly endeavors. By and large, ordinary people do not see their stories of repression and resistance reflected in the historiography of the post-transition era that preceded the memory boom.

The law also divided international scholars of the Civil War with notable figures weighing in on both sides. American historian Stanley Payne, in a wide-ranging interview with the conservative newspaper *ABC* that raised eyebrows everywhere, noted that "the objective of the Law of Historical Memory is to demarcate a rigid line between good Spaniards and bad ones."[54] Payne also accused the Zapatero administration of acting in a "Francoist mode without admitting it" by not treating all the victims of the Civil War equally, as the law only recognizes the victims on one side of the war. These comments were widely seen by Spanish liberals as providing ideological cover to conservative intellectuals like Moa. Payne's comments stand in contrast to those of other leading international scholars of the Civil War, including British historian Paul Preston. In comments at a 2008 conference in Santiago de Compostela, Preston criticized the right for its "interested manipulation" in projecting the view that the current debate about the past places the nation on the brink of another civil war.[55] According to Preston, neither domestic nor international conditions provide the basis for history repeating itself; in any case, he argued, the Spanish people are more interested in making ends meet at the end of the month than in reliving the Civil War.

On the Road to a Settled Past?

Notwithstanding the divisive rhetoric coming from the political class and the intelligentsia, there are reasons to believe that in the long term the Law of Historical Memory will have achieved some type of settlement or accommodation about the past. Since the law's passage, the issue of historical memory appears to have lost much of the potency and edge that it once possessed, at least as suggested by the fact that today the issue generates relatively few headlines. A 2012 article in the opinion pages of *El País* with the tile of "The Forgetting of Memory" aptly captured the new mood of the nation regarding its tortured past.[56] Surely, tensions remain that ensure that the past will continue to resonate in national politics for years to come. Human rights activists have complained about the slow pace of compliance with some of the stipulations of the law; mayors of some municipalities controlled by the PP have resisted the law by dragging their feet in fulfilling the mandate to remove memorials to Franco, such as changing the names of streets honoring individuals or acts associated with the dictatorship. Scholars have complained about limitations on access to military archives.

Among the factors that explain the apparent lessening of the past's importance in the national agenda, are several changes in the political environment. The 2008 elections served as a natural pause for discussions of the past (at least at the elite level) in at least two ways. Since elections served as a referendum on Zapatero's first term in office, the PSOE's decisive victory over the PP served to mute the conservative argument that Zapatero's policies lacked legitimacy because of the manner in which his government had entered office. Much about the PP criticism of the government in 2004–2008 had as much to do with genuine indignation about the government's policies as with the sense that Zapatero had robbed the party of another term in office.[57] In the 2008 elections, the PSOE increased its representation in the Congress of Deputies by 2.2 percent and its share of the popular vote over 2004 by 1.2 percent. On the other hand, having secured an important victory in 2008, to say nothing of much of his social and cultural agenda, Zapatero was less compelled to push the issue of the past back into the spotlight to mobilize his left-wing constituency.

Since the global financial crisis of 2008, which sent the Spanish economy reeling, the economy has taken center stage and pushed all other issues to the side (Royo 2013). It is telling that the wave of protests that rocked Spain in the spring of 2011—otherwise known as the "M-15 movement" and "Days of Indignation," which featured the occupation of such major public places as Madrid's Plaza del Sol and Barcelona's Plaza de Catalunya and tense confrontation between a wide range of civil society organizations and the police—made little if any reference to the issue of the past. Instead, the focus was on addressing mounting economic problems (especially skyrocketing unemployment), ending corruption, and reforming the political system (Encarnación 2013). Undoubtedly, the most important political consequence of the protests was to force the Zapatero administration to call for early elections in 2011. Even though Zapatero decided against a third term for himself, the PSOE took a severe beating at the polls, winning only 28.8 percent of the popular vote, the party's worst showing since the democratic transition.

Despite an electoral promise to undo the 2007 memory law, the new conservative government headed by Rajoy has made few waves with respect to the politics of the past. The most notable actions regard the status of El Valle de los Caídos. The new government reopened the monument to the public in 2012 (it had been closed by the Zapatero administration in 2009 claiming safety concerns), and shortly thereafter shelved a report by a "commission of experts" on the future of the monument organized by the Zapatero administration. In keeping with the goal of turning El Valle into "a memory center that honors and rehabilitates the victims of the Civil War and the subsequent Franco regime," the report recommended that Franco's remains be transferred to a private burial site chosen by his family, with the intention of reserving El Valle as a burial site for individuals who actually died in the Civil War. In explaining its decision to ignore the recommendations, the Rajoy administration argued that the report lacked validity since it was created unilaterally by the previous administration, and that the country had more pressing matters to attend to such as the present economic crisis. "Let the dead bury the dead" and "let us return to dealing with the problems of the living," announced PP Senator Alejandro Muñoz-Alonso when rationalizing why his party had no interest in further delving into the politics of the past.[58]

Yet the Law of Historical Memory itself deserves much credit for creating a less contentious climate with respect to the past. For starters, there is the symbolic importance of the law, a rarely acknowledged fact. Much of what the law stipulates could have been accomplished by a government decree, but the Zapatero administration recognized the importance of a law addressing the issue of historical memory and a public debate about the merits of such a law. As noted by Torres Mora in the second plenary debate, a law has "symbolic value" because while "a decree would be exclusively a governmental measure, we all participate in the making of a law. The more we support the law the more value it will have."[59] Moreover, for all its shortcomings with respect to accountability, the law radically changed the landscape of memory politics by addressing many of the demands of memory advocates, such as government responsibility for the exhumation of Civil War graves and more generous reparation provisions. The law also changed official discourse about the past, especially with respect to the victims of the Civil War and the dictatorship, which ultimately was the main purpose of the law. After the parliamentary vote, Zapatero proclaimed that the Law of Historical Memory had met his goal of "rehabilitating the memory of the vanquished."[60]

Zapatero's words find support in the fact that the law condemns the Franco regime for its human rights abuses, that it recognizes and compensates those victimized by the violence of the Civil War and the dictatorship, and that it acknowledges a new class of victims, those who suffered building democracy during the last years of the dictatorship. Less evident is that the law ushered in a more frank conversation about historical events. The interministerial commission to study the situation of the victims of the Civil War and Francoism was the first public body to speak honestly about the suffering of thousands of Spaniards because of their political beliefs and/or commitment to democratic values. The law itself vanquished some of the euphemisms that for years had been employed to avoid making direct references to the Civil War and that underwrote the rise and maintenance of the politics of forgetting, most notably the notion of collective culpability for the Civil War. Even the draft version of the bill included the euphemistic phrase "the conflict between the Spaniards," instead of a more specific reference of the "Civil War" which was included in the final version of the bill.

With the left's revisiting of the past seemingly done, some conservative sectors of Spanish society appear to have softened their stance toward the issue of historical memory.[61] While the PP at the national level remains resolute in its opposition to any revisiting of the past, at the regional level the situation is much less hostile. In Catalonia, for example, the PP has supported the CiU agenda on historical memory, including the removal from public spaces of Francoist monuments and the establishment of a Democratic Memorial Center devoted to educating the public about the struggle for democracy in Catalonia from the Republican period to the present. Relations between the Zapatero administration and the hierarchy of the Catholic Church experienced a thawing after the memory law was enacted. As a kind of olive branch from the Zapatero administration, Spain's foreign minister attended the beatification for the 498 Catholic clergy killed by the Republicans, held in Rome in October 2007. The church has complied with the memory law by, among other things, covering church plaques that feature Francoist iconography and ending the practice of conducting a funeral mass to the memory of Franco at El Valle on the anniversary of the dictator's death. Even more important, the church leadership has hinted at its willingness to accept alternative versions of what it perceives to be the truth. Monsignor Ricardo Blásquez Pérez, president of the Spanish Conference of Bishops, has noted that "every social group" reserves the right to "recall its history."[62] Collective history, he added, cannot be selective. "It is possible for different evaluations of the same events to exist side by side. If a genuine desire to discover what happened exists, these accounts will be reconciled and the ghosts of the Civil War will be laid to rest at last."

Public Opinion: A Reconciled Past?

The most important cues about the apparent retreat of the past from national politics, however, come from the general public, which appears quite accepting of the treatment of the past introduced by the Law of Historical Memory. A CIS survey from 2005, summarized in Table 11, which was conducted just before the parliament began to debate the merits of the law, found that the issue of historical memory—while certainly controversial among the public—was nowhere near as polarizing as it was within the political class. A clear majority of the public (54.1 percent) supported the idea of recognizing all the victims of the Civil War. Another impressive percentage of the public (44.8) thought that government measures could help repair the suffering of the victims of the Civil War. These findings suggest that for the public, the issue of addressing the past was clearly not the zero-sum game that it became within the political class, with the left in favor of it and the right dead set against it.

Table 12, based on the 2008 CIS survey conducted just after the Law of Historical Memory was enacted, shows a clearer picture of the public's satisfaction with the law. A solid majority of Spaniards who professed awareness of the law (50 percent), rate it either "very good" or "good," with an additional 17.1 percent deeming it "average." Curiously, the evaluation of the law in the nationalist regions of the Basque Country and Catalonia, where the issue of political memory has been especially contentious, mirrors closely the national findings.

What explains the apparent discrepancy between the politicians and the general public on their perceptions of the law? One potential theory is that the public as a whole is not that interested in the past, an explanation that would support the right's contention that Zapatero seized on this issue to rally the left and to attack the right. Interestingly, despite its high profile in national politics since at least the mid-1990s, the issue of historical memory has never been one of great concern to the public as a whole. The CIS general surveys on Spanish public opinion for much of Zapatero's first term (2005–2008) rank unemployment, drugs, personal safety, terrorism (ETA), infrastructure, and health care as the issues of greatest concern to the

Table 11. Public Attitudes on What to Do About the Past (2005) (percent)

Question/ statement	*More or less in agreement*	*More or less in disagreement*	*Neither agreement nor disagreement*	*Don't know*	*No answer*
Do you support initiatives designed to recognize the victims of the Civil War?	54.1	24.8	11.4	8.6	1.1
Can government measures help to repair the suffering of the victims of the Civil War?	44.8	33.9	11.0	8.6	1.8
It does not make any sense to debate or take action over things that are already history	43.4	40.0	8.0	7.2	1.4
The victims of the Civil War have been forgotten and it is time to repair this injustice	53.3	24.0	11.2	9.9	1.6
The victims of the Civil War belong to both sides and any recognition should include both	72.9	9.9	6.3	8.8	2.1
The victims have been recognized differently according to the political side to which they belonged	65.9	7.6	6.7	17.8	2.0

Source: CIS (2005).

Table 12. Public Opinion on the 2007 Law of Historical Memory (percent)

	National	*Basque Country*	*Catalonia*
Very good	12.8	14.9	11.6
Good	39.7	39.8	47.3
Average	17.1	20.9	17.2
Bad	10.2	5.8	7.0
Very bad	5.4	2.3	2.4
I don't know it sufficiently	10.6	12.1	12.6
Don't know	3.6	4.0	1.8
No answer	0.6	0.3	–

Source: CIS (2008).

public.[63] Historical memory appears nowhere in these national surveys (which list up to thirty issues or problems), not even during October 2007, when the final vote on the Law of Historical Memory was held.

A more persuasive theory is that the law has correctly gauged how the general public wants to deal with the past; in other words, the law conforms to the public's idea of coming to terms with the past. This point gives credence to Zapatero's argument that his policies aim at "following rather than guiding the will of the people."[64] For the public, as for Zapatero, the main purpose of the memory law was to acknowledge and offer reparation to those victimized by the political crimes of the past rather than to bring justice to those responsible for those crimes. This sentiment appears to be conveyed in the 2008 CIS survey, which shows a clear majority of Spaniards (72 percent) in agreement with the statement that "under Franco the victims of the Civil War were recognized differently according to their political affiliation" alongside some reservation about the most aggressive measures of transitional justice.

As seen in Table 13, when asked whether Spain should create a commission to investigate the human rights abuses of the Civil War and the Franco regime, a majority of Spaniards disapproved. Even in the nationalist regions of Catalonia and the Basque Country, support for a truth commission did not reach 50 percent. Oddly enough, a higher percentage of the general public approved of trials for those responsible for human rights abuses. This support did not reach 50 percent in the national sample, although it did go beyond 50 percent in Catalonia and the Basque Country. Only the removal of monuments to the Franco regime garnered over 50 percent approval by the public. Clearly, the public did not regard this component of the law as especially controversial since it did not entail any serious digging into the past. Less apparent is the complex memory about the Franco dictatorship. Certainly, Spaniards do not regret the passing of Francoism, nor do they worship Franco's memory. As shown in Table 14, which shows public attitudes toward Franco's legacy, 79.6 percent of the public agreed that under Franco "basic human rights were violated," and 88.2 percent concurred with the statement that "under Franco people did not express their opinions for fear of retribution." Yet the most fascinating finding in this table is the stunning 58.8 percent of the public that credited Franco "with both good and bad things," a dramatic increase from the evaluation of the regime through the 1980s and 1990s, which generally hovered in the mid-40s (see CIS 1985).[65] At some level, the public remains quite reluctant to view the dictatorship as deserving of a harsh indictment, even as it acknowledges the need to honor and recognize its victims.

Table 13. Public Opinion on Transitional Justice Mechanisms (percent)

	National Sample	*Basque Country*	*Catalonia*
Should the human rights violations of the Civil War be investigated?			
Yes	38.9	49.5	46.6
No	44.8	27.6	43.5
Don't know	15.5	22.3	9.4
No answer	0.8	0.6	0.6
Should the human rights violations committed under Franco be investigated?			
Yes	40.8	49.8	47.9
No	42.2	27.2	41.7
Don't know	16.1	22.2	9.7
No answer	0.9	0.9	0.7
Should former Franco officials be prosecuted for human rights violations?			
Yes	48.7	66.7	65.9
No	27.7	12.2	21.4
Don't know	14.4	13.6	6.1
No answer	1.0	0.4	0.9
Should monuments to the Franco regime be removed?			
Yes	56	64.9	63.4
No	22	16.8	11.6
Don't know	10	12.7	17.2
No answer	10	0.7	0.6

Source: CIS (2008).

Table 14. Public Opinion on Franco's Legacy (percent)

	On the whole in agreement	*Neither agreement nor disagreement*	*On the whole in disagreement*	*Don't know*	*No answer*
One of the great achievements of Francoism was keeping Spain unified	37.6	8.4	39.4	13.9	0.7
Under Franco basic human rights were violated	79.6	3.4	4.3	12.3	0.3
Under Franco there was more peace than today	35.1	13.0	42.2	8.8	1.0
Under Franco fear inhibited people's opinions	88.2	4.3	2.6	4.7	2.0
Francoism contributed to the economic modernization of Spain	23.8	10.5	48.2	16.8	0.7
Francoism had good and bad things	58.8	10.5	48.2	16.8	0.7

Source: CIS (2008).

Finally, it is hard to avoid the conclusion that the success of the democratic transition seems to have influenced a great deal how the Spaniards have constructed their idea of coming to terms with the past. In other words, the very success of democracy in the post-Franco period, premised on forgetting rather than confronting the past, has to some extent convinced the Spaniards that their course of action with respect to the past was the correct one. Certainly, there appears to be no shame among the Spaniards in embracing the view that forgetting is a legitimate response to dealing with the past; even in the nationalist regions of Catalonia and the Basque Country over 30 percent of the public agree that in the particular case of Spain "it is best to forget the past" (CIS 2008). But more telling still is the overwhelming majority of Spaniards (73.8 percent) who take pride in how the transition was organized (CIS 2008). Interestingly, this very high level of pride in the democratic transition has remained virtually the same since the question was first posed to the public in 1985 on the tenth anniversary of Franco's death (CIS 1985). Apparently, for most Spaniards, the success of democracy more than compensates for the lack of transitional justice.

CHAPTER 7

Coping with the Past: Spanish Lessons

Spain's experience with "democratization without justice" affords much food for thought about how nations in real life contend with the burden of a difficult and painful past and the consequences for democracy of whatever decisions are made about that past. Three broad lessons are offered and examined in this concluding chapter. The first is that the roots of forgetting in Spain in the traumas of the Civil War and the Franco dictatorship and the nature and legacy of the democratic transition suggest the extent to which domestic circumstances can take precedence over international human rights norms in shaping how states settle a dark past. This lesson appears to transcend the Spanish experience since, despite the near hegemonic influence of the transitional justice movement, there is no global consensus on how nations are dealing with the political crimes of a departed regime. As will be seen shortly, Spain is hardly alone among cases of late twentieth-century democratization in having subverted justice to the exigencies of politics. From Latin America to the former communist world, a marked discrepancy can be appreciated between what the transitional justice movement preaches and what individual countries practice. Instead of clear-cut cases of retribution and reconciliation, we find approaches that incorporate practices generally thought of as antithetical to the transitional justice movement, such as temporary or partial amnesties; deferred, abandoned, or abridged prosecutions; reparations and restitutions; pardons and forgiveness; and outright impunity. These political solutions for coping with the past ensue from countries' attempts to balance the desire to bring justice against the old authoritarian regime against conditions on the ground that militate against justice, such as the need to protect the stability of the new democratic regime.

The second lesson is that while the success of democracy in Spain in the absence of transitional justice does not negate the positive impact transitional justice can have on the process of democratization, the Spanish experience nonetheless suggests the seldom-acknowledged ambiguous relationship between transitional justice and democratization. A transition to democracy can in fact succeed without transitional justice; moreover, alternatives to transitional justice, such as amnesty, forgetting, and moving on, can be complementary to democratization by promoting some of the very goals transitional justice is intended to accomplish, such peace and democracy itself. Not surprisingly, well before the Spanish experience there was a long tradition (nowadays forgotten) of nations availing themselves of amnesty and forgetting to construct a democratic future. On the other hand, other national experiences examined in this chapter reveal that transitional justice can itself become an obstacle to democratization. In sum, there is no predestined outcome for democracy to the effort of holding an old regime accountable for its past misdeeds.

Third and last, the three decades Spain took to begin to confront the legacy of its dark history, with the 2007 Law of Historical Memory, reveal that coming to terms with the past is not as static or formulaic a process as the transitional justice movement would suggest. Although we have been conditioned into thinking that coping with a difficult and painful past can be conveniently dealt with during the transition (at the very least soon thereafter), through universal, one-size fits all models, in reality this process can hardly be confined to the transition. Indeed, settling the past appears to depend on a host of social, political, and historical factors unique to each case that make it very difficult to generalize about the scope and timing of this process. One variable that is hard to predict are societal impulses toward justice and accountability. There is a tendency to believe that societies coming out of long periods of repression are invariably predisposed toward transitional justice. But as the Spanish experience clearly shows, this is not always the case.

The Primacy of Politics over Justice

A good departure point for our comparative discussion of the politics of coping with the past are the cases of Portugal and Greece, which together with Spain launched the so-called "third wave of democratization" in the mid-1970s (see Di Palma 1990; Huntington 1991; Linz and Stepan 1996; Diamond and Plattner 1996). The Portuguese transition, begun in 1974 with a coup by military officers opposed to Portugal's colonial wars in Africa, simultaneously ended Western Europe's longest-standing dictatorship (the Salazar-Caetano regime, in place since 1932) and put Southern Europe on the path toward democracy. Facilitated by the collapse of the authoritarian regime and the rise to power of a democratic opposition dominated by the Portuguese Communist Party, transitional justice in Portugal was anchored in a comprehensive process of lustration designed to purge both the state and society of all traces of authoritarian influence. The aptly named policy of *saneamento* (cleansing) began with uprooting the ruling elite that had been in power since the 1930s, led by dictator Marcelo Caetano, who fled to Brazil to escape prosecution, and gradually expanded to the civil service, media, church, leading universities, and business community. By November 1975, some 20,000 people had been purged from their official posts on charges of "collaboration" with the dictatorial regime (Costa Pinto 2001: 73).

But cleansing quickly deteriorated into a virtual political witch-hunt, placing Portugal's emerging democracy in great peril by polarizing the political class and raising the specter of civil war. Soon after their inception, the purges acquired a "savage" nature, with many lustration tribunals operating with arbitrary definitions of "collaborator," such as people suspected of harboring "authoritarian attitudes" (Costa Pinto 2001: 73). This capricious application of the law, with people being punished for political beliefs rather than political crimes, contributed to a chaotic political environment that led directly to a counter-revolutionary military coup. The coup halted transitional justice altogether and forced the introduction of a process of "reconciliation and pacification." This new policy overturned most of the sentences handed down by the purge committees, provided reparation for those purged, including those forced into exile, and dismissed all pending cases. Military officers convicted of serious offenses, including murder, had their sentences reduced and in some cases rescinded.

In Greece, the right-wing government of Constantine Karamanlis that followed the Colonels' regime (1967–1974) was, on the whole, reluctant to prosecute the military and proceeded only after private suits were launched against the old regime. Although the prosecutions resulted in convictions for the leaders of the military coup of April 1967, the whole affair was "minimized" by the fact that the trials were "short in duration and—with the exception of the junta's ring leaders—the meted out punishments were lenient" (Sotiropoulos 2010: 461). By the end of 1975, less than two years after the collapse of the dictatorship, the government had settled most transitional justice issues. This hasty approach to handling the political misdeeds of the old regime—which included not only shutting down democracy in 1967, but also the ill-fated military intervention in Cyprus in 1974 intended to establish a military regime, and the violent suppression of political dissidents—reflected the priority given to "political stability" and "foreign affairs" over transitional justice (Sotiropoulos 2010: 462).

Tense Greco-Turkish relations over the debacle in Cyprus were a major reason why the Karamanlis government was reluctant to prosecute the military throughout the period of democratic transition and consolidation (1975–1981). Turkey responded to the Greek intervention in Cyprus with an intervention of its own intended to protect the island's Turkish minority, and for subsequent years the fear of war with Turkey dominated Greek politics. In this context, punishing the military, which was expected to defend the country against Turkey, seemed foolhardy. The Karamanlis government was also less than keen on taking on conservative sectors of society that had supported or collaborated with the military regime because of "the erstwhile ideological affinity between some members of Karamanlis' post-1974 cabinets and the junta's military officials" (Sotiropoulos 2010: 452). Such affinities led the government in the post-war years to encourage a narrative about the past that put the blame for the breakdown of democracy in 1967 on external actors (the United States in particular), rather than on domestic actors, and on a very small group of military officers.

Across Latin America, amnesty and justice have awkwardly coexisted for decades in governments' attempts to balance the public's desire for retroactive justice and the need to protect political stability, especially from the military, the target of most attempts at retribution. A case in point is Argentina, which made history in the mid-1980s by staging Latin America's first military trials on charges of human rights abuses linked to the dirty war against political dissidents carried out between 1976 and 1983. But the early impulse to enact vigorous retributive policies rapidly gave way to more pragmatic approaches once the military trials began to threaten the stability of the new democratic regime. Under the presidency of Raúl Alfonsín, whose center-right Radical Party made human rights the cornerstone of its political program, Argentina's Federal Appeals Court convicted nine generals and admirals on charges of murder and kidnapping related to the disappearance of some 10,000 individuals while in the custody of the state police.[1] The federal court action came after the court overturned an earlier verdict by the Armed Forces Supreme Council that found nothing objectionable about the actions undertaken by the military junta.

While popular with the public and human rights activists, the trials had a destabilizing effect on the process of democratization by triggering multiple military rebellions. Between 1987 and 1990, Argentina experienced four major military uprisings, forcing Alfonsín to dramatically reverse course on transitional justice by enacting a set of amnesty laws in 1986 and 1987, including the Ley de Punto Final (the Full Stop Law), which abruptly ended all investigations and prosecutions of people accused of political crimes during the military dictatorship. The law served as a prelude for a full pardon of the military in 1990 by President Carlos Menem. In rationalizing an amnesty process, Alfonsín (1993: 18) cited the need for pragmatism in handling the military: "It should be irrational to impose a punishment when the consequences of doing so, far from preventing future crimes, might cause greater social harm than that caused by the crime itself or by the absence of punishment." Those yearning for justice had to wait until 2005, when the Argentine Supreme Court annulled the amnesty laws enacted in the 1980s, allowing for the continuation of trials of military and police officers accused of human rights violations. By then, the threat of a military coup had all but disappeared and the new democracy had achieved considerable political stability.

In Uruguay, support for punishment for those convicted of human rights abuses was very high (a whopping 73 percent) by the time the military retreated from governing. This enthusiasm for retribution was hardly a surprise considering that Uruguay had endured a military regime between 1973 and 1985 that according to one study detained one of every 50 Uruguayans, giving the country the ugly distinction of having the world's highest proportion of political prisoners (Huntington 1991: 211). In 1987, after the military threatened to ignore summonses issued by civilian courts investigating charges of murder and disappearances by the military, the newly democratically elected president, Julio María Sanguinetti, proposed a blanket military amnesty. In making the case for amnesty for the military, the president argued that the political stability of the new democracy had to be considered, as well as the fact that terrorist groups were also covered by the amnesty. The amnesty law was later endorsed in two referendums (1989 and 2009), both garnering over 50 percent of the vote.

Justice for the old regime came to Uruguay in the late 2000s, under the left-wing presidency of Tabaré Vásquez, in response to complaints from human rights activists about the lack of justice for former authoritarian leaders. Without overturning the amnesty process of the transition, the courts have allowed individual cases of human rights abuses to proceed. The most prominent prosecution was that of Gregorio Conrado Álvarez, who fronted Uruguay's military government in 1981–1985. In 2009, he was sentenced to 25 years in prison for 37 counts of murder and human rights violations. In 2010, former president Juan María Bordaberry, widely regarded as a military-sponsored dictator after he dissolved the General Assembly in 1973 and began to rule by decree, was sentenced to 30 years in prison (the maximum allowed by Uruguayan law) in connection with the murder of two senators during Bordaberry's presidency (1972–1976). In both cases, however, justice served largely a symbolic function given the advanced age of those prosecuted.

Hamstrung by a negotiated transition to democracy, which like Spain's left almost no room for retribution against the old regime, Chilean President Patricio Aylwin entered office embracing what his government called a policy of "justice within the limits of the possible," which in essence meant setting clear boundaries on how far the government would go in its pursuit of justice against the old authoritarian regime (Zalaquett 1992). In words meant to assure military officers that his government posed no threat to them, shortly after assuming the presidency, on March 11, 1990, Aylwin announced, "The idea of trials is not in my mind . . . I am not in the mood to persecute or to antagonize General Pinochet or anyone else" (Huntington 1991: 217). Aylwin quickly followed with legislation designed to foreclose the possibility of military trials and did little to undermine the infamous laws (the so-called *leyes de amarre*) purposely designed by Pinochet to limit the discretionary power of the incoming democratic regime to prosecute human rights abuses. Among other things, these nefarious laws granted Pinochet and his henchmen lifetime tenure as military officers (Pinochet himself retained the title of commander in chief of the armed forces until 1998), prevented the new congress from investigating the crimes of the previous regime, and set limits on how far the new government could reform state institutions (including the judiciary).

Not until the Spaniards' ironic decision to indict Pinochet on crimes against humanity, followed by the general's arrest in London in 1998, were the Chileans emboldened to begin the process of freeing themselves from the grip of Pinochet's political legacy. On his return to Chile from Britain, Pinochet was charged with a host of crimes including torture, enforced disappearances, and tax evasion. He died of a heart attack in December 2006 while under house arrest. Since Pinochet's passing, Chilean courts have shown a willingness to chip away at the 1978 amnesty declared by the military by accepting the argument that the amnesty process does not apply to war crimes and crimes against humanity and that these crimes cannot be subjected to a statute of limitation. Yet this willingness to prosecute the old regime has hardly made for a wholesale embrace of transitional justice. Chilean court rulings (including those from the country's highest court) apply only to those cases under review. Since 2008, many military personnel indicted on human rights abuses have benefited from a law that offers a sentence reduction for crimes committed more than thirty years ago. For some already convicted, this has meant escaping time in prison altogether.

In Brazil, impunity has reigned supreme since the end of military rule in 1985. As in Spain, the dearth of transitional justice reflects the dynamics of the political transition. Brazil's transition to democracy was imposed from the top down by military officers bent on retaining as much power as possible in the post-transition era and on avoiding Argentine-style prosecutions for their political misdeeds. Although the Brazilian military was considerably less violent than its Southern Cone counterparts, human rights abuses were nonetheless widespread. According to Human Rights Watch, between 1964 and 1985, the military was responsible for "systematic human rights violations, including extrajudicial killings, forced disappearances, torture, detention, and the curtailment of free expression."[2] *Brasil: Nunca Mais*, the report of human rights abuses by the military compiled by the archbishop of São Paulo, accounted for 1,918 cases of torture. Local human rights groups claim the military is responsible for as many as 400 politically motivated killings.

A comprehensive amnesty law passed by the military in 1979, well before political liberties were restored, prevents prosecution of any crimes by the Brazilian military during the period of military rule. Ever since, even the mildest attempts at revisiting the past have been resisted, such as the opening of military archives, by a military establishment regarded as the most politically influential in all Latin America. In 2009, the left-wing administration of Luiz Inacio "Lula" da Silva, a former prisoner of the military regime, prodded by the Inter-American Human Rights Commission and local human rights organizations, proposed creation of a truth and reconciliation commission to examine the human rights violations of the dictatorial period. Such a modest proposal created a serious crisis in the Lula administration with the minister of defense and the secretaries of the navy, army, and air force threatening to resign if plans for the commission proceeded. In the face of such stiff opposition from the military establishment, Lula recanted his proposal, leaving it to the Supreme Federal Court to decide if and when Brazil would ever undertake any revisiting of its dictatorial past.

In Eastern and Central Europe in the wake of the collapse of Communism, a variety of approaches for dealing with the past prevailed, from political trials, to disqualifying people from serving in public office, to Spanish-style forgetting. Given the Nuremberg precedent, it is hardly surprising that the former East Germany underwent the most extensive experience prosecuting former communist leaders. But politics, not ethics and the law, informed the actions of public officials, a priority reflected in the prosecutions themselves. As noted by Garton Ash (2002: 272), the prosecution of former East German communist leaders was characterized by "radical, arbitrary and political selection of the accused." When charges were brought against members of the old regime, the arrests were not for the crimes the world knows about, such as the shoot-to-kill policy at the Berlin Wall, but for crimes often unrelated to communist rule that were easier to prosecute and gain a conviction. Erich Mielke, former director of the infamous Stasi secret police, was prosecuted not for spying and repressing his countrymen (which was legal and in fact lauded under communist rule), but for the murder of a policeman in 1931, years before the rise of communism in East Germany.

In Poland, where the wave of democratic revolutions in the former communist world began, we find the closest analogy to the Spanish experience. Tadesusz Mazowiecki, Poland's first noncommunist leader in more than forty years, famously declared in his first speech to parliament that "we draw a thick line (*gruba linia*) under the past," which was widely interpreted to stand "for a whole Spanish approach to the past" (Garton Ash 2002: 267). The general attitude at the time was to "let bygones be bygones, look to the future, to democracy and Europe, as Spain had done" (268). Unlike Spain, however, the will to forget quickly collapsed, as the political class found it difficult to resist the temptation of using the past (especially membership in communist organizations) as a political weapon. Hungary abandoned any meaningful attempt at transitional justice after the country's constitutional court struck down the Law of Treason that the Hungarian parliament had passed to prosecute former communist oppressors on grounds that it amounted to "retroactive justice."

The former Czechoslovakia deemed political trials too difficult to organize and potentially destabilizing, and instead settled on a policy of lustration that banned high functionaries of the Communist Party, members of the state security agency (StB), and the People's Militia (the party's private army, as well as their collaborators) from holding senior administrative positions in government for five years. Legal experts have criticized this law as undemocratic by having created an entire class of people denied rights available to others. After all, the law is based on the principle of collective rather than individual culpability by considering whole categories of people guilty through their association with the institutions of the old regime. Moreover, the law makes no distinction in degrees of guilt, since it covers anyone from police agents to those who studied at certain academies in the former Soviet Union.

Even in cases held by the transitional justice movement as paradigmatic of justice in times of transition, political concerns have greatly limited the extent to which justice has been delivered. In South Africa, which gave "reconciliation" its global renown, justice was seriously abridged for the sake of protecting political stability and advancing democratization. Full-scale prosecution of human rights abuses by the apartheid regime was the preferred option of many South Africans, including many leaders in the African National Congress, after decades of brutal oppression by a white minority. But in the end Nelson Mandela had to abandon this goal for the more pragmatic one of moving on with the new democracy. As reported by one analyst (Nagy 2002: 325): "State military and security forces posed a considerable threat to peaceful elections and there was a very real risk of civil war. Thus, there was a compromise between the outgoing National Party's demand for blanket amnesty and the African National Congress desire for Nuremberg-style trials: limited amnesty, partial accountability, and the fullest truth possible."

An Ambiguous Relationship

For the transitional justice movement, justice in times of transition can only mean good things for democratization (and hence the common assumption that the more robust the transitional justice the better the democratization outcome) and its absence nothing but trouble for the emerging regime. In Spain, however, there is little doubt that a well-functioning democracy consolidated without retribution or reconciliation; moreover, the absence of transitional justice did not hinder democratization. Such a turn of events in Spain underscores what Schmitter (2001: 5) has identified as the phenomenon of "equifinality" in democratic transitions—countries arriving at the same point of democratic maturity without having experienced a common political journey.

Arguably, the most compelling evidence of democracy's success in the post-Franco period is the high level of legitimacy Spanish democracy has enjoyed since the transition.[3] This point powerfully contradicts the expectation of transitional justice theorists that forgoing justice for the authoritarian regime would lead citizens to lose faith in democracy.[4] The most respected research on democratic legitimacy in Spain in the post-Franco era notes that "the new system enjoyed a high level of legitimacy from the first stages of the transition," with at least two thirds of the public expressing strong support for democracy as "the best system of governance for a country like ours" (Montero 1993: 144). As seen in Table 15, this early support for democracy has remained constant in the post-transition period. Interestingly enough, the public's satisfaction with democracy in Spain has routinely

Table 15. Public Appraisals of Democracy in Spain, 1978–2008 (percent)

	1978	*1980*	*1985*	*1990*	*1995*	*2000*	*2005*	*2008*
Democracy is always preferable to any other kind of government	78	65	65	80	80	85	85	85
In some circumstances an authoritarian regime could be preferable to democracy	10	9						5.9
For people like me, the kind of regime does not make a difference	10	8						5.3
Don't know		33						2.2

Source: CIS (2008).

exceeded that of Portugal and Greece, two countries that engaged in high profile attempts by the post-transition government to hold the old regime accountable for its political excesses. A 1990 CIS survey that asked the Spaniards, Portuguese, and Greeks to rank the quality of their own democracy on a 1–10 point scale revealed a mean score of 6.8 for Spain, 5.8 for Greece, and 5.7 for Portugal (Montero 1993: 149).

Democracy's legitimacy in Spain makes it possible to understand why the move to overturn the Pact of Forgetting is not generally seen as having anything to do with correcting weaknesses in the existing democracy, but rather as a sign of democratic maturity. Vincent (2007: 241) has pointedly argued that "The current concern about historical memory in Spain is not about democracy. There is no serious suggestion that these issues represent a flaw in the fabric of Spanish democracy; rather it has become commonplace to assert that, as only now has it become possible to address the question of the repression, so historical memory actually attests to the robustness of consolidated democracy." In the end, what mattered most to the success of democracy in Spain was not how the transgressions of the authoritarian regime were handled but how the new democratic regime responded to the public's desire for construction of viable and effective governing institutions. In this respect, Spain had a leg up on other states in Latin America and post-communist Europe as a result of the modernization of the state and the economy that took place during the late Franco period. It succeeded in creating a cross-class consensus on democracy well before the actual dismantling of the authoritarian regime.

Ironically, the case of Spain reveals that forgetting and democratization can be mutually supporting. Certainly, this assertion does not negate the fact that the Pact of Forgetting exacted a high price on Spanish democracy. It did, and none more obvious than prolonging the suffering of Franco's victims. As observed by Davis (2005: 867), whether the pact of silence was "necessary or legitimate, its effect was in many ways to perpetuate the historical injustice suffered by the victims of Francoism." Another cost of forgetting was to have distorted the collective memory about the past, since the pact drew a very problematic moral equalization across both sides of the Civil War on several fronts. The false premise of collective culpability used to rationalize forgetting the past implied that the suffering of the defeated Republicans was the same as that of the victorious Nationalists, a point contradicted by all objective research. The Pact of Forgetting was also underwritten by the myth that all sectors of Spanish society were similarly affected by the Franco dictatorship. This was clearly not the case, with the left and its allies (labor, intellectuals, and regional nationalists) bearing the brunt of Franco's violence and repression, to say nothing of the political and economic benefits that the right and its allies (the Catholic Church, rural oligarchs, and urban industrialists) derived from the long Francoist period.

But the Pact of Forgetting is recognized, whether explicitly or implicitly as critical to Spain's successful democratic transformation (see Share 1986; Gunther 1992; Linz and Stepan 1996; Gunther, Montero and Botella 2004; Encarnación 2008a).[5] Interestingly, the pejorative terms Pacto del Olvido or Pacto del Silencio appear nowhere in this literature. Instead, the willingness of the political class to set aside a divisive history while working to consolidate a new democracy is seen as a sign of political maturity. These assessments about the pact to forget suggest the counterintuitive insight that democratization succeeded in Spain not in spite of the absence of confronting the past through trials and truth commissions but rather because of it. But how precisely did the pact to forget serve to facilitate democratization in Spain?

First and foremost, forgetting aided democratization by minimizing political uncertainly—widely regarded by the literature on democratic transitions as the most urgent task for democratizing elites (O'Donnell and Schmitter 1986). Much of the uncertainty in Spain around the time of Franco's death centered on the residual power of the authoritarian state left in place by the state-controlled transition to democracy, and embodied most prominently by the military. As noted by Pi-Sunyer (1977: 189), during the democratic transition the army, as the one "strong institution" to have survived Franco, "could, if conditions deteriorated, re-emerge as a potent political force, and Spaniards are well aware of this potential." Therefore, by keeping a tight lid on the past, the political class, especially the left, intended to purchase the acquiescence of those who had the means to derail the process of democratization.

Another advantage of forgetting was to allow the political class to focus on the tasks of democratic consolidation, which in Spain, in sharp contrast to other new democracies such as those of Latin America, entailed building a democratic regime from scratch without much of a democratic heritage. As Linz and Stepan (1996: 89) have argued, given that in Spain the authoritarian regime had lasted thirty-six years, "it was not possible to use the existing institutions by filling them with democratic content or proceeding to a restoration of the pre-dictatorship institutions." With the highly contentious and potentially explosive subject of the past conveniently tucked away, the political class could focus their energies on creating a new constitutional regime that addressed many of the challenges that for centuries had made democracy so elusive in Spain, especially how to accommodate demands for regional autonomy in the confines of a centralized state.

Forgetting also boosted Spain's historically weak and fragmented sense of nationhood, a long-standing obstacle to democratization. The link between forgetting and nation-building is intriguing, and has been popularized in recent years by Benedict Anderson in his work on "imagined communities," which borrows directly from the work of the nineteenth-century French philosopher Ernest Renan. Anderson (1991: 11) quotes Renan as having said that "the essence of a nation is that all its people have a great deal in common, and also that they have forgotten a great deal. Forgetting is a crucial factor in the creation of a nation, which is why progress in historical studies often constitutes a danger for nationality." Renan's words apply, with great accuracy, to the Spanish experience in light of how the deliberate repression and distortion of the memory of the events leading to the Civil War and the Franco dictatorship facilitated Spain's reimagining of itself as a modern, European state. It is difficult to conceive this reimagining with the nation preoccupied with matters concerning a very divisive past.

The world beyond Spain also suggests that the role of transitional justice in the process of democratization is neither as straightforward nor as positive as currently presumed. Forgetting the past has not always worked to the detriment of democracy and transitional justice has hardly been the unmitigated blessing its advocates make it out to be. The successful democratization of Europe in the postwar period reveals that notwithstanding the commitment to human rights born after World War II, a deliberate attempt at forgetting was a democratic building block. An emphasis on forgetting the past as part of Europe's postwar political reconstruction was famously set by Winston Churchill's 1946 "Zurich Speech," in which the former British Prime Minister urged the Europeans to set the rancor of the past aside by embracing the spirit of forgetting: "If Europe is to be saved from infinite misery, and indeed from final doom, there must be an act of faith in the European family and an act of oblivion against all crimes and follies of the past."[6]

Individual states appear to have taken Churchill's advice to heart. Garton Ash (2002: 267) reminds us that much of postwar West European democracy was constructed "on a foundation of forgetting." He adds that "the postwar

French Republic was built, after the first frenzy of the *épuration*, on more or less a policy of supplanting the painful memory of collaboration in Vichy and occupied France with de Gaulle's unifying national myth of a single, eternally resistant, fighting France." Of Austria, Garton Ash notes that under Kurt Waldheim the country was "happily restyled, with the help of the allies, as the innocent victim of Nazi aggression." Poggiolini (2002: 232) has argued that "the new Italy" emerged from "the tunnel of poverty and destruction," determined to secure "its security, stability and wealth" anchored in "a regime of national amnesia."

Then there is the German experience, in many people's eyes the paradigmatic example of coming to terms with the past, as well as the preeminent symbol of post-war democratic and economic success. Although the Nazi regime was subjected to a comprehensive process of transitional justice at the hands of the Nuremberg International Tribunal, this did not preclude deliberate attempts on the part of the Germans to try to set the past aside as they sought to rebuild political institutions from the ruins of World War II. From the 1950s through at least the 1980s, the lack of frank confrontation with the past in Germany was deemed by many as "a moral black mark on the country that needed to be rectified for the country to be truly rehabilitated" (Langenbacher 2010: 28). Such indictments about how Germany faced its Nazi past are generally associated with the Adenauer era (the 1950s and 1960s), the peak years of the consolidation of West German democracy. For much of this period, a great sense of denial about the past was rooted in the presumption that that the horrors of the interwar period were somewhat detached from the real Germany. Langenbacher writes (2010: 28):

> The responsible and rabid Nazi elite, most of whom were conveniently dead, were contrasted with innocent "ordinary Germans" and honourable Wehrmacht soldiers. Abstract, agent-less historical conceptions implied that the "German catastrophe" fell out of thin air and portrayed the Nazi period as an aberration from "real" German traditions. Theories of totalitarianism compounded the problem by stressing the affinities between Nazi Germany and Soviet Russia, relativising German crimes in the process. Moreover, this willed gap with the past "was, to a certain extent filled by the manic achievements of the 'economic miracle'—that has been responsible for much of the psychic and political immobility of large segments of the German population."

An attachment to forgetting is also evident in the ways the German experience with transitional justice falls quite short of what is nowadays generally demanded of nations confronting their dark pasts. It was not until 1998 that Germany passed the Law to Nullify Nationalist-Socialist Sentences, which declared the entire Nazi judicial apparatus null and void by contending that between 1933 and 1945 laws were designed "to upkeep a system of injustices fueled by racist, political, military, religious and ideological reasons."[7] This law does not provide reparations for those unjustly sentenced, but it allows for certification from the country's highest court about the unjust nature of the sentencing. A total of 500,000 sentences were automatically annulled. Also suggestive is that a memorial honoring the victims of the Holocaust, intended to remind the German people of the enormity of Hitler's crimes, was not inaugurated in Berlin until 2005, sixty years after the end of World War II.

On the other hand, notable examples of transitional justice are themselves difficult cases of democratization, in no small part due to the attempt to hold the old regime accountable. Argentina's military trials of the 1980s are held by the international human rights community as a major triumph for democracy and the rule of law (Sikkink 2008). Among Argentines, the view is decidedly less sanguine. Jaime Malamud-Goti, a senior aide to the Alfonsín administration and one of the architects of the Argentine military trials, has argued in his fascinating book *Game with No End* (1995) that the trial of military officers did not advance democracy because they failed to treat all citizens as equal before the law and thus perpetuated the us-versus-them mentality that enabled the junta to establish authoritarian rule in the first place. Malamud-Goti goes further, contending that the trials played an anti-democratic role by contributing to the new mode of authoritarianism. In his view, the back and forth between justice and amnesty begun by the military trials suggests that Argentina is persisting in turning logic on its head: multitudes of Argentinians respond to authoritarianism by playing political and judicial hardball, inciting a response in kind.

Elsewhere around the world, transitional justice has morphed into "transitional revenge," with devastating consequences for democratization. The most recent and compelling example is that of Iraq. To say that transitional justice has been more of a curse than a blessing is something of an understatement, considering that it has been blamed for rising sectarian violence and bringing the country to the brink of civil war. To accompany the toppling of the Saddam Hussein regime in March 2003, the Americans introduced an ambitious policy of "de-Baathification" designed to cleanse Iraq of the influence of 35 years of Baathist dictatorship. By almost any measure, this was a paradigmatic example of "victor's justice," with the Iraqi government exacting nothing short of revenge against the defeated regime. Under a preponderance of influence by the American occupying forces, the Iraqi government disbanded its army, purged as many as 50,000 members of Saddam Hussein's ruling political apparatus, and put Saddam himself on trial. He was sentenced to death by hanging, an act characterized by human rights activists as "a legal lynching."[8] For the Iraqi government, however, protecting human rights was the rationale for killing Saddam. "Our respect for human rights requires us to execute him, and there will be no review or delay in carrying out the sentence," explained president Nouri al-Maliki, in response to a chorus of complaints about the trial's numerous irregularities, such as admission of hearsay evidence and failure of the prosecutors to disclose evidence to the defense.[9]

Today, Iraq's policy of de-Baathification is widely regarded as one of the most serious missteps in the American intervention in Iraq by creating a power vacuum in government, dividing Iraqi political society, fueling sectarian violence and insurgency against the Americans, and tarnishing the dignity of the law (Packer 2005). A 2008 law passed by the Iraqi parliament promised to reverse de-Baathification by permitting former members of the Baath party to return to their government jobs and by allowing those who have reached retirement age to claim their pensions. This law was one of the key recommendations of the Iraqi Study Group, a bipartisan commission created by the U.S. Congress in 2006 to examine American policy in Iraq and introduce new approaches intended to facilitate political reconciliation.[10]

Coming to Terms with the Past Spanish-Style

Spain's delayed encounter with its past suggested by the 2007 Law of Historical Memory reveals the deeply contextual nature of coming to terms with a difficult and painful history. This stands in striking contrast to the perception that emerges from much of the transitional justice literature, whereby countries make the leap to democracy while simultaneously confronting the past—independent of the conditions in which they undertake democratization and the historical events that brought them into conflict prior to the democratic transition. In Spain, for instance, the mass violence of the Civil War, which left citizens from all corners of society traumatized and with blood on their hands, created a stiff resistance about delving into the past. Moreover, this violent past has made the Spanish public more desirous of peace and stability than anything else. Decades after the end of the Civil War, a clear majority of Spaniards (39.3 percent) believe that "maintaining peace and order" trumps all other government priorities, including protecting civil and political liberties (28.4 percent), fighting inequality (10.9 percent), reducing unemployment (9.7 percent), and guaranteeing economic prosperity (9.5 percent) (CIS 2008).

Curiously, in Spain the desire to confront the past has become more pronounced since the consolidation of democracy than it was before, quite in contrast to what is generally expected. The passing of societal fears that encouraged the culture of forgetting after Franco's death, paired with the advent of a new generation of politicians not beholden to the political compromises of the transition, have proved auspicious for a more honest treatment of the past. This sequencing of confronting the past after the transition to democracy is firmly in place has been termed "post-transitional justice" by some scholars (Aguilar 2009), since it indicates the desire to hold the old regime accountable for its misdeeds well past the point when democratic institutions have reached some semblance of stability and/or maturity.

In Spain and elsewhere (South America, for instance), the emergence of post-transitional justice challenges the popular view that the failure to confront the past during the transition precludes confronting the past at a later juncture. Yet the revisiting of the past introduced by the 2007 Law of Historical Memory after three decades of self-imposed silence, demonstrates that decisions about the past made during the transition are not written in stone; they can be renegotiated and even discarded after they have outlived their purpose. All that said, Spain's coming to terms with the past remains very much rooted in domestic realities rather than in international norms of transitional justice.

Arguably, the most distinctive aspect of Spain's coming to terms with the past is the commitment to amnesty, which largely rules out human rights prosecutions and even a truth commission. Protecting the amnesty law of 1977 was one of the few points of consensus among the political class during the deliberations of the new memory law, with virtually no one suggesting that the country should entertain the notion of prosecuting anyone associated with the old regime. Although human rights groups have called for a truth commission to investigate the political crimes of the Civil War and the Francoist period, no major political party has ever endorsed this idea, which means that any future attempt at truth-telling will likely be a private rather than a public project. At this point, the closest thing to a truth commission we find in Spain is Todos los nombres (All the Names), a voluntary national registry that aims to identify by name all victims of the Civil War.[11]

Why amnesty persists in Spain is an interesting question to ponder, especially in light of recent decisions by the courts in South America to rescind or modify transition-era amnesty laws. Two points are worth noting. The first is that amnesty in Spain is intimately linked to the country having overcome the political divisions of the Civil War, a point that was explicitly made by the left during the transition that still resonates to this day. "In Spain there is a willingness for amnesty, not amnesia," declared the renowned historian Javier Tussell just before he passed away in 2005 (Elkin 2006: 3). Less apparent, but arguably more compelling, is that whereas in South America amnesty is seen as an authoritarian relic, in Spain it is regarded as a democratic touchstone. Amnesty laws in several South American countries were passed by the military as they were retreating from power in an obvious attempt to escape prosecution, and hence the traditional association of amnesty with abuses of power; in Spain, by contrast, the political class agreed to amnesty voluntarily. The 1977 amnesty law was the first piece of legislation enacted by the new parliament. Clearly, the democratic origin of the amnesty process in Spain makes it difficult for either the politicians or the courts to seek to undermine it.

Also characteristic of Spain is an apparent resistance to memorializing the past, at least publicly. Aside from the creation of a national Civil War archive, the 2007 Law of Historical Memory is remarkably silent on the issue of memorializing the victims of the Civil War (El Valle de los Caídos with its close association with the Franco dictatorship is not regarded as a legitimate memorial to the war dead), the massive Republican exile created by the Civil War, and the Franco regime, and those whose lives were lost as part of the Francoist resistance. All of this stands in striking contrast to the memory boom that coming to terms with the past has generated in other post-authoritarian democracies, especially in Latin America (Hite 2011). Argentina may well be the paradigmatic case. After the fall of the military dictatorship, the country undertook important memory projects, such as Buenos Aires's Memory Park, an expansive slice of the de la Plata River where many of the bodies of the "disappeared" were dumped by the police, and the Memory Museum in Rosario, which honors the memory of those detained and tortured by the military government. Buenos Aires's Escuela Superior de Mecánicos de la Armada, a military institution that served as a principal site for torturing political prisoners, was converted into a center for the promotion of memory and human rights.

Equally telling is that no significant efforts have been made to recover the memory of the political leaders associated with the Republican period, quite remarkable considering the many years since Franco's death that the country has been ruled by left-wing governments. The remains of the two Republican ex-presidents, Niceto Alcalá-Zamora and Manuel Azaña, both of whom died in exile, are a case in point. The remains of Alcalá-Zamora were moved from Buenos Aires to Madrid by his relatives in a private (and secret) operation that took place in 1977 after the government refused to honor him with a state funeral. Azaña's remains, the last president of the Republic, are buried in a cemetery in the French town of Montauban. As of 2010, there was no monument honoring Azaña's memory in the Spanish capital, although a bust can be found at his birthplace, the city of Alcalá de Henares.

The contrast with Chile, whose politics under Allende are often compared to those of the Second Republic, is telling. Since the fall of the Pinochet regime, much has been done to restore Allende's memory. In 1990, under the center-left presidency of Patricio Aylwin, Allende's remains were moved from a private burial site to the national cemetery where all of Chile's past democratic presidents rest. This operation included an elaborate funeral procession leading to a ceremony honoring Allende's memory at the Santiago Cathedral attended by notable domestic and international personalities. In 2000, the Salvador Allende monument was unveiled in front of the National Palace of la Moneda, the very building where Allende is believed to have committed suicide while under siege by Pinochet's military rebels. Other figures associated with the Allende regime have also been given official recognition, including Orlando Letelier, the Chilean Ambassador to the United States, who was assassinated in downtown Washington DC by Pinochet's secret police (the DINA). Chile's Estadio Nacional, a place filled with infamy for the human rights abuses it witnessed following Pinochet's attack on the Allende government, today features a permanent exhibit on political repression.

The apparent disinterest on the part of the Spaniards in publicly memorializing the past responds to several factors, beginning with the lack of consensus in Spanish society about the roots of the Civil War and who is ultimately responsible for it. Whatever consensus there is about the Civil War—for instance, that it should never be repeated—lends itself better to forgetting than to remembering. There is also the issue of memory fatigue, exemplified by the excessive (some might say obsessive) memorializing of the past that was so characteristic of the Franco regime. No other authoritarian regime in either Southern Europe or Latin America comes close to Franco's Spain in having so cynically employed history to legitimize its rule, and no other dictator in either region matches Franco's megalomaniac tendencies. Finally, there is the nature of the transition in Spain, which lacked a heroic narrative behind it. As observed by Humlebaek, (2011: 186), "Franco was not ousted by the democratic opposition, but died of old age in his bed . . . .There was no revolutionary upheaval or tradition of opposition in which to feel pride and through which to construct a new democratic community."

A less apparent aspect of coming to terms with the past in Spain is the dearth of reconciliation rhetoric, especially religious rhetoric, a commonality in contemporary discourses about coming to terms with the past intended to facilitate closure about an anguished past. Instead, the 2007 memory law adheres to strict secularist language. This is not surprising considering the polarizing role that religion played in twentieth-century Spanish history. Anti-clericalism was a hallmark of the Republican period and the Franco regime essentially drew no demarcation line between church and state when it made Catholicism the state's official religion and outsourced many state functions, especially education, to the church. In any case, religious authorities played no role whatsoever in crafting the course of reconciliation in Spain—quite in contrast to other nations such as South Africa. The Catholic Church opposed the new memory law believing that forgetting provided the best means for addressing the past.

The absence of religious rhetoric in Spain's coming to terms with the past also mirrors the almost radical secularism of the post-Franco era, itself a reaction to the hyper-religiosity of the Franco regime. Many Spanish left-wing leaders are self-declared agnostics, including former Prime Minister Zapatero, who in 2004 became the first president of the government in the post-transition era to swear his oath of allegiance not on the Bible, but on a copy of the Spanish constitution, making it very difficult for concepts such as contrition, repentance, and forgiveness to be incorporated into the debates about reconciliation in Spain. Civil society also appears hesitant to incorporate religion into discussions of reconciliation. Interestingly, there have been very few calls from memory advocates for repentance or contrition from those responsible for past political crimes, although some have called for an apology from the Catholic Church for its behavior during the dictatorship. Even ideas such as dignity have been resisted. In questioning the wisdom of tinkering with the past, the editorial page of *El País* took exception to the notion that in Spain, punishing the perpetrators of state violence could advance reconciliation by bringing "dignity" to the victims. "Francoism deprived victims of their lives or freedom, but never of their dignity. It is difficult to restore dignity to those who never lost it."[12] Rather, the paper contended, the oppressors were the ones "who lost their dignity by taking arms against a popularly elected government and by killing those that defended it."

Taken as a whole, Spain's peculiar experience with coming to terms with the past suggests the need for a more pragmatic understanding of how nations confront their dark histories, one that questions whether the one-size-fits-all model promoted by the transitional justice movement—premised on justice and accountability in all cases at the time when democracy is inaugurated—is realistic considering the wildly divergent political experiences that countries bring to the process of democratization. It may well be that different democratizing contexts demand different approaches. In some cases, as in Spain, the past is best addressed not as an ethical and/or legal problem but as a political dilemma. This point echoes Max Weber's contention (1946) that notions of absolute justice need to be tempered by the realities of what is possible and what is not, and the belief that ethical political judgment has to allow for some degree of pragmatism. It is regrettable that much of the debate concerning what to do about an anguished past has failed to appreciate these key insights about justice and politics.

NOTES

Introduction

1. A broader view of Franco's material legacy is provided in Chapter 1.

2. "Escasos incidentes," *Pueblo*, May 14, 1977.

3. "Spain's Civil War: Painful Memories," *Economist*, December 23, 2006, 73.

4. Garzón's reputation is owed to the prominent cases his court has heard. Aside from the Pinochet case, these cases include international drug trafficking, human rights abuses by the Spanish government in its fight against Basque terrorists, and Italian prime minister Silvio Berlusconi's involvement in the Spanish media. These high-profile cases have made Garzón the object of numerous death threats and one of Spain's best-protected citizens. They also explain the charge that Garzón is more interested in self-promotion than in the pursuit of justice. See "Charlemagne: Baltazar Garzón," *Economist*, June 22, 2001.

5. Garzón was cleared of the charge of illegally prosecuting former Francoist officials, but convicted of ordering illegal wiretaps of lawyers' conversations about a case concerning political corruption. His suspension from the bench for eleven years effectively ended his celebrated judicial career in Spain, since the verdict cannot be appealed. He has defended his prosecution of former Francoist officials by arguing that Spanish law cannot contravene international human rights law (Urbano 2000; Zapico 2010). For many in Spain and abroad, Garzón's trial represents a "deficit of justice" and a rebuke to those seeking justice for those victimized by human rights violations. See Lydia Vicente, Alicia Moreno, and Javier Chinchón, "España y el déficit de justicia," *El País*, January 17, 2012, and "A Chilling Verdict in Spain," *New York Times*, February 13, 2012.

6. In 2009, the Spanish Congress put the brakes on universal jurisdiction by determining that crimes committed outside Spain were prosecutable in Spanish courts only if Spanish citizens were affected. This intervention by the Congress was widely seen as reflecting external pressures by many nations, including the United States, which feared investigations of claims of human rights abuses at the Guantánamo base.

7. Natalia Junquera, "Las ONG afirman que el texto de la ley de memoria no cierra heridas si no que las abre," *El País*, March 23, 2007.

8. Carmen Pérez-Lanzac, "Human Rights Watch critica la ley Española de amnistía," *El País.com*, Madrid, March 19, 2010.

9. Natalia Junquera, "Las ONG afirman que el texto de la ley de memoria no cierra heridas si no que las abre."

10. According to Judt (2002: 161), a lot of "selectivity and apparent hypocrisy" were at work in the staging of the Nuremberg trials, a reflection of the politics of the day. For instance, having Soviet judges sentencing Nazi criminals for some of the same acts Stalin was perpetrating back home in the Soviet Union limited the trial's capacity to delve into moral and judicial questions, since the Soviet authorities presiding over the trials carefully sought to avoid them in order not to draw attention to the Soviet Union's own practices. Soviet participation was "regrettable but unavoidable," a Faustian bargain the U.S. and Britain made in order to bring the Nazis to justice (Hirsch 2008: 701). Also, only the Nazis were prosecuted for the excesses of World War II, prompting West Germany to reject the Nuremberg trials as "enforced victor's justice."

11. The world's first truth commission was created in Uganda in 1974 to investigate accusations of disappearances at the hands of the military during the first years of the Idi Amin government. To date, according to the United States Institute for Peace, more than two dozen truth commissions have been organized in places as diverse as Argentina, Chile, Uruguay, Brazil, East Timor, Liberia, Sierra Leone, El Salvador, Guatemala, and South Korea. National governments have organized the bulk of them, with the rest created or assisted by the UN and nongovernmental organizations.

12. This phrase is found in Santayana's *The Life of Reason* (1906).

13. David Rieff, "Against Remembrance," Lecture to Bard College Human Rights Project, October 19, 2010.

14. International Center for Transitional Justice, "What Is Transitional Justice," December 2008, http://www.ictj.org/en/tj/, accessed January 31, 2011. This criticism by the ICTJ has given a big boost to "reparation" as a third rail of transitional justice, notwithstanding the troubled notion that a monetary price can be put on human suffering and the fear of the spread of a victim culture. Barkan (2001: xxii) writes that restitution can be part of "negotiating recognition of historical injustices as part of their revised national identity in order to facilitate closure of a conflict." The impetus for reparation stems from the view that prosecutions and truth commissions are by and large "inconsequential" to the victims of the political excesses of an oppressive regime (De Greiff 2006: 1). What is needed, it is argued, is a broader policy of social and economic justice that includes concrete material compensation for those victimized by political repression and violence and acknowledges that a key legacy of authoritarian repression is often deep economic and social inequality and indeed injustice.

15. Santos Juliá, "Acuerdo sobre el pasado," *El País*, November 24, 2002.

16. Other political commentators in Spain have taken a less sanguine view of the legacy of the politics of forgetting. See Vicenç Navarro, "Los costes de la desmemoria histórica," *El País*, June 6, 2001.

17. Ricardo García Cárcel, "La memoria histórica y la transición," *ABC*, May 25, 2009.

18. PSOE, "Declaraciones de Cristianos Sociales para el diario The Times," http://www.psoe.es/ambito/cristianos/news/index.do?action=View&id=167011, accessed July 15, 2009.

19. Carlos Castresana Fernández, "Secretos de familia," *El País*, July 16, 2007.

Chapter 1. History, Politics, and Forgetting in Spain

1. Not everyone agrees with this view. Francisco Espinosa has complained about limited access to archives, especially military records. See his "La investigación del pasado reciente: un combate por la historia," http://biblioteca2.uclm.es/biblioteca/ceclm/websCECLM/transición/PDF/02-02.%20Texto.pdf, accessed March 26, 2010.

2. The electoral results of the last election of the Republican period (1936) suggest how politically divided the country was at the onset of the Civil War. The Popular Front, comprised of left-wing parties, won 48.06 percent of the vote, the right-wing National Front 46.60 percent. The center, dominated mainly by regional-nationalist parties, garnered 5.42 percent.

3. The Spanish "revolution" was staged most dramatically in Catalonia, Spain's historic industrial center, where the CNT and other workers' organizations seized hundreds of factories, but it spread to other parts of the country such as Asturias, Valencia, and Andalusia. Malefakis (1970: 372) reports that by 1933 one third of all land and two-thirds of all arable land had been seized by anarchist groups in Republican Spain.

4. According to Payne (1970: 275), the Spanish Civil War divided public opinion to a greater degree than anything in England since the Great Reform Bill and in France since the Dreyfus Affair. In the United States, the majority favored what was known as the "Republican" or "Loyalist" cause, though the great bulk of \ opinion opposed any direct American intervention.

5. It is widely accepted that Soviet Union had little interest in the survival of democracy in Spain. Its support for the Second Republic rested on the hope that a Republican victory over Franco would lead to the establishment of a communist regime in Spain (Payne 2011).

6. The figure 7,937 (cited by Beevor 1982: 70) is not too far from the one provided by Jackson (1965: 533), which makes note of "6,800 priests" assassinated by the Republican side.

7. This neglect of Republican graves is generally attributed to the Francoist repression, and after 1977, to the politics of forgetting. But some analysts (Treglown 2009: 25–26) have challenged this view by arguing that the state of Republican graves during and after the Franco regime also suggests realities such as people being too busy surviving to mind the dead and people feeling that the remains of their killed relatives

were best off left with their friends. Both points, according to Treglown (2009: 25), reflect Spanish attitudes toward the dead "which have always included a paradoxical mix of reverence and casualness."

8. See the works of novelist Jorge Semprún, especially *Le grand voyage*, which describes the inhumane conditions experienced by Spanish exiles in French concentration camps.

9. This information is based on *Más allá de la Alambrada: La memoria del horror*, a documentary by Pau Vergara, who interviewed twenty-three survivors of the camp, many of whom spent the rest of their lives in exile (mainly France), unable to return to Spain after the end of World War II.

10. According to one estimate by Javier Rodrigo cited by Faber (2007: 142), 367,000–500,000 people passed through the more than 100 concentration camps created by the Franco regime after the end of the Civil War.

11. This characterization of the Franco regime as "genocidal," popular in some quarters, has not gone unchallenged (see Ruiz 2005).

12. Leslie Crawford, "Franco's Slaves," *Financial Times*, 5 July 2003.

13. Ibid. For a broader view of Franco's labor camps see Torres (2004)

14. In recent years, this issue has exploded in Spain with reports indicating that state officials were stealing babies well into the democratic period. It appears that in the 1940s babies were taken from their parents for ideological reasons; by the 1960s, however, this had evolved into a money-making scheme. Babies were taken from unsuspecting parents directly from the hospitals where they were born, after hospital administrators informed their parents that the babies were born dead and the hospital had proceeded to bury the remains, and sold to families willing to pay for the babies. In several notable cases, parents who had been told their babies were born dead have discovered them alive as adults. For an early report on this story see Jesús Duva, "Hijos del Olvido: La fábrica de bebés," *El País*, February 22, 2009.

15. On the rise of ETA see Clark 1988; Muro 2005.

16. An in-depth look at ETA's violent campaign is provided in the next chapter.

17. Quoted passages from this section are from Valls (2007: 157–58).

18. Like other facts about the Civil War, the number of people killed in the bombing of Guernica remains in dispute. The figure cited here comes from Beevor (1982: 166). The generally accepted figure in Spain is 1,500 people, owing largely to its adoption by the Basque government. These figures have been questioned by recent scholarship, however, which places the number of dead at around 250. See Arias Ramos (2003).

19. Alongside Guernica, Aguilar (2008: 163) regards Belchite as "mythical places of the defeated."

20. The main basilica at El Valle would be larger than St. Peter's basilica were it not for a partition wall that creates a large entryway left unconsecrated.

21. How many Republican prisoners actually worked in building El Valle remains in dispute. The Franco regime always minimized the use of prisoners' labor, a claim

based on the statement by the monument's main architect, Diego Méndez, that only eighty prisoners were employed on the site (Aguilar 2002: 75).

22. This close association with Francoism accounts for the rather difficult relationship of ordinary Spaniards and El Valle. Generally speaking, only devoted Franquistas, such as members of the Falange, frequent the site. The monument is also a favorite target of terrorists, most recently in May 2005, when someone planted a homemade bomb under the bridge of one of the gardens.

23. "La prensa de los Estados Unidos da relieve de acontecimiento international al acto del Valle de los Caídos," *ABC*, April 3, 1959.

24. According to Aguilar (2008: 120), NODO produced 4,016 newsreels (excluding documentaries) from 1943 to 1981, when the agency was disbanded. In 1943–1946, the agency averaged one weekly newscast, expanding to two through the 1960s. With the economic boom of the 1960s, NODO accelerated production, averaging three weekly editions. In 1978–1981, the agency produced a Catalan version of its newscasts.

25. *El Camino de la paz*, reel 7, NODO Archive, author's translation.

26. This accounting of Madrid streets with names associated with the Franco regime comes from interviews by the author with officials from the Spanish Socialist Party in 2004.

27. In December 2008, the last remaining statue to Franco in the Spanish mainland was removed from Santander's town square, leaving the statue in Melilla, a Spanish colonial enclave in Northern Africa, the only one standing in a city under Spanish jurisdiction. The justification for a statue to Franco in Melilla is that it is a tribute for defending the city against Moroccan rebels in 1921.

28. Interview with Miguel A Muñoz Molina, president, Foros por la Memoria (Madrid, July 2, 2009).

Chapter 2. Regime Transition and the Rise of Forgetting, 1977–1981

1. Renwick McLean, "Spain's Dilemma: To Toast Franco or Banish His Ghost," *New York Times*, October 8, 2006.

2. The king's support for democracy was critical to legitimization of the monarchy. In a survey marking the tenth anniversary of Franco's death, 40 percent of Spaniards regarded the role of the king during the transition to democracy as "very important," while 30 percent agreed with the statement that without the monarchy democracy would not have been possible (CIS 1985).

3. Perhaps owing to his background as a prosecutor during the early Franco years, Arias Navarro was especially fond of political executions. In March 1974, his government ordered the execution of Catalan anarchist Salvador Puig Antich for his presumed involvement in the assassination of a Guardia Civil guard, an event that drew condemnation of the Franco regime throughout Europe and South America.

In September 1974, much to the horror of international observers and against threats of a boycott from its democratic neighbors and pleas from the Vatican, the Arias Navarro government executed five people suspected of terrorism, a clear sign that the old political order remained very much in place.

4. "La oposición, pesimista; la derecha, exultante," *Cuadernos para el Diálogo*, July 10, 1976.

5. The 1976 Law of Political Reform did not legalize the PCE for fear of upsetting the military. This exclusion was corrected on April 9, 1977.

6. The idea for a provisional government reflected the communists' desire for rapid inclusion into the political establishment. Because of Carrillo's demonization by the Franco regime, the public regarded the communists as more radical than the socialists.

7. Carrillo clearly stood to benefit from amnesty since he was officially banned from entering Spain (a policy he brazenly violated numerous times) and his party remained illegal until 1977.

8. "Carrillo: Los comunistas llevarán a las Cortes la voz del pueblo," *Pueblo*, May 30, 1977.

9. "El PSOE comenzará hoy a presentar su programa legislativo," *Ya*, September 21, 1977.

10. These figures included not only socialists but also nationalist leaders from Catalonia and the Basque Country. Although generally "conservative" in their political orientation, nationalist leaders from both regions worked closely with the PSOE while in exile, brought together by the common experience of being forced out of Spain and by their opposition to Franco.

11. Octavio Cabezas, "Enrique Múgica: El optimismo socialista," *El País*, December 5, 1976.

12. Santiago Álvarez cited by Encarnación (2008a: 29). I first encountered this quote in the Juan Linz Archives of the Juan March Institute in Madrid.

13. The main accuser of Santiago Carrillo's involvement in the Paracuellos killings is the Irish historian Ian Gibson in his 1983 book *Paracuellos: cómo fue*. See also "Entrevista: Ian Gibson Hispanista," *El Pais.com*, September 22, 2005. In this interview Gibson characterizes the killings at Paracuellos as "terrible but understandable," given the chaos of the era and the fears of what the prisoners might do on being freed. Carrillo has disputed Gibson's charges.

14. This quote is extracted from the film *Rejas en la Memoria* (Bars in the Memory) by Manuel Palacios (2004).

15. As might be expected, trading the chance to confront the old regime's political sins for political legality made Carrillo and González vulnerable to the charge that they had sold their principles for political gain. According to Morán (1991: 186–88): "the first ethical defeat of the democratic opposition was to consider that the only way that it could incorporate itself into political life was to guarantee impunity to the other side."

16. "Projecto de Manifesto-Programa del PCE, 1973," in *El PCE y sus documentos, 1920–1977.*

17. "Comentario," *Mundo Obrero*, April 25, 1975.

18. *El País digital*, "Aquel año de un muerto cada 60 horas," August 27, 2000.

19. Pablo Lucas Verdú, "Suárez y el nuevo juego político," *Diaro 16*, April 25, 1977.

20. "Disparidad de criterios," *Informaciones*, September 16, 1976.

21. Poll cited by López-Pintor (1980: 15).

22. Interview with Joaquín Estefanía, managing editor of *El País*, Madrid, February 11, 1994.

23. Francisco Espinosa Maestre, "La investigación del pasado reciente: un combate por la historia," http://biblioteca2.uclm.es/biblioteca/ceclm/websCECLM/transición/PDF/02-02.%20Texto.pdf, accessed March 26, 2010.

24. The text of this law is available on the Equipo Niznor website, http://www.derechos.org/nizkor/espana/doc/amnistia.html, accessed August 27, 2008.

25. "No deseo continuar en la presidencia si no tengo el respeto necesario," *El País*, June 12, 1977.

26. This sentence is pieced together from Suárez (1978).

27. The quotes from this section are taken from Julia Navarro, "Al paso de los protagonistas," *Pueblo*, October 10, 1977.

28. "La amnistía entra en vigor el lunes o el martes," *El Alcázar*, October 15, 1977.

29. "Editorial: Amnistía al fín," *El País*, October 15, 1977.

30. This quote and subsequent ones from Fuejo Lagos come from Aguilar (2002: 196).

31. La amnistía entra en vigor el lunes o el martes," *El Alcázar*, October 15, 1977.

32. "Todos apoyaron la amnistía excepto AP," *El País*, October 15, 1977.

33. The economic boom of the late Franco years came to a screeching halt around the time of the transition. GDP declined 6.7 percent in 1973 and by 1975 the economy had stopped growing altogether; unemployment soared from 2.6 percent in 1974 to 5.7 percent by 1977 (Encarnación 2008a: 113).

34. "La moderación de hoy frente a los viejos choques," *Informaciones*, July 14, 1977.

35. See "Ley 35/1980, de 26 Junio, sobre pensiones a los mutilados excombatientes de la zona republicana," available on the Equipo Nizkor website.

36. Author's interview (Madrid, February 9, 1994).

37. Electronic correspondence with the author, September 19, 2008.

Chapter 3. Socialist Rule and the Years of "Disremembering," 1982–1996

1. For a broader overview of this period see Newton and Donaghy 1997; Royo 2000; Méndez-Lago 2006; Gunther, Montero and Botella 2004; Encarnación 2008a.

2. "La ruptura moral," *Diaro 16*, February 1, 1983.

3. See "Ley 37/22 de octubre de reconocimiento de derecho y servicios prestados," Equipo Nizkor website, http://www.derechos.org/nizkor/espana/doc/ley37.html, accessed August 27, 2008.

4. This recognition was not spared controversy. By 1996, when the citizenship ceremony took place, Spain had undergone a change to a conservative government less than enthusiastic about the idea. Private funds had to be raised to finance the trip of the surviving Brigade members, and much was made of the fact that Prime Minister Aznar refused to greet the honorees.

5. "Declaración del gobierno: Una guerra fraticidia no es un acontecimiento conmemorable," *Ya*, July 19, 1986.

6. "Editorial: Amnistía al fín," *El País*, October 15, 1977.

7. Gálvez Biesca (2006: 33–34) notes that the 1993 elections were "the partial end" by the political parties of the commitment not to use the memory of the dictatorship to score political points.

8. Author's interview, Madrid, February 14, 1994.

9. Felipe González, "Chile, Argentina y las comisiones de la verdad," *El País*, April 23, 2001.

10. Francisco Espinoza Maestre, "La investigación del pasado reciente: un combate por la historia," http://biblioteca2.uclm.es/biblioteca/ceclm/websCECLM/transición/PDF/02-02.%20Texto.pdf, accessed March 26, 2006.

11. Spain's effort to join the EEC began in 1962 when the minister of foreign affairs petitioned the opening of negotiations for incorporation. The request was denied because of the absence of democratic freedoms in Spain. On July 28, 1977, when the first democratic parliament of the new democracy convened, Spain presented a formal request for membership.

12. Javier Pradera, "Vísperas Republicanas," *El País*, December 4, 1990.

13. Felipe González, "Europa, frontera de nuestra ambición," *El País*, January 29, 1999.

14. The full quote reads: "To feel the ills of Spain is to desire to be European. Regeneration is the desire, Europeanization is the means to satisfy it. It was clearly seen from the beginning that Spain was the problem and Europe the solution" (Jáuregui 1999: 275).

15. Leading thinkers of Hispanismo included ultra-right-wing writer Ramiro de Maeztu, who popularized the concept as "the community of Hispanic nations founded on the religious spirit of Spanish colonization, a specifically anti-liberal and traditionalist idea that was adopted by the Francoist regime as one of its ideological pillars" (Aguilar and Humlebaek 2002: 137).

16. Author's interview with José M. Maravall, Madrid, February 21, 1994.

17. "Esperanza Aguirre deplora el estado de los estudios de historia," *El Mundo*, October 11, 1996.

18. Tom Burns, "Spain Divide over History," *Financial Times*, December 18, 1997.

19. Ibid.

20. This quote comes from Nuñez Seixas 2005: 134. The complete report can be found at www.ppvizcaya.com/pages/patrio.html.

21. "El PP tira tanto de la bandera que quiere dejar la mitad de España a la intemperie," *El Mundo*, October 20, 2003.

22. Toni Comín, "Sobre el patriotismo constitucional," *El Mundo*, October 1, 2003.

23. See, for example Carlos Gurméndez, "Los recuerdos y la memoria," *El País*, May 11, 1996; Antonio Elorza, "El regreso de la memoria," *El País*, January 4, 1997; Antonio Munoz Molina, "La historia y el olvido," *El País*, November 9, 1997; Vicenç Navarro, "Los costes de la desmemoria histórica," *El País*, June 6, 2001.

24. Vicenç Navarro, "Los costes de la desmemoria histórica," *El País*, June 6, 2001.

25. Author's interview, December 10, 2009.

26. Ibid.

27. Agustín Yanel, "El PP y los demás grupos condenan la represión de la dictadura franquista," *El Mundo*, November 21, 2002.

28. Giles Tremlet, "Spain Torn on Tribute to Victims of Franco," *The Guardian*, December 1, 2003.

Chapter 4. A Silent Accomplice: Civil Society and the Persistence of Forgetting

1. By "civil society" I mean the sector of society that stands apart from the state and marketplace in which the citizenry come together to pursue common interests and goals (see Encarnación 2006).

2. The intention was to emulate the 1966 Russell Commission, convened by European intellectuals to examine human rights abuses by the American government during the Vietnam War.

3. The source of these data is a survey from *Cambio 16*, December 1, 1975.

4. Interview with the author, June 16, 2009.

5. Interview with the author, July 3, 2009.

6. The Fundamental Laws were meant to substitute for a constitution, which Franco never enacted, believing a constitution smacked of republicanism.

7. Francisco Espinoza Maestre, "La investigación del pasado reciente: un combate por la historia," http://biblioteca2.uclm.es/biblioteca/ceclm/websCECLM/transición/PDF/02-02.%20Texto.pdf, accessed March 26, 2006.

8. Juan C. de la Cal, "La Guerra Civil de esquelas se dispara," *El Mundo*, September 3, 2006.

9. The new accounting of the Civil War killings is discussed in Chapter 6 as part of the movement to restore the historical memory.

10. The Basque repression explains why the myth of equal blame for the Civil War resonates less in the Basque Country than in the rest of Spain. As argued by Aguilar (1998), for many Basques, the Civil War was a conflict between "the Spaniards" in which the Basque people were unwillingly dragged into to protect their interests.

11. Author's interview with Joaquín Estefanía, Managing Editor of *El País*, cited in Encarnación (2005: 190).

12. Interview, Luís Berlinches Raso, spokesperson, Associación de Ex-presos y Represaliados Políticos Anti-franquistas (Madrid, June 25, 2009).

13. "Franco, el hombre más olvidado del Franquismo, *El País*, November 21, 1976.

14. "Primer Aniversario," *Ya*, November 20, 1976.

15. This same source reports that the media were very slow to report on the exhumation of graves that triggered the "return" of the historical memory in the early 2000s. It is noted that the earliest reports came about one year after the exhumations had begun.

16. Interview with author, July 2, 2009.

17. Independent investigations have concluded that while the German Condor Legion conducted the air raids that destroyed Guernica, Franco bore moral responsibility for the attack (Viñas 1978). In 1997, German president Roman Herzog apologized on behalf of the German people for his country's role in the Spanish Civil War. The German parliament ratified the apology in 1998.

18. Basque Nationalists Want Picasso's Guernica," *ARTINFO*, January 23, 2007.

19. Under Franco, the media were tightly regulated by the state. After the Civil War, the regime shut down all privately owned newspapers except for a handful, including Madrid's *ABC* and Barcelona's *La Vanguardia*, whose owners agreed with the regime's policies, and *Ya*, owned by the Catholic Church, which supported the regime. The state also controlled the national radio network, the news agency EFE, and developed a monopoly on television service (TVE) introduced during the late Franco period.

20. Reported in "Spain and Europe," *El País*, August 22, 2006.

21. The quotes cited in this section come from Solís (2003).

22. "The Eurogeneration Comes of Age," *El País*, August 22, 2006.

Chapter 5. Pinochet's Revenge: Awakening the Memory of Civil War and Dictatorship

1. The first case to reach the Audiencia Nacional was a suit by the Unión Progresista de Fiscales, charging the Argentine military with genocide, heard by García-Castellón in June 1996. The second, filed in July 1996 by the human rights branch of the IU and the Salvador Allende Foundation on behalf of victims of the Pinochet regime, was heard by Garzón.

2. These laws are discussed in some detail in Chapter 7.

3. For a more detailed overview of the technical aspects of Pinochet's arrest see Wilson (1999).

4. The role of the United States in the fall of the Allende government remains hotly debated, with many observers agreeing that the Nixon administration played a part, but uncertain how decisive this role was.

5. The Clinton administration did, however, release previously classified information detailing the involvement of the U.S. government in the fall of Chilean democracy in 1973. See "Chile and the United States: Declassified Documents Relating to the Military Coup, September 11, 1973," http://www.gwu.edu/~nsarchiv/NSAEBB/NSAEBB8/nsaebb8i.htm, accessed August 12, 2008.

6. This headline from the Chilean newspaper *El Mercurio* is taken from a summary of international reactions to Pinochet's arrest gathered by the U.S. Information Agency, Office of Research and Media Reaction, December 4, 1998, http://www.fas.org/irp/news/1998/12/wwwh8d04.html, accessed May 4, 2008.

7. Marisa Cruz, "Frei pide que se trate a Pinochet como a los dirigentes franquistas," *El Mundo*, October 20, 1998. Frei's reference to the GAL regards the death squads employed by the Spanish government to fight ETA during the 1980s (see Chapter 4).

8. F. Frechoso and J. I. Irigaray, "El PSOE mantiene la petición de que Pinochet sea extraditado," *El Mundo*, October 25, 1998.

9. "Spain Digs Up Civil War Graves," *BBC News Online*, July 18, 2002.

10. "La obligación de Aznar, la sin razón de Frei," *El Mundo*, October 20, 1998.

11. Felipe González, "Chile, Argentina y las comisiones de la verdad," *El País*, April 23, 2001.

12. Antonio Candilejos, "González no quiere precedentes," *El Mundo*, October 31, 1998.

13. Jordi Solé Tura, "Franco y Pinochet," *El País Digital*, September 27, 1999.

14. For a detailed accounting of the many twists and turns of Pinochet's legal case, see "Timeline: The Pinochet Legal Saga," *BBC Online*, December 14, 2006.

15. Frechoso and Irigaray, "El PSOE mantiene la petición de que Pinochet sea extraditado."

16. This process of right-wing modernization entailed reconversion of the neo-Francoist Alianza Popular (AP), created by Manuel Fraga in 1977, into the PP, under Aznar's leadership in 1989. On this transformation see Balfour (2005).

17. One wonders what any potential trial of Pinochet would have revealed about Franco and Pinochet. It is widely known, for instance, that Franco was supportive of the so-called "Caravan of Death," in which 75 political prisoners were killed shortly after the 1973 coup that ousted Allende. Approximately 3,000 people, including these prisoners, were reported killed or "disappeared" under Pinochet's regime, as chronicled by the Rettig Commission, which provided the official tally of Pinochet's victims. The deaths associated with the Caravan of Death are especially noteworthy because many of those killed died while in police custody and had no history of violent behavior.

18. M. Cruz, A. Rubio and C. Cerdan, "Aznar reclama a Garzón "fundamentos reales" para tramitar la extradicion," *El Mundo*, October 19, 1998.

19. On his return to Chile, Pinochet was indicted on murder and disappearance charges. These charges were subsequently reduced to accessory to the crime, but all legal proceedings stopped once he was deemed mentally unfit to stand trial. Pinochet died December 10, 2006. He was denied a state funeral.

20. Frechoso and Irigaray, "El PSOE mantiene la petición de que Pinochet sea extraditado."

21. "Almunia pide a Aznar que no interfiera," *El Mundo*, October 20, 1998.

22. Adela Gooch, "Spain: Clamor for Prosecution," *The Guardian*, March 25, 1999.

23. "Almunia pide a Aznar que no interfiera," *El Mundo*, October 20, 1998.

24. Enrique Gimbernat, "La situación jurídical de Pinochet, *El Mundo*, October 19, 1998.

25. Luis Solana, "Aznar sin suerte," *El Mundo*, October 20, 1998.

26. "Fraga defiende a Pinochet," *El Mundo*, October 21, 1998.

27. "Spanish Fight over Poet's Remains," July 18, 2002, *BBC News*.

28. Author's interview with Emilio Silva, July 9, 2009.

29. Emilio Silva Barrera, "Mi abuelo fué un desaparecido," *derechos.net*, http://www.derechos.net/algomas/silva.html, accessed March 31, 2010.

30. "La ONU pide que se investigue donde estan enterrados republicanos fusilados tras la guerra," *El País*, November 16, 2002.

31. This report is available at http://www.es.amnesty.org/paises/espana/victimas-de-la-guerra-civil-y-del-franquismo/, accessed March 31, 2010.

32. "Second Declaration of the ARMH Before the UN Working Group on Forced Disappearances," ARMH 2002, http:/www.memoriahistorica.org, accessed September 21, 2007.

33. Carlos E. Cué, "La tierra devuelve a sus muertos," *El País*, July 1, 2002.

34. Issac Rosas, "Empacho de memoria," *El País*, July 6, 2006.

35. This tale was made famous worldwide by the film *El laberinto del fauno* (Pan's Labyrinth, 2005), by Mexican director Guillermo del Toro.

36. During the 1970s, Moa was a member of the Maoist organization Grupos de Resistencia Antifascista Primero de Octobre (GRAPO), the terrorist wing of the Spanish Communist Party.

37. "Reabrir cicatrizadas heridas," *ABC*, September 15, 2006.

38. "Pio Moa: No condeno a Franco," *La Nación*, April 23, 2008.

39. This work has been savagely criticized by Spanish academics as "propagandist," "trash," "factually wrong," and Moa himself as a "pseudo-historian" (see Reig 2006; Gálvez Biesca 2006). Prominent historians, however, have come to Moa's defense, most notably Stanley Payne. In a review of Moa's work on "the myths of the Spanish Civil War," Payne notes that "each and every one of Moa's theses are defended seriously in terms of the evidence that is available," and that Moa's work is "based on direct investigation, and generally, on a careful revisiting of the sources and historiography." He added: "It is lamentable that among the historians and reviewers who have examined Moa's work, the most notable thing about their work is the absence of debate and the reluctance to discuss the many themes that Moa's work provokes." See "Stanley Payne elogia la obra de Pío Moa," La Esfera de los Libros, http://www.esferalibros.com/noticias/notdetalle.html?notID=223, accessed April 1, 2010.

40. Moa, however, has had a contentious relationship with the Spanish right, which he has accused of not defending Franco and his modernizing legacy for fear of being branded "Francoist."

41. Antonio Feros, "Civil War Still Haunts Spanish Politics," *New York Times*, March 20, 2004.

42. See "El Patriotismo Constitucional del Siglo XXI, http://www.ppvizcaya.com/pages/patrio.html, accessed September 8, 2008.

43. Author's interview with William Chislett, September 22, 2008.

44. Juan C. de la Cal, "La guerra de esquelas se dispara," *El Mundo*, 3 September 2006.

45. "Interview with Carlota Leret O'Neill," October 17, 2006, ARMH, http://www.memoriahistorica.org/modules.php?name=News&file=print&sid=333, accessed October 3, 2008.

46. These are taken from a sample of obituaries published by Juan C. de la Cal, "La guerra de esquelas se dispara," *El Mundo*, September 3, 2006.

47. Nuria Tesón, "Esquelas de las dos España." *El País*, October 10, 2006.

48. "Guerra de esquelas," *ABC.es*, September 9, 2000.

49. de la Cal, "La guerra de esquelas se dispara."

50. Tesón, "Esquelas de las dos España."

51. Ibid.

52. "La Guerra Civil revive viejos fantasmas con la publicación constante de esquelas en la prensa," *20 Minutos*, September 17, 2006, *20 Minutos.es*, http://www.20minutos.es/noticia/152958/0/esquelas/guerra/civil/, accessed September 27, 2008.

Chapter 6. Post-Transitional Justice in Zapatero's Second Transition

1. In the weeks prior to the elections, national polls consistently showed the PP enjoying a 2- to 5-point lead over the PSOE (CIS 2004). This polling had led PP party leaders to confidently predict a safe if narrow victory.

2. It did not help the PP case that days before the elections Rajoy attacked young people as "anti-democratic" and threatened to haul them to jail for breaking the law by protesting during the so-called *jornada de reflexión* (day of reflection), a provision in Spain's electoral law that bans campaigning the day before a national election.

3. PSOE, "Merecemos una España mejor: Programa Electoral Elecciones Generales 2004," PSOE website, www.psoe.esinfosoe, accessed August 25, 2004.

4. Lisa Abend and George Pingree, "Farewell to Franco," November 13, 2005, Time Online website.

5. This phrase comes from reports of an interview Zapatero gave to journalists Marco Calamai and Aldo Garzia for their 2005 book *Zapatero: El mundo de los Ciudadanos*, http://www.lukor.com/literatura/index-22.htm, accessed May 4, 2008.

6. Luis R. Aizpeolea, "Zapatero planea una sucesión natural," *El Pais.com*, 5 May 2008.

7. Ibid.

8. Renwick Mclean, "Spain's Zapatero Shows Backbone in his Soft Power," *International Herald Tribune*, December 6, 2006.

9. "Discurso de investidura," 2004, Office of the Spanish President of the Government website, http://www.la-moncloa.es/Presidente/Discursodeinvestidura/default.htm, accessed September 21, 2007.

10. "The Party's Over: A Special Report on Spain," *Economist*, November 11, 2008, 4.

11. Pettit has also served as an advisor to the Zapatero government; toward the end of Zapatero's first term in office he offered a very positive assessment noting the progress the government had made in pursuit of social equality. See Pettit (2008).

12. Diario de Sesiones del Congreso de los Diputados, 296, Sesión del 31/X/2007.

13. Cited by Paul Stuart, "Spain: Law of Historical Memory Continues Cover-up of Franco's Crimes," World Socialist website, http://www.wsws.org/articles/2006/sep2006/spai-s11.shtml, accessed December 19, 2007.

14. See Informe General de la Comisión Interministerial para el estudio de la situación de las víctimas de la Guerra Civil y el Franquismo, July 28, 2006.

15. This is one of the least-known stories, at least outside Spain, about the post-Civil War Republican repression. An excellent overview of the events at Mauthausen is provided by the documentary *Más allá de la Alambrada: La memoria del horror*, by Pau Vergara, which interviews 23 of the then living survivors of the camp, many of whom lived the rest of their lives in exile (mainly France), unable to return to Spain after the end of the World War II. Of the 8,000 Republicans interned at the camp, only 2,000 are believed to have come out alive.

16. "Rodriguez Zapatero rinde homenaje a los españoles que murieron en el campo nazi de Mauthausen," *El Mundo*, May 9, 2005.

17. "Ley de la Memoria Histórica," 2007, Boletín Oficial del Estado (BOE), http://www.mpr.es/NR/rdonlyres/D03898BE-21B8-4CB8-BBD1-D1450E6FD7AD/85567/boememoria.pdf, accessed June 20, 2008.

18. A curious inclusion in this opening article is persecution and violence for religious reasons. It is possible to read this as recognition of the violence of the Republicans toward the Catholic Church, but more accurately, it reflects the desire on the part of Catalan nationalists that the law recognizes the suffering of those repressed because of their Catholic faith and despite their support of the Republic.

19. Carlos E. Cué, "De la Vega frena la ley de memoria histórica para acoger a ambos bandos," *El País*, September 12, 2005.

20. "El rechazo de IU y ERC pone en peligro el projecto del Ejecutivo," *El País*, August 25, 2006.

21. Abend and Pingree, "Farewell to Franco."

22. Author's interview with Luís Berlinches Raso, spokesperson, Associación de Ex-presos y Represaliados Políticos Anti-franquistas, Madrid, June 25, 2009.

23. "Carta Abierta a la Vicepresidenta del Gobierno y Presidenta de la Comisión Interministerial para el Estudio de la Situación de las Víctimas de la Guerra Civil y el Franquismo, María Teresa Fernández de la Vega," November 12, 2004, http://www.derechos.org/nizkor/, accessed March 27, 2010.

24. Carlos E. Cué, "Las asociaciones se impacientan y exigen una solución definitive," *El País*, September 12, 2005.

25. For a detailed overview of these efforts see, Jorge Errandonea, "Estudio Comparado de la anulación de sentencias injustas en España," ICTJ Website, http://ictj.org/sites/default/files/ICTJ-Spain-Amnesty-Justice-2008-Spanish_0.pdf.

26. Cué, "Las asociaciones se impacientan y exigen una solución definitiva."

27. Quoted by Stuart, "Spain: Law of Historical Memory Continues Cover-up of Franco's Crimes."

28. So far the courts have been reluctant to revise Francoist sentences. Indeed, only one such case exists to date, that of an individual who was given the death sentence twice for the same crime, which prompted the Constitutional Court to annul the second sentence. In refusing to tamper with the legacy of the Francoist legal system, both the government and the courts have generally subscribed to the view that while the Franco regime came into being through illegitimate means, its procedures were not themselves illegitimate. This stance harkens back to the restoration of democracy in 1976 with the Law of Political Reform, which employed the legal mechanisms of the Franco regime to end the dictatorship and launch the new democracy.

29. Diario de Sesiones del Congreso de los Diputados, 222, Sesión del 14/XII/2006.

30. "El projecto de ley de memoria historica divide el congreso," *El País*, December 14, 2006.

31. Ibid.

32. These quotes come from an interview that Fraga gave to the Italian newspaper *Corriere della Sera* on the thirtieth anniversary of Franco's death. The interview is available on *20 Minutos*, http://www.20minutos.es/66363/4/4, accessed March 27, 2010.

33. "Acusa al PSOE de cobarde por abrir tumbas de la Guerra Civil y no las del Gal," *ABC.es*, 19-05-2007.

34. "Las estatuas como cortina de humo," *ABC*, August 15, 2006.

35. Anne Roy, "The Conspiracy of Silence Around Franco's Spain Has Finally Been Broken," *L'Humanité in English*, November 4, 2007.

36. This estimate comes from Bess Twiston Davis, "Sacred Law of Historical Memory," *Times*, November 23, 2007.

37. Carmen Del Riego, "El apoyo de ERA pasa por Companys," *La Vanguardia*, August 25, 2006.

38. Carlos E. Cué, "El gobierno quitó de la ley de la memoria el consejo de suprimir símbolos franquistas," *El País*, August 25, 2006.

39. Interview with Emilio Silva, president, Associación para la Recuperación de la Memoria Histórica, July 9, 2009.

40. Author interview with Pedro A. García Bilbao of Foro por la Memoria, June 14, 2009.

41. Interview with Ludivina García Arias, spokesperson, Asociación de Descendientes del Exilio Español. Madrid, July 3, 2009.

42. Author interview with Gregorio Ortíz Ricoll, spokesperson, Asociación de Expresos y Represaliados Anti-Franquistas, June 25, 2009.

43. Equipo Nizkor, "The Question of Impunity in Spain and Crimes Under Franco," Madrid, 2004, http:/www.derechos.org, accessed December 10, 2010.

44. Carlos E. Cué, "La ley de memoria se aprueba entre aplausos de invitados antifranquistas," *El País*, November 1, 2007.

45. Ibid.

46. Agustín Yanel, "Ningún otro grupo apoya la ley de la memora historica," *El Mundo*, December 16, 2006.

47. "Rajoy promete bajar los impuestos si gana la elecciones," *El País*, October 7, 2007.

48. Ibid.

49. "Entrevista con Alberto Reig Tapia," December 25, 2006, Foro por la Memoria website, http://www.foroporlamemoria.es/pl.php?id=202, accessed September 27, 2008.

50. Vicenç Navarro, "Los costes de la memoria histórica," *El País*, June 16, 2001.

51. Author interview with ARMH president Emilio Silva, July 9, 2009.

52. Santos Juliá, "Memorias en lugar de memoria," *El País*, July 2, 2006.

53. "Antonio Muñoz Molina critica que la actualidad española este centrada en "Guerra civil y toros," *RTVE*, Febuary 8, 2010, RETV website, http://www.rtve.es/noticias/20100802/antonio-munoz-molina-critica-actualidad-espanola-este-centrada-guerra-civil-toros/343475.shtml, accessed March 20, 2011.

54. "El objetivo de la ley de memoria histórica es trazar una linea tajante entre buenos y malos," *ABC.es*, December 17, 2006.

55. "Preston señala que la gran lección de la Guerra Civil es no querer repetirla," *ABC.es*, June 4, 2008.

56. Araceli Manjón-Cabeza Olmeda, "El olvido de la memoria," *El País*, March 6, 2012.

57. The PP attacks on the Zapatero administration were unprecedented in the democratic period. Several PP leaders and their cheerleaders in the media, such as the daily *El Mundo* and the radio network *La Cope* disgraced themselves by peddling conspiracy theories linking the PSOE to the 2004 bombing of Atocha station. The best known has the PSOE plotting with the national security forces to leave Spain vulnerable to a terrorist attack by Islamic radicals before the 2004 elections, to ensure a socialist victory. See Encarnación (2009).

58. "El PP rechaza convertir el Valle de los Caídos en un centro de memoria," *ABC.es*, October 11, 2012.

59. Diario de Sesiones del Congreso de Diputados, 296.

60. Roy, "The Conspiracy of Silence Around Franco's Spain Has Finally Been Broken."

61. This is not to say that the left has given up altogether on revisiting the past. In May 2013 the leftwing and regional-nationalist parties proposed that July 18, the start of the Civil War, be declared "the day of condemnation of Francoism." The effort was defeated by the PP, which currently enjoys a majority of seats in the Congress of Deputies.

62. Quoted by Bess Twiston Davis, "Sacred Law of Historical Memory."

63. See especially CIS survey 2735, October 2007, CIS website, http://www.cis.es.

64. Renwick McLean, "Spain's Zapatero Shows Backbone in His Soft Power," *International Herald Tribune*, December 6, 2006.

65. To be sure, this mixed verdict is not universally shared in Spain. As the CIS 2008 survey reveals, in the Basque Country the picture is decidedly more negative, with only 24 percent of Basques crediting Franco with "good and bad things."

Chapter 7. Coping with the Past: Spanish Lessons

1. The 10,000 figure is noted in the National Report of the Disappeared. Unofficial reports by human rights NGOs place the tally of the casualties in the dirty war at 30,000.

2. "Brazil: Prosecute Dictatorship-Era Abuses," Human Rights Watch, April 14, 2009.

3. For a more comprehensive view of democracy in Spain, based on the criteria set by the NGO Freedom House, see Encarnación 2013.

4. Democratic legitimacy is generally understood to represent "the belief that despite its shortcomings and failures, the existing political institutions are better than any others that might be established" (Linz 1978: 16).

5. This literature by and large avoided the complicated issue of the repression of memory during the transition, leading some in more recent years to criticize it for its "celebratory" tone. See especially Resina (2000).

6. See Winston Churchill, "The Zurich Speech," Churchill Society, http://churchill-society-london.org.uk/astonish.html, accessed May 15, 2011.

7. Jorge Errandonea, "Estudio comparado de la anulación de sentencias injustas en España," ICJ website.

8. This view of Hussein's killing has been enhanced by videotape evidence that shows him being taunted by his Shiite executioners right before he was hanged. These images, recorded for posterity by onlookers on their cell phones, were circulated around the world, reinforcing the view that killing Saddam was a spectacle of revenge rather than the product of justice.

9. "Comments on the Death Penalty for Saddam," *Washington Post*, December 29, 2006.

10. This report is available at the U.S. Institute for Peace website.

11. See http://www.todoslosnombres.org.

12. "Editorial: Memoria de ley," *El País*, October 20, 2007.

REFERENCES

Ackerman, Bruce (1991). *We the People*. Vol. 2, *Transformations*. Cambridge, Mass.: Harvard University Press.

Aguilar, Paloma (1996a). *Memoria y olvido de la Guerra Civil Española*. Madrid: Alianza.

——— (1996b). "Collective Memory of the Spanish Civil War: The Case of the Political Amnesty in the Spanish Transition to Democracy." Estudios/Working Paper 85, Juan March Institute, Madrid.

——— (1998). "The Memory of the Civil War in the Transition to Democracy: The Peculiarity of the Basque Case," *West European Politics* 21 (4): 88–109.

——— (2001). "Justice, Politics and Memory in the Spanish Transition." In Alexandra Barahona de Brito, Carmen González-Enriquez, and Paloma Aguilar, eds., *The Politics of Memory: Transitional Justice in Democratizing Societies*. Oxford: Oxford University Press.

——— (2002). *Memory and Amnesia: The Role of the Spanish Civil War in the Transition to Democracy in Spain*. New York: Berghahn.

——— (2008). *Políticas de la memoria y memoria de la política*. Madrid: Alianza.

——— (2009). "Transitional or Post-Transitional Justice: Recent Developments in the Spanish Case." *Southern European Society and Politics* 13 (4): 417–33.

——— (2013). "Judiciary Involvement in Authoritarian Repression and Transitional Justice: The Spanish Case in Comparative Perspective," *International Journal of Transitional Justice* 7: 1–22.

Aguilar, Paloma, Laila Balcells and Héctor Cebolla-Boado (2011). "Determinants of Attitudes Toward Transitional Justice: An Empirical Analysis of the Spanish Case," Comparative Political Studies 44 (10): 1397–1430.

Aguilar, Paloma, and Carsten Humlebaek (2002). "Collective Memory and National Identity in the Spanish Democracy." *History and Memory* 14: 121–64.

Akhavan, Payam (2001). "Beyond Impunity: Can International Criminal Justice Prevent Future Atrocities?" *American Journal of International Law* 95 (1): 7–31.

Alfonsín, Raúl (1993). "Never Again in Argentina." *Journal of Democracy* 4 (1): 15–19.

Alted, Alicia (2003). *Historia y memoria de los niños de la guerra en el siglo XX*. Madrid: Universidad de Mayores Experiencia Recíproca.

——— (2005). *La voz de los vencidos: el exilio republicano de 1939*. Madrid: Aguilar.

Amell, Samuel, ed. (1990). *Literature, the Arts, and Democracy: Spain in the Eighties.* Madison, N.J.: Fairleigh Dickinson University Press.

Amodia, José (1977). *Franco's Political Legacy.* London: Penguin.

Amnesty International (1985). *España: La cuestión de la tortura.* London: AI.

Anderson, Benedict (1991). *Imagined Communities: Reflections on the Origins and Spread of Nationalism.* London: Verso.

Angell, Alan (2003). "The Pinochet Factor in Chilean Politics." In Madeleine Davis, ed., *The Pinochet Case: Origins, Progress and Implications.* London: ILAS.

Arendt, Hannah (1958). *The Human Condition.* Chicago: University of Chicago Press.

Arias Ramos, Raúl (2003). *La legion Condor en la Guerra Civil.* Madrid: Esfera de los Libros.

Aukerman, Miriam (2002). "Extraordinary Evil, Ordinary Crime." *Harvard Human Rights Journal* 15: 39–98.

Augé, Marc (2004). *Oblivion.* Minneapolis: University of Minnesota Press.

Ballbé, Manuel (1983). *Orden público y militarismo en la España constitucional (1812–1983).* Madrid: Alianza.

Balcells, Laila (2007). "Rivalry and Revenge: Killing Civilians in the Spanish Civil War." Estudios Working Paper 233. Madrid: Instituto Juan March.

Balfour, Sebastian (2005). "The Reinvention of Spanish Conservatism: The Popular Party Since 1989." In Balfour, ed., *The Politics of Contemporary Spain.* New York: Routledge.

Balfour, Sebastian, and Alejandro Quiroga (2007). *The Reinvention of Spain: Nation and Identity Since Democracy.* Oxford: Oxford University Press.

Barahona de Brito, Alexandra, Carmen González-Enriquez, and Paloma Aguilar, eds. (2001), *The Politics of Memory: Transitional Justice in Democratizing Societies.* Oxford: Oxford University Press.

Barkan, Elazar (2001). The Guilt of Nations: Restitution and Negotiating Historical Injustices. Baltimore: Johns Hopkins University Press.

Barreiro, Belén, and Ignacio Sánchez-Cuenca (1998). "Analysis del cambio de voto hacio el PSOE en las elecciones de 1993." *Revista Española de Investigaciones Sociológicas* 82.

Beevor, Antony (1982). *The Spanish Civil War.* New York: Penguin.

Benedicto, Jorge (2004). "Cultural Structures and Political Life: The Cultural Matrix of Democracy in Spain." *European Journal of Political Research* 43: 287–307.

Benhabib, Seyla (2009). "Claiming Rights Across Borders: International Human Rights and Democracy Sovereignty." *American Political Science Review* 104 (4): 691–704.

Benomar, Jamal (1993). "Justice After Transitions." *Journal of Democracy* 4 (1): 3–14.

Bermeo, Nancy (1992). "Democracy and the Lessons of Dictatorship." *Comparative Politics* 24 (3): 273–91.

Bermeo, Nancy, with José García-Durán (1994). "Spain: Dual Transition Implemented by Two Parties." In Stephan Haggard and Steven B. Webb, eds., *Voting for Reform:*

Democracy, Political Liberalization, and Economic Adjustment. New York: Oxford University Press.

Bernecker, Walter (2007). "The Change in Mentalities during the Late Franco Period." In Nigel Townson, ed., *Spain Transformed: The Late Franco Dictatorship*. New York: Palgrave.

Besas, Peter (1985). *Behind the Spanish Lens: Spanish Cinema under Fascism and Democracy*. Denver: Arden Press.

Blakeley, Giorgina (2005). Digging Up Spain's Past: Consequences of Truth and Reconciliation." *Democratization* 12 (1): 44–59.

Bookchin, Murray (1977). *The Spanish Anarchists: The Heroic Years, 1868–1936*. New York: Free Life Editions.

Boraine, Alexander L. (2006). Transitional Justice: A Holistic Interpretation." *Journal of International Affairs* 60 (Fall/Winter): 17–27.

Borneman, John (1997). *Settling Accounts with the Past: Violence, Justice and Accountability in Post-Socialist Europe*. Princeton, N.J.: Princeton University Press.

Boyd, Carolyn P. (1997). *Historia Patria: Politics, History and National Identity in Spain*. Princeton, N.J.: Princeton University Press.

——— (1999). "History, Politics, and Culture, 1936–1975." In David Gies, ed., *The Cambridge Companion to Modern Spanish Culture*. Cambridge: Cambridge University Press.

———. (2005). *De la memoria oficial a la memoria histórica: La Guerra Civil y la dictadura en los textos escolares, 1939 al presente*, Manuscript, University of California, Irvine.

——— (2008). "The Politics of History and Memory in Democratic Spain." *Annals of the American Academy of Political and Social Science* 133: 133–48.

Braithwhite, John (2002). *Restorative Justice and Responsive Regulation*. New York: Oxford University Press.

Brasslof, A. (1998). *Religion and Politics in Spain: The Spanish Church in Transition, 1962–1996*. London: Macmillan.

Brett, Sebastien (1999). *When Tyrants Tremble: The Chile Case*. Human Rights Watch Chile 11, 1. New York: Human Rights Watch.

Brysk, Alison (1993). "From Above and Below: Social Movements, the International System, and Human Rights in Argentina." *Comparative Political Studies* 26 (3), October: 259–85.

Buck, Marcus (1998). "The exemplary transition from authoritarianism: Some notes on the legacy of undemocratic decision-making in Spain." In Stein Ugelvik Larsen, ed., *Modern Europe After Fascism, 1943–1980s*. Boulder, Colo.: Social Science, East European Monographs.

Calvo, Kerman (2005). "Pursuing Membership in the Polity: The Spanish Gay and Lesbian Movement in Comparative Perspective." Doctoral thesis, Center for Advanced Study in the Social Sciences, Juan March Institute, Madrid.

Calvo-Sotelo, Leopoldo (1990). *Memoria viva de la trancisión*. Barcelona: Plaza y Janes/Cambio 16.

Campillo Madrigal, Oscar (2004). *Zapatero: Presidente a la primera*. Madrid: Esfera de los Libros.

Cardus i Ros, Salvador (2000). "Politics and the Invention of Memory: For a Sociology of the Transition to Democracy in Spain." In Joan Ramon Resina, ed., *Disremembering the Dictatorship: The Politics of Memory in the Spanish Transition to Democracy*. Amsterdam: Rodop.

Carr, Raymond, and Juan Pablo Fussi (1981). *Spain: Dictatorship to Democracy*. London: Allen & Unwin.

Carrillo, Santiago (1965). *Después de Franco, Qué?* Paris: Éditions Sociales.

——— (1967). *Nuevo enfoques a problemas de hoy*. Paris: Éditions Sociales.

——— (1977). *Eurocomunismo y Estado*. Barcelona: Crítica.

——— (1983). *Memoria de la transición*. Barcelona: Grijalbo

Casanova, José (1994). *Public Religion in the Modern World*. Chicago: University of Chicago Press.

Casanova, Julián, ed. (1992). *Morir, matar, sobrevivir: La violencia en la dictadura de Franco*. Barcelona: Crítica.

Castells, Manuel (1977). *Los procesos políticos: De la cárcel a la amnistía*. Madrid: Fundamentos.

——— (1983). *The City and the Grassroots: A Cross-Cultural Theory of Urban Social Movements*. Berkeley: University of California Press.

Cazorla, José (1993). "The Theory and Reality of the Authoritarian Regime, Thirty Years Later." In Richard Gunther, ed., *Politics, Society and Democracy: The Case of Spain*. Boulder, Colo.: Westview Press.

Cazorla-Sánchez, Antonio (2005). "They Shall Not Pass: How the Experience of Violence Reshaped Political Values in Franco's Spain." *Journal of Contemporary History* 40/3 (July): 503–20.

Cenarro, Ángela (2008). "Memories of Repression and Resistance: Narratives of Children Institutionalized by Auxilio Social in Postwar Spain." *History & Memory* 20 (2) (Fall/Winter): 39–59.

Centro de Investigaciones Sociológicas (1985). Survey on the 10th Anniversary of Franco's Death (November).

——— (2000). *Veinticinco años después: La memoria del franquismo y de la transición a la democracia en los Españoles en el año 2000*. Madrid: CIS.

——— (2004). "Estimación de Voto." *Estudio* 2555 (January–February).

——— (2008). "Memorias de la Guerra Civil y el Franquismo." Estudio 2760 (April).

Chuliá, Elisa (2007). "Cultural Diversity and the Development of a Pre-Democratic Civil Society in Spain." In Nigel Townson, ed., *Spain Transformed: The Late Franco Dictatorship*. New York: Palgrave.

Clark, Robert P. (1988). *The Basque Insurgents*. Madison: University of Wisconsin Press.

Closa, Carlos, and Paul M. Heywood (2004). *Spain and the European Union*. London: Palgrave.

Cole, Elizabeth A. (2007). "Reconciliation and History Education." In Elizabeth A. Cole, ed., *Teaching the Violent Past*. Lanham, Md.: Rowman and Littlefield.

Colomer, Josep M. (1998). *La transición a la democracia: el modelo español*. Anagrama: Barcelona.

Comisiones Obreas (1989). *De los pactos de la Moncloa al ASE*. Madrid: CCOO.

Cooper, Belinda (2009). "The Limits of International Justice." *World Policy Journal* (Fall): 99–101.

Costa Pinto, Antonio (2001). "Setting Accounts with the Past in a Troubled Transition to Democracy: The Portuguese Case." In Alexandra Barahona De Brito et al., *The Politics of Memory: Transitional Justice in Democratizing Societies*. Oxford: Oxford University Press.

——— (2006). "Authoritarian Legacies, Transitional Justice and State Crisis in Portugal's Democratization." *Democratization* 13 (2) (April).

Crespo, Julio (2000). *Spain and the Process of European Integration*. London: Basingstoke.

Crocker, David (1999). "Reckoning with Past Wrongs: A Normative Framework." *Ethics & International Affairs* 13: 43–64.

——— (2000). "Retribution and Reconciliation." *Philosophy and Public Policy* 20 (1): 23–31.

Crow, John A. (1985). *Spain: The Roots and the Flower*. Berkeley: University of California Press.

Crozier, Brian (1967). *Franco*. Boston: Little, Brown.

Davis, Madeleine (2004). "The Indictment of Pinochet: Pursuing Justice in Chile, 1973–2003." *Hispanic Research Journal* 5 (3): 264–71.

Davis, Madeleine (2005). "Is Spain Recovering Its Memory? Breaking the *Pacto del Olvido*." *Human Rights Quarterly* 27: 858–80.

De Brito, Alexandra Barahona (2001). "Truth, Justice, Memory, and Democratization in the Southern Cone." In Alexandra Barahona De Brito, Carmen González Enríquez, and Paloma Aguilar, eds., *The Politics of Memory: Transitional Justice in Democratizing Societies*. Oxford: Oxford University Press.

De Greiff, Pablo (2006). "Repairing the Past: Reparations for Victims of Human Rights Violations." In Pablo De Greiff, ed., *Handbook on Reparations*. Oxford: Oxford University Press.

Dent Coad, Emma (1995). "Designer Culture in the 1980s: The Price of Success." In Helen Graham and Jo Labanyi, eds., *Spanish Cultural Studies: An Introduction*. New York: Oxford University Press, 1995.

de Riquer i Permanyer, Borja (1995). "Social and Economic Change in a Climate of Political Immobilism." In Helen Graham and Jo Labanyi, eds., *Spanish Cultural Studies: An Introduction*. New York: Oxford University Press.

Diamond, Larry, and Mark F. Plattner, eds. (1996). *The Global Resurgence of Democracy.* Baltimore: Johns Hopkins University Press.

Díaz-Plaja, Fernando (1966). *La Guerra de España en sus documentos.* Barcelona: Ediciones de Marte.

Di Palma, Giuseppe (1990). *To Craft Democracies: An Essay on Democratic Transitions.* Berkeley: University of California Press.

Elkin, Mike (2006). "Opening Franco's Graves." *Archeology* (September/October): 38–43.

Ellwood, Sheelagh (1995). "The Moving Image of the Franco Regime." In Helen Graham and Jo Labanyi, eds., *Spanish Cultural Studies: An Introduction.* New York: Oxford University Press.

Encarnación, Omar G. (1997). "Social Concertation in Democratic and Market Transitions: Comparative Lessons from Spain." *Comparative Political Studies* 30 (4): 387–419.

——— (2001a). "Labor and Pacted Democracy: Spain in Comparative Perspective." *Comparative Politics* 33 (3): 337–59.

——— (2001b). "Civil Society and the Consolidation of Democracy in Spain." *Political Science Quarterly* 116 (1): 53–79.

——— (2005). "Do Political Pacts Freeze Democracy? Spanish and South American Lessons." *West European Politics* 28 (1): 182–203.

——— (2006). "Civil Society Reconsidered." *Comparative Politics* 38 (3): 357–76.

——— (2007). "Democracy and Dirty Wars in Spain." *Human Rights Quarterly* 29 (4): 950–72.

——— (2008a). *Spanish Politics: Democracy After Dictatorship.* Cambridge: Polity Press.

——— (2008b). "Reconciliation After Democratization: Coping with the Past in Spain." *Political Science Quarterly* 123 (3): 435–59.

——— (2009). "Spain Remade, Again." *Current History* 108 (March): 117–23.

——— (2010). "Spain's New Left Turn: Society Driven or Party Instigated?" *South European Society and Politics* 14 (4): 399–415.

——— (2012). "Justice in Times of Transition: Lessons from the Iberian Experience." *International Studies Quarterly* 56 (1): 179–92.

——— (2013). *Democracy at the Crossroads 2012: Spain.* Washington, D.C.: Freedom House.

Evans, Peter (1995). "Cinema, Memory and the Unconscious." In Helen Graham and Jo Labanyi, eds., *Spanish Cultural Studies: An Introduction.* New York: Oxford University Press.

Faber, Sebastiaan (2006). "The Price of Peace: Historical Memory in Post-Franco Spain, A Review Article." *Revista Hispánica Moderna* 58 (June–December): 205–19.

——— (2007). "Revisiting the Past: Truth, Justice, and Reconciliation in Post-Franco Spain, A Review Article (Second Part)." *Revista Hispanica Moderna* 59 (June–December): 141–54.

——— (2009). "Contestación a Santos Juliá." *Colorado Review of Hispanic Studies* 7 (Fall).

Farrell, Mary (2005). "Spain in the New European Union." In Sebastian Balfour, ed., *The Politics of Contemporary Spain*. London: Routledge.

Field, Bonnie (2010). "A Second Transition in Spain? Policy, Institutions and Interparty Politics under Zapatero." In Bonnie Field, ed., *Spain's Second Transition: The Socialist Government of José Luis Rodríguez Zapatero*. New York: Routledge.

Fishman, Robert (1990). *Working Class Organizations and the Return of Democracy in Spain*. Ithaca, N.Y.: Cornell University Press.

——— (2013). "On the Significance of Public Protest in Spanish Democracy." In Jacint Jordana, Vicenç Navarro, Francesc Pallarés, and Ferran Requejo eds., *Democràcia, política i societat: Homenatge a Rosa Virós*. Barcelona: Universitat Pompeu Fabra and Avenç.

Foweraker, Joe (1989). *Making Democracy in Spain*. Cambridge: Cambridge University Press.

Friedman, Max Paul and Padraic Kenney, eds. (2005). *Partisan Histories: The Past in Contemporary Global Politics*. New York: Palgrave.

Gálvez Biesca, Sergio (2006). "El proceso de la recuperación de la 'memoria histórica' en España: Una aproximación a los movimientos sociales por la memoria." *International Journal of Iberian Studies* 19 (1): 25–51.

Garton Ash, Timothy (1998). "The Truth About Dictatorship." *New York Review of Books* (February): 35–40.

——— (2002). "Trials, Purges and History Lessons: Treating a Difficult Past in Post–Communist Europe." In Jan-Werner-Müller, ed., *Memory and Power in Post-War Europe*. New York: Cambridge University Press.

Gibson, Ian (1983). *Paracuellos: Cómo fue*. Madrid: Argos Vergara.

Gies, David T. (1999). "Modern Spanish Culture: An Introduction." In David T. Gies, ed., *The Cambridge Companion to Modern Spanish Culture*. Cambridge: Cambridge University Press.

Gillespie, Richard (1989). *The Spanish Socialist Party: A History of Factionalism*. Oxford: Clarendon.

Gil, Alicia (2009). *La justicia de transición en España*. Barcelona: Atelier.

Gilmore, David (1985). *The Transformation of Spain*. London: Quartet.

Gironella, José María, and Rafael Borrás (1979). *100 Españoles y Franco*. Barcelona: Planeta.

Golob, Stephanie (2002). "The Pinochet Case: Forced to be Free Abroad and at Home." *Democratization* 9 (4): 25–57.

——— (2008). "Volver: The Return of/to Transitional Justice in Spain." *Journal of Spanish Cultural Studies* 9 (2): 127–41.

González Duro, Enrique (2003). *El miedo en la posguerra*. Madrid: Oberon.

González Márquez, Felipe (1976). "La unidad de los socialistas." *Sistema* 15: 45–51.

——— (1978). *España y su Futuro*. Madrid: Cuadernos para el Diálogo.

——— (1989). *European Union Speeches*. Madrid: Ministerio del Portavoz del Estado.

González Márquez, Felipe, and Alfonso Guerra (1977). *Partido Socialista Obrero Español*. Bilbao: Albia.

González Navarro, Francisco (1977). *La nueva ley fundamental para la reforma política*, Madrid: Servicio Central de Publicaciones, Secretaría General Técnica.

Graham, Helen (2002). *The Spanish Republic at War, 1936–1939*. Cambridge: Cambridge University Press.

——— (2004a). "Coming to Terms with the Past: Spain's Memory Wars." *History Today* 54 (5).

——— (2004b). "The Spanish Civil War, 1936–2003: The Return of the Republican Memory." *Science and Society* 68 (3): 313–28.

Graham, Helen, and Jo Labanyi (1995). "Democracy and Europeanization: Continuity and Change." In Helen Graham and Jo Labanyi, eds., *Spanish Cultural Studies: An Introduction*. New York: Oxford University Press.

Grigory Sevostianov, ed. (2000). *Spain Betrayed: The Soviet Union in the Spanish Civil War*. New Haven, Conn.: Yale University Press.

Grugel, Jean, and Tim Rees (1997). *Franco's Spain*. London: Arnold.

Guarnieri, Carlo, Pedro C. Magalhaes, and Yorgos Kaminis (2006). "Democratic Consolidation, Judicial Reform, and the Judicialization of Politics in Southern Europe, in Richard Gunther, P. Nikiforos Diamandouros, and Dimitri A. Sotiropoulos, eds., *Democracy and the State in the New Southern Europe*. Oxford: Oxford University Press.

Gunther, Richard (1986a). "The Spanish Socialist Party: From Clandestine Opposition to Party of Government." In Stanley Payne, ed., *The Politics of Democratic Spain*. Chicago: Chicago Council on Foreign Relations.

——— (1986b). "The Parties in Opposition: The Prospects for Change and Electoral Success." In Stanley Payne, ed., *The Politics of Democratic Spain*. Chicago: Chicago Council on Foreign Relations.

———(1992). "Spain: The Very Model of an Elite Settlement." In Richard Gunther and John Higley, eds., *Elites and Democratic Consolidation in Latin American and Southern Europe*. New York: Cambridge University Press.

——— (2007). "The Spanish Model Revisited." Paper presented at Conference, New Perspectives on the Spanish Transition, King's College London, May 18–19.

——— (2011). "The Spanish Model Revisited." In Diego Muro and Gregory Alonso, eds., *The Politics and Memory of the Democratic Transition: The Spanish Model*. New York: Routledge.

Gunther, Richard, José María Montero, and Joan Botella (2004). *Democracy in Modern Spain*. New Haven, Conn.: Yale University Press.

Gunther, Richard, Hans-Jürgen Puhle, and P. Nicos Diamandouros (2005). "Introduction." In Richard Gunther, Hans-Jürgen Puhle, and P. Nicos Diamandouros, eds., *The Politics of Democratic Consolidation: Southern Europe in Comparative Perspective*. Baltimore: Johns Hopkins University Press.

Hagopian, Frances (1992). "The Compromised Consolidation: The Political Class in the Brazilian Transition." In Guillermo O'Donnell and J. Samuel Valenzuela, eds., *Issues in Democratic Consolidation: The New South American Democracies in Comparative Perspective*. Notre Dame, Ind.: University of Notre Dame Press.

Halbwachs, Maurice (1992). *On Collective Memory*. Chicago: University of Chicago Press.

Hayner, Priscilla (2001). *Unspeakable Truths: Confronting State Terror and Atrocity*. New York: Routledge.

——— (1994). "Fifteen Truth Commissions—1974–1994: A Comparative Study." *Human Rights Quarterly* 16 (4): 597–655.

Helmke, Gretchen, and Steven Letvisky, eds. (2006). *Informal Institutions and Democracy: Lessons from Latin America*. Baltimore: Johns Hopkins University Press.

Herf, Jeffrey (1997). *Divided Memory: The Nazi Past in the Two Germanies*. Cambridge, Mass.: Harvard University Press.

Herr, Richard (1971). *An Historical Essay on Modern Spain*. Berkeley: University of California Press.

Heywood, Paul (2005). "Corruption, Democracy and Governance in Contemporary Spain." In Sebastian Balfour, ed., *The Politics of Contemporary Spain*. London: Routledge.

Hipsher, Patricia L. (1996). "Democratization and the Decline of Urban Social Movements in Chile and Spain." *Comparative Politics* 28 (3): 273–99.

Hite, Katherine (2008). "The Valley of the Fallen: Tales from the Crypt." *Forum for Modern Language Studies* 43 (2): 110–27.

——— (2011). *Politics and the Art of Commemoration: Memorials to Struggle in Latin America and Spain*. New York: Routledge.

Hite, Katherine, and Paola Cesarini, eds. (2004). *Authoritarian Legacies and Democracy in Latin America and Southern Europe*. Notre Dame, Ind.: University of Notre Dame Press.

Hirsch, Francine (2008). "The Soviets at Nuremberg: International Law, Propaganda, and the Making of the Postwar Order." *American Historical Review* (June 2008): 701–30.

Hopewell, John (1986). *Out of the Past: Spanish Cinema After Franco*. London: British Film Institute.

Hopper, John (1986). *The Spaniards: A Portrait of the New Spain*. London: Penguin.

Humlebaek, Carsten (2005). "Political Uses of the Recent Past in the Spanish Post-Authoritarian Democracy." In Max Paul Friedman and Padraic Kenney, eds., *Partisan Histories: The Past in Contemporary Global Politics*. New York: Palgrave.

——— (2007). "Revisiting the so-called 'Pacto del Olvido.'" Paper presented at Conference, New Perspectives on the Spanish Transition, King's College London, May 18–19.

——— (2011). "The "Pacto de Olvido." In Diego Muro and Gregory Alonso, eds., *The Politics and Memory of the Democratic Transition: The Spanish Model*. New York: Routledge.

Huntington, Samuel (1991). *The Third Wave: Democratization in the Late Twentieth Century*. Norman: Oklahoma University Press.

Ignatieff, Michael (1996). "Articles of Faith." *Index on Censorship* 25 (5): 110–22.

Jarausch, Konrad (2006). *After Hitler: Recivilizing Germans, 1945–1995*. New York: Oxford University Press.

Jackson, Gabriel (1965). *The Spanish Republic and the Civil War*. Princeton, N.J.: Princeton University Press.

Jaúregui, Fernando y Manuel Ángel Menéndez (1995). *Lo que nos queda de Franco. Símbolos, personajes, leyes y costumbres veinte años después*. Madrid: Temas de Hoy.

Jaúregui, Pablo (1999). "National Price and the Meaning of Europe: A Comparative Study of Britain and Spain." In Dennis Smith and Sue Wrights, eds., *Whose Europe? The Turn Towards Democracy*. Oxford: Blackwell.

Jelin, Elizabeth (2003), *State Repression and the Struggles for Memory*. Minneapolis: University of Minnesota Press.

Jordan, Barry (1995). "The Emergence of a Dissident Intelligentsia." In Helen Graham and Jo Labanyi, eds., *Spanish Cultural Studies: An Introduction*. New York: Oxford University Press.

Judt, Tony (2002). "The Past is another Country: Myth and Memory in Post-War Europe." In Jan-Werner-Müller, ed., *Memory & Power in Post-War Europe*. New York: Cambridge University Press.

——— (2005). *Postwar: A History of Europe Since 1945*. New York: Penguin.

Juliá, Santos (1999a). "History, Politics, and Culture, 1975–1996." In David Gies, ed., *The Cambridge Companion to Modern Spanish Culture*. Cambridge: Cambridge University Press.

———, ed. (1999b). *Las víctimas de la Guerra Civil*. Madrid: Temas de Hoy.

——— (2003). "Echar al olvido, memoria y amnistía en la transición." *Claves de Razón Política* 129 (January/February): 14–24.

——— (2004). *Historia de las dos España*. Madrid: Taurus.

——— (2006a). "Bajo el imperio de la memoria." *Revista de Occidente* 302–3 (July–August): 7–19.

———, ed. (2006b). *Memoria de la guerra y del franquismo*. Madrid: Fundación Pablo Iglesias/Tauros.

Kamen, Henry (2007). *The Disinherited: Exile and the Making of Spanish Culture, 1492–1975*. New York: HarperCollins.

Karl, Terry L. (1987). "Petroleum and Political Pacts: The Transition to Democracy in Venezuela." *Latin American Research Review* 22 (1): 63–94.

Keck, Margaret, and Kathryn Sikkink (1998). *Activists Beyond Borders: Advocacy Networks in International Politics*. Ithaca, N.Y.: Cornell University Press.

Kennedy, Paul (2007). "Phoenix from the Ashes. The PSOE Government under Rodríguez Zapatero 2004–2007: A New Model for Social Democracy." *International Journal of Iberian Studies* 20 (3): 187–206.

Kinder, Marsha (1993). *Blood Cinema: The Reconstruction of National Cinema in Spain*. Berkeley: University of California Press.

——— (1997). "Reconfiguring Socialist Spain: An Introduction." In Marsha Kinder, ed., *Reconfiguring Spain: Cinema/Media/Representation*. Durham, N.C.: Duke University Press.

Kissane, Bill, and Nick Sitter (2005). "Civil Wars, Party Politics and the Consolidation of Regimes in Twentieth Century Europe." *Democratization* 12 (2): 183–201.

Kritz, Neil J., ed. (1995). *Transitional Justice: How Emerging Democracies Reckon with Former Regimes*. Washington, D.C.: U.S. Institute of Peace Press.

Labanyi, Jo (1995). "Postmodernism and the Problem of Cultural Identity." In Helen Graham and Jo Labanyi, eds., *Spanish Cultural Studies: An Introduction*. New York: Oxford University Press.

——— (2007). "Memory and Modernity in Democratic Spain: The Difficulty of Coming to Terms with the Spanish Civil War." *Poetics Today* 28 (1): 89–116.

——— (2008). "The Politics of Memory in Contemporary Spain." *Journal of Spanish Cultural Studies* 9 (2): 119–25.

Laiz, Consuelo (1995). *La lucha final: Los partidos de la izquierda radical durante la transición española*. Madrid: Libros de La Catarata.

Langenbacher, Eric (2005). "*Moralpolitik* Versus *Moralpolitik*: Recent Struggles over the Construction of Cultural Memory in Germany." *German Politics and Society* 23 (3): 106–34.

——— (2010). "Still the Unmasterable Past? The Impact of History and Memory in the Federal Republic of Germany." *German Politics* 19 (1): 24–40.

León Solís, Fernando (2003). "The Transition(s) to Democracy and Discourses of Memory." *International Journal of Iberian Studies* 16 (1): 48–64.

Lind, Jennifer (2008). *Sorry States: Apologies in International Politics*. Ithaca, N.Y.: Cornell University Press.

Linz, Juan (1978). "Crisis, Breakdown and Reequilibration." In Juan J. Linz and Alfred Stepan, eds., *The Breakdown of Democratic Regimes*. Baltimore: Johns Hopkins University Press.

Linz, Juan and Alfred Stepan (1996). *Problems of Democratic Transition and Consolidation*. Baltimore: Johns Hopkins University Press.

Linz, Juan, Miguel Jerez, and Susana Corzo (2001). "Ministers and Regimes in Spain: From First to Second Restoration, 1874–2001." Center for European Studies Working Paper 191. Cambridge, Mass: Harvard University.

Llera, Francisco J. (1993). "Conflicto en Euskadi Revisited." In Richard Gunther, ed., *Politics, Society and Democracy: The Case of Spain*. Boulder, Colo.: Westview Press.

López-Pintor, Rafael (1985). "Transition Toward Democracy in Spain: Opinion Mood and Elite Behavior." Working Paper 80. Washington, D.C.: Wilson Center.

MacDonald, Ross B. (2006). "The Politics of Victimhood: Historical Memory and Peace in Spain and the Basque Region." *Journal of International Affairs* 60 (Fall/Winter): 173–96.

Magalgaes, Pedro C., Carlos Guarnieri, and Yorgor Kaminis (2006). "Democratic Consolidation, Judicial Reform and the Judicialization of Politics in Southern Europe." In Richard Gunther, P. Nikiforos Diamandouros, and Dimitri Sotiropoulos, eds., *Democracy and the State in Southern Europe*. Oxford: Oxford University Press.

Maier, Charles (1988). *The Unmasterable Past: History, Holocaust and German National Identity*. New York: Cambridge University Press.

Malamud, Carlos (2003). "Spanish Public Opinion and the Pinochet Case." In Madeleine Davis, ed., *The Pinochet Case: Origins, Progress and Implications*. London: ILAS.

Malamud-Goti, Jaime (1995). *Game with No End: State Terror and the Politics of Justice*. Norman: University of Oklahoma Press.

Malefakis, Edward (1970). *Agrarian Reform and Peasant Revolution in Spain*. New Haven, Conn.: Yale University Press.

——— (1982). "Spain and its Francoist Heritage." In John H. Herz, ed., *From Dictatorship to Democracy: Coping with the Legacies of Authoritarianism and Totalitarianism*. Westport, Conn.: Greenwood Press.

——— (1995). "The Political and Socioeconomic Contours of Southern European History." In Richard Gunther, P. Nikiforos Diamandouros, and Hans-Jürgen Puhle, eds., *The Politics of Democratic Consolidation: Southern Europe in Comparative Perspective*. Baltimore: Johns Hopkins University Press.

Mamdani, Mahmood (1996). "Reconciliation Without Justice." *Southern African Political and Economic Monthly* 10: 21–25.

Magone, José (2011). "The Role of the EEC in the Spanish, Portuguese and the Greek Transitions." In Diego Muro and Gregorio Alonso, eds., *The Politics and Memory of Democratic Transition: The Spanish Model*. New York: Routledge.

Maravall, José M. (1985). "The Socialist Alternative: The Policies and Electorate of the PSOE." In Howard R. Penniman and Eusebio M. Mujal-León, eds., *Spain at the Polls, 1977, 1979, and 1982*. Durham, N.C.: Duke University Press.

——— (1978). *Dictatura y disentimiento político: obreros y estudiantes bajo el franquismo*. Madrid: Alfaguara.

——— (1981). *La política de la transición*. Madrid: Tauros.

——— (1979). "Spain: Eurocommunism and Socialism." *Political Studies* 27 (June): 218–35.

Marías, Julián (1981). *Cinco años en España*. Madrid: Calpe.

Marti, José Luis and Philip Pettit (2010). *A Political Philosophy in Public Life: Civic Republicanism in Zapatero's Spain*. Princeton, N.J.: Princeton University Press.

Martínez, Robert (1993). "The Business Sector and Political Change in Spain." In Richard Gunther, ed., *Politics, Society and Democracy: The Case of Spain*. Boulder, Colo.: Westview Press.

Martínez-Torrón, Javier (2006). "Religious Freedom and Democratic Change in Spain." *Brigham Young University Law Review* (3).

Martín Cortéz, Irene (2007). "Political Parties and Interest in Politics in Greece and Spain." Paper presented at Conference, New Perspectives on the Spanish Transition to Democracy, King's College, London.

Maxwell, Richard (1995). *The Spectacle of Democracy: Spanish Television, Nationalism and Political Transition.* Minneapolis: University of Minnesota Press.

McDonough, Peter, Samuel H. Barnes, and Antonio López Pina (1998). *The Cultural Dynamics of Democratization in Spain.* Ithaca, N.Y.: Cornell University Press.

Mendeloff, David (2004). "Truth-Seeking, Truth-Telling, and Post-Conflict Peacebuilding: Curb the Enthusiasm?" *International Studies Review* 6: 355–80.

Méndez-Lago, Mónica (2006). "Turning the Page: Crisis and Transformation of the Spanish Socialist Party." *South European Society and Politics* 11 (3–4): 419–37.

Michnik, Adam (1993). "Justice or Revenge?" *Journal of Democracy* 4 (1): 20–27.

Mínguez Villar, José Carlos (2004). "El miedo del recuerdo." In Emilio Silva, Pancho Salvador, Asunción Esteban, and Javier Castán, eds., *La memoria de los olvidados.* Madrid: Ambito.

Moa, Pío (2003). *Los mitos de la Guerra Civil.* Madrid: Esfera de los Libros.

——— (2006). *El Iluminado de la Moncloa y otras plagas.* Madrid: Libros Libre.

Montero, José R. (1993). "Revisiting Democratic Success: Legitimacy and the Meanings of Democracy in Spain." In Richard Gunther, ed., *Politics, Society and Democracy: The Case of Spain.* Boulder, Colo.: Westview Press.

Moran, John P. (1994). "The Communist Torturers of Eastern Europe: Prosecute or Forgive or Forgive and Forget?" *Communist and Post-Communist Studies* 27 (1): 95–109.

Morán, Gregorio (1991). *El precio de la transición.* Barcelona: Planeta.

Moreno, Juliá Xavier (2005). *La División Azul: Sangre española en Rusia, 1941–1945.* Barcelona: Crítica.

Moulian, Tomás (1999). "The Arrest and Its Aftermath." *NACLA Report on the Americas* 32 (6): 12–17.

Müller, Jan-Werner (2002). "Introduction: The Power of Memory, the Memory of power, and the Power over Memory." In Jan-Werner-Müller, ed., *Memory and Power in Post-War Europe.* New York: Cambridge University Press.

Mujal-León, Eusebio (1985). "The Spanish Communist Party and the Search for Political Space." In Howard R. Penniman and Eusebio M. Mujal-León, eds., *Spain at the Polls, 1977, 1979, and 1982.* Durham, N.C.: Duke University Press.

Muro, Diego (2005). "Nationalism and Nostalgia: The Case of Radical Basque Nationalism." *Nations and Nationalisms* 11 (4): 571–89.

——— (2008). *Ethnicity and Violence: The Case of Radical Basque Nationalism.* New York: Routledge.

——— (2009). "The Politics of War Memory in Basque Radical Nationalism." *Ethnic and Racial Studies* 32 (4): 659–78.

Muro, Diego, and Alejandro Quiroga (2005). "Spanish Nationalism: Ethnic or Civic?" *Ethnicities* 5 (1): 9–29.

Nagy, Rosemary (2002). "Reconciliation in Post-Commission South Africa: Thick and Thin Accounts of Solidarity." *Canadian Journal of Political Science* 35 (2): 323–46.

Navarro, Marysa (1989). "The Personal is Political: Las Madres de la Plaza de Mayo." In Susan Eckstein, ed., *Power and Popular Protest: Latin American Social Movements*. Berkeley: University of California Press.

Newton, Michael T., and Peter J. Donaghy (1997). *Institutions of Modern Spain: A Political and Economic Guide*. New York: Cambridge University Press.

Nietzsche, Friedrich (1983). *Untimely Meditations*. Trans. R.J. Hollingdale. Cambridge: Cambridge University Press.

Nuñez Seixas, Xosé–Manoel (2005). "From National Catholic Nostalgia to Constitutional Patriotism: Conservative Spanish Nationalism Since the Early 1990s." In Sebastian Balfour, ed., *The Politics of Contemporary Spain*. New York: Routledge.

O'Donnell, Guillermo and Philippe Schmiter (1986). *Tentative Conclusions About Uncertain Democracies*. Baltimore: Johns Hopkins University Press.

Oglesby, Elizabeth (2007). "Historical Memory and the Limits of Peace Education: Examining Guatemala's Memory of Silence and The Politics of Curriculum Design." In Elizabeth A. Cole, ed., *Teaching the Violent Past*. Lanham, Md.: Rowman and Littlefield.

Olsen, Tricia, Leigh Payne, and Andrew G. Reiter (2011). *Transitional Justice in Balance: Comparing Processes, Weighing Efficacy*. Washington, D.C.: U.S. Institute for Peace.

Osiel, Mark (1995). "Ever Again: Legal Remembrance and Administrative Massacre." *University of Pennsylvania Law Review* 1 (144): 463–680.

Packer, George (2005). *The Assassins' Gate: America in Iraq*. New York: Farrar, Strauss.

Partido Socialista Obrero Español (2004). *Merecemos una España Mejor: Programa electoral*, Elecciones Generales 2004.

Payne, Stanley (1970). *The Spanish Revolution*. New York: Norton.

——— (1984). *Spanish Catholicism*. Madison: University of Wisconsin Press.

——— (1985). "Representative Government in Spain." In Howard R. Penniman and Eusebio M. Mujal-León, eds., *Spain at the Polls, 1977, 1979, and 1982*. Durham, N.C.: Duke University Press.

———, ed. (1986). *The Politics of Democratic Spain*. Chicago: Chicago Council on Foreign Relations.

——— (1993). *Spain's First Democracy: The Second Republic*. Madison: University of Wisconsin Press.

——— (2006). *The Collapse of the Spanish Republic, 1936–1936: The Origins of the Spanish Civil War*. New Haven, Conn.: Yale University Press.

——— (2011). *The Spanish Civil War: The Soviet Union, and Communism*. New Haven, Conn.: Yale University Press.

Pendas, David (2008). "Transitional Justice and Just Transitions: The German Case, 1945–1950." *European Studies Forum* (Spring): 57–64.

Pérez-Díaz, Victor (1980). *Clase obrera, orden social y conciencia de clase.* Madrid: Fundación del Instituto Nacional de Industria.

——— (1993a). La primacía de la sociedad civil: el proceso de la formación de la España democrática. Madrid: Alianza.

——— (1993b). *The Return of Civil Society and the Emergence of Democratic Spain.* Cambridge, Mass.: Harvard University Press.

Pettit, Philip (1997). *Republicanism: A Theory of Freedoms and Government.* New York: Oxford University Press.

——— (2008). *Examen a Zapatero: Balance del gobierno socialista.* Madrid: Temas de Hoy.

Philpott, Daniel (2007). "Religion, Reconciliation, and Transitional Justice: The State of the Field." Social Science Research Council Working Paper, October 17.

Pión-Berlin, David (1994). "To Prosecute or to Pardon? Human Rights Decisions in the Latin American Southern Cone." *Human Rights Quarterly* 16 (1): 105–30.

Piqueras, José A. and Vicent Sanz Rozalén (2007). "Traditional History and the New Social History of Labour in Spain." In José A. Piqueras and Vicent Sanz Rozalén, eds., *A Social History of Spanish Labour: New Perspectives on Class, Politics and Gender,* trans. Paul Edgar. New York: Berghahn.

Pi-Sunyer, Oriol (1977). "Political Humor in a Dictatorial State: The Case of Spain." *Ethnohistory* 24 (2): 179–80.

Podolny, Joel (1992). "The Role of Juan Carlos I in the Consolidation of the Parliamentary Monarchy." In Richard Gunther, ed., *Politics, Society and Democracy: The Case of Spain.* Boulder, Colo.: Westview Press.

Poggiolini, Ilaria (2002). "Translating Memories of War and Co-belligerency into Politics: The Italian Post-war Experience." In Jan-Werner-Müller, ed., *Memory and& Power in Post-War Europe.* New York: Cambridge University Press.

Preston, Paul (1991). *The Politics of Revenge: Fascism and the Military in Twentieth Century Spain.* London: Unwin Hyman.

——— (1995). "The Urban and Rural Guerilla of the 1940s." In Helen Graham and Jo Labanyi, eds., *Spanish Cultural Studies.* New York: Oxford University Press.

Przeworski, Adam (1991). *Democracy and the Market.* New York: Cambridge University Press.

Quiroga, Alejandro (2011). "Salvation by Betrayal: The Left and the Spanish Nation." In Gregory Alonso and Diego Muro, eds., *The Politics and Memory of the Democratic Transition: The Spanish Model.* New York: Routledge.

Rabkin, Jeremy (1999). "Nuremberg Misremembered." *SAIS Review* 19 (2): 81–96.

Reig Tapia, Alberto (2006). *Anti-Moa.* Barcelona: Ediciones B.

Reinares, Fernando (1990). "Sociogénesis y evolución del terrorismo en España." In Salvador Giner, ed., *España: sociedad y política.* Madrid: Espasa-Calpe.

Resina, Joan Ramon ed. (2000). *Disremembering the Dictatorship: The Politics of Memory in the Spanish Transition to Democracy.* Amsterdam: Rodopi:.

Richards, Michael (1996). "Constructing the Nationalist State: Self-Sufficiency and Regeneration in the Early Franco Years." In Clare Mar-Molinero and Angel Smith, eds., *Nationalism and the Nation in the Iberian Peninsula*. Oxford: Berg.

——— (2006). "Between Memory and History: Social Relationships and Ways of Remembering the Spanish Civil War." *International Journal of Iberian Studies* 19 (1): 84–94.

Richardson, Dan (1976). "Foreign Fighters in the Spanish Militias: The Spanish Civil War 1936–1939." *Military Affairs* 40 (1): 7–11.

Ricoeur, Paul (2004). *Memory, History, Forgetting*. Chicago: University of Chicago Press.

Rigby, Andrew (2000). "Amnesty and Amnesia in Spain." *Peace Review* 12 (1): 73–79.

Risse, Thomas and Kathryn Sikkink (1999). "The Socialization of International Human Rights Norms into Domestic Practices: Introduction." In Thomas Risse and Kathryn Sikkink, eds., *The Power of Human Rights: International Norms and Domestic Change*. New York: Cambridge University Press.

Robinson, Richard A. H. (1971). *The Origins of Franco's Spain: The Right, the Republic and Revolution, 1931–1936*. Pittsburgh: University of Pittsburgh Press.

Rodden, John (2008). "Heuristics, Hypocrisy and History Without Lessons: Nuremberg, War Crimes, and 'Shock and Awe,'" *Journal of Human Rights* 7 (1): 34–43.

Roldán Ros, Juan (1985). "The Media and the Elections." In Howard R. Penniman and Eusebio M. Mujal-León, eds., *Spain at the Polls, 1977, 1979, and 1982*. Durham, N.C.: Duke University Press.

Rosenberg, Tina (1996). *The Haunted Land: Facing Europe's Ghosts After Communism*. New York: Vintage Books.

Rotberg, Robert and Dennis Thompson, eds. (2000). *Truth v. Justice: The Morality of Truth Commissions*. Princeton, N.J.: Princeton University Press.

Royo, Sebastián (2000). *From Social Democracy to Neo-Liberalism: The Consequences of Party Hegemony in Spain*. New York: St. Martin's.

——— (2013). *Lessons from the Economic Crisis in Spain*. New York: Palgrave.

Rubio, Javier (1977). *La emigración de la guerra civil de 1936–1939: historia del exodo que se produce con el fin de la II Republica Española*. Madrid: Libreria Editorial San Martín.

Ruiz, Julius (2005). *Franco's Justice: Repression in Madrid After the Spanish Civil War*. Oxford: Oxford University Press.

Ruiz-Vargas, José María (2002). *Memoria y olvido*. Madrid: Trotta.

——— (2006). "Trauma y memoria de la guerra civil y la dictadura franquista." *Hispania Nova: Revista de Historia Contemporanea* 6. http://hispanianova.rediris.es/6/dossier/6d012.pdf.

Sánchez-León, Pablo (2006). "La objetividad como ordoxía: Los historiadores y el conocimiento de la Guerra Civil Española." In Julio Aróstegui and François Godicheau, eds., *Guerra Civil: Mito y memoria*. Madrid: Marcial Pons.

Santayana, George (1906). *The Life of Reason*. Reprint Amherst, N.Y.: Prometheus, 1998.

Schmitter, Philippe (2001). *Contrasting Approaches to Political Engineering: Constitutionalization and Democratization*. Florence: European University Institute.

Seiman, Michael (2002). *Republic of Egos: A Social History of the Spanish Civil War*. Madison: University of Wisconsin Press.

Serra, Narcís (2010). *The Military Transition: Democratic Reforms of the Armed Forces*. New York: Cambridge University Press.

Shaklar, Judith (1963). *Legalism: Law, Moral and Political Trials*. Cambridge, Mass.: Harvard University Press, 1963.

Share, Donald (1986). *The Making of Spanish Democracy*. New York: Praeger.

Shnayerson, Robert (1996). "Judgment at Nuremberg." *Smithsonian* (October): 124–41.

Sikkink, Kathryn (2008). "From Pariah State to Global Protagonist: Argentina and the Struggle for International Human Rights." *Latin American Politics & Society* 50 (1): 1–29.

——— (2011). *The Justice Cascade: How Rights Prosecutions Are Changing World Politics*. New York: Norton.

Simmons, Beth (2009). *Mobilizing for Human Rights: International Law in Domestic Politics*. New York: Cambridge University Press.

Skarr, Elin (1999). "Truth Commissions, Trials or Nothing? Policy Options in Democratic Transitions." *Third World Quarterly* 20 (6) (December).

Smith, Paul Julian (2000). *The Moderns: Time, Space and Subjectivity in Contemporary Spanish Culture*. Oxford: Oxford University Press.

——— (2003). *Contemporary Spanish Culture: TV, Fashion, Culture, Art and Film*. Cambridge: Polity Press.

Sotiropoulos, Dimitri A. (2010). "The Authoritarian Past and Contemporary Greek Democracy." *Southern European Society and Politics* 15 (3): 449–65.

Stein, Louis (1979). *Beyond Death and Exile: The Spanish Republicans in France, 1939–1955*. Cambridge, Mass.: Harvard University Press.

Storm, Eric (2004). "The Problems of the Spanish Nation-Building Process around 1900." *National Identities* 6 (2): 143–56.

Suárez, Adolfo (1978). *Un nuevo horizonte para España: Discursos del Presidente del Gobierno, 1976–1978*. Madrid: Boletín Oficial del Estado.

Tarrow, Sidney (1994). *Power in Movement*. New York: Cambridge University Press.

Theidon, Kimberly (2009). "Editorial Note." *International Journal of Transitional Justice* 3 (3): 1–6.

Teitel, Ruti (2000). *Transitional Justice*. Oxford: Oxford University Press.

Threlfall, Monica (2008). "Reassessing the Role of Civil Society Organizations in the Transition to Democracy in Spain." *Democratization* 15 (5): 930–51.

Torreblanca, José I. (2008). "Ideas, Preferences, and Institutions: Explaining the Europeanization of Spanish Foreign Policy." Arena Working Papers, November 8.

Torres, Rafael (2004). *Los esclavos de Franco*. Madrid: Oberón.

Townson, Nigel (2002). *La república que no pudo ser: La política de centro en España (1931–1936)*. Madrid Taurus.

———, ed. (2007). *Spain Transformed: The Late Franco Dictatorship, 1959–1975*. New York: Palgrave Macmillan.

Treglown, Jeremy. (2009). "The Memory Moment." *Granta* 105 (Spring): 17–43.

Tussell Gomez, Javier (1985). "The Democratic Center and Christian Democracy in the Elections of 1977 and 1979." In Howard R. Penniman and Eusebio M. Mujal-León, eds., *Spain at the Polls, 1977, 1979, and 1982*. Durham, N.C.: Duke University Press.

Tutu, Desmond (1999). *No Future Without Forgiveness*. London: Random House.

Urbano, Pilar (2000). *Garzón: El hombre que veía amanecer*. Madrid: Plaza & Janes.

Valls, Rafael (2007). "The Spanish Civil War and the Franco Dictatorship: The Challenges of Representing a Conflict Past in Secondary Schools." In Elizabeth Cole, ed., *Teaching the Violent Past: History Education and Reconciliation*. Lanham, Md.: Rowman and Littlefield.

Vincent, Mary (2007). *Spain 1833–2002: People and State*. New York: Oxford University Press.

Viñas, Ángel (1978). "Guernica: Las responsabilidades." *Historia* 16 (25): 127–43.

Weber, Max (1946). "Politics as a Vocation." In Weber, *From Max Weber: Essays in Sociology*, ed. H. H. Gerth and C. Wright Mills. New York: Oxford University Press.

Wert Ortega, José Ignacio (1985). "The Transition from Below: Public Opinion Among the Spanish Population from 1977 to 1979." In Howard R. Penniman and Eusebio M. Mujal-León, eds., *Spain at the Polls, 1977, 1979, and 1982*. Durham, N.C.: Duke University Press.

Wiarda, Howard (1973). "Toward a Framework for the Study of Political Change in the Iberic-Latin Tradition: The Corporative Model." *World Politics* 25 (2): 206–35.

Wilde, Alexander (1999). "Irruptions of Memory: Expressive Politics in Chile's Transition to Democracy." *Journal of Latin American Studies* 31 (2): 473–500.

Wilson, Richard J. (1999). "Prosecuting Pinochet: International Crimes in Spanish Domestic Law." *Human Rights Quarterly* 21 (4): 927–79.

Zalaquett, José. (1992). "Balancing Ethical Imperatives and Political Constraints: The Dilemma of New Democracies Confronting Past Human Rights Violations." *Hastings Law Journal* 43: 1425–37.

Zapico Barbeito, Monica (2010). "Investigating the Crimes of the Franco Regime: Legal Possibilities, Obligations of the Spanish State and Duties Towards the Victims." *International Criminal Law Review* 10 (2): 243–74.

INDEX

ACKNOWLEDGMENTS

While writing this book, I have accumulated numerous intellectuals debts that I am happy to record here.

First, and foremost, I am indebted to fellow students of contemporary Spanish politics, especially Paloma Aguilar, Richard Gunther, Robert Fishman, Stephanie Golob, Katherine Hite, Sebastiaan Faber, Bonnie Field, and Diego Muro, for the insight provided by their own research and their willingness to discuss and comment on my own work. I am most grateful to Diego for his very generous reading of the entire manuscript at almost the very last minute. I am also indebted to Sebastián Royo and Sofía Pérez for organizing a very timely presentation of this work at its earliest and most formative stage at Harvard University's Minda de Gunzburg Center for European Studies in 2008, from which I drew tremendous inspiration. Special thanks also go to the anonymous referees of *Political Science Quarterly* and *International Studies Quarterly*, two journals that have published essays of mine inspired by this book, and the University of Pennsylvania Press, for insightful and helpful commentary, Peter Agree, my editor at Penn Press, has been a source of constant support during the long and turbulent gestation of this project.

Over the years, several research assistants at Bard College undertook work related to this project, including Gabriel Sub, Rachel Meyer, and Rosana Zarza Canova, who conducted many of the interviews cited in this study. Financial support from the Program for Cooperation between Spain's Ministry of Culture and North American University and Bard's Research Council made interviews and archival work in Spain possible.

As always, John and Amos provided invaluable emotional support, especially at times when they were far from aware of it.

This book is dedicated to the memory of my father, Guillermo Encarnación Betancourt.